PRINCIPLES FOR
A CATHOLIC MORALITY

PRINCIPLES FOR A CATHOLIC MORALITY

TIMOTHY E. O'CONNELL

1817

Harper & Row, Publishers, San Francisco
Cambridge, Hagerstown, New York, Philadelphia
London, Mexico City, São Paulo, Singapore, Sydney

Library of Congress Catalog Card Number: 78-17884

ISBN: 0-86683-885-6

Printed in the United States of America

5   4   3

Harper & Row, Publishers, Inc.
10 East 53d Street
New York, NY 10022

To the priests of Chicago
From whom I come,
For whom I work,
With whom I minister to God's people;

And in particular to
that priest who taught me
the dignity and privilege
of doing moral theology:
Father John F. Dedek.

Acknowledgments

The author gratefully acknowledges permission to use material on which the following hold copyright:

Chicago Studies, for Chapter Eight, which originally appeared in their pages under the title "The Theology of Conscience" (vol. 14 [1976]: 149–66).

Liturgy Training Program of the Archdiocese of Chicago for portions of Chapters Two and Twelve which originally appeared as a pamphlet entitled "Identification of Sin," *Reconciliation Background Papers* (1976).

Confraternity of Christian Doctrine for all scriptural quotations that are taken from the *New American Bible*.

CONTENTS

PART III
THE MORAL WORLD

PART IV
CONCLUDING ESSAYS

FOREWORD

Timothy O'Connell has done a great service in providing a popular textbook in contemporary Catholic moral theology. This is the first textbook written in the United States which strives to incorporate the recent developments in moral theology. The older textbooks used in Catholic colleges and seminaries before Vatican II were based on the manuals of moral theology. These texts, most often written originally in Latin, came into existence in the seventeenth century and continued as the staple fare in moral theology until very recently.

The differences between O'Connell's work and the former textbooks illustrate the great changes that have occurred in moral theology. Not only the discipline of moral theology but also the life of the Church shows the discussions and disagreements existing in the area of moral theology. These tensions brought about by new developments in moral theology are being experienced throughout the world, but perhaps in the United States the import of these approaches has been felt even more acutely than elsewhere.

Although there is a great difference in the two approaches, the new developments in moral theology did not just appear overnight. In European countries the shift toward the newer approaches began in the 1950s. If one compares the moral theology written in the United States in the 1950s with the moral theology being written in Europe, the differences are startling. Obviously, hindsight gives us a much better vantage point, but in the United States and probably in the whole English-speaking Catholic world there was little or no preparation for the changes which came in so quickly and apparently unexpectedly in the post–Vatican II Church.

There was no writing in the United States in the 1950s comparable to the work being done by Häring, Fuchs, Gilleman, and members of the neo-Thomist school in Europe (all of whom are mentioned and used by O'Connell). In these writings, which themselves are somewhat dependent on earlier developments, one sees the beginnings of the changes that have occurred and have been accepted by many more moral theologians today.

What were the developments which were occurring in Europe in the 1950s and were not yet apparent in the United States?

The very purpose and nature of moral theology was changing. The manuals of moral theology and the periodical literature in the United States in the 1950s viewed moral theology as preparing confessors for the sacrament of penance with a great emphasis on the role of the judge in determining degrees of guilt. Consequently, the emphasis was on specific acts, and whether or not these acts were mortally or venially sinful. The newer European developments saw moral theology as reflecting on the whole life of the Christian including the call to the fullness of love and not merely as addressing the minimum of what constitutes sin. This different perspective greatly influenced the approaches to moral theology.

Perhaps the most significant and fundamental question in moral theology is the model of the Christian life. The manuals generally use a law model which sees the moral life primarily in terms of obedience to law—divine law, natural law, and human law. The Thomist renewal continually rejected a law model and called for the teleological model of Aquinas. Aquinas understood the moral life in the light of the ultimate end of human beings. Those things are good which bring us closer to our ultimate end and those things are wrong which prevent our arriving at the ultimate end. Gilleman insisted on the primacy of charity as the formal element in moral theology and as present in every single moral act. Häring and Fuchs introduced a more relational model. The Christian responds to the gift and call of God. The basic model for understanding the moral life of the Christian is bound to have significant ramifications. The incipient renewal of moral theology in Europe in the 1950s insisted on the intrinsic character of morality as opposed to the extrinsicism of the manuals. For the Thomists, primacy has always been given to reason and not to the will. In such a view, something is commanded because it is good. The will of the legislator must be conformed to the reality itself. For the extrinsicists, something is good because it is commanded.

The act-centered approach of the manuals was also criticized. Christian morality involved more than mere external actions. Again it is obvious that in a law model the external action receives the primary importance. The Thomistic tradition insisted on the importance and significance of the virtues. Every single act for the Christian is a mediation of charity and cannot be reduced merely to an act against the fifth or sixth commandment. Here one finds the seeds of the theory of fundamental option which has become very significant in contemporary moral theology.

The importance of historicity characterizes much of contemporary Catholic moral theology and its emerging importance can be found in the 1950s. Josef Fuchs reminded Catholics of the fact that human nature exists in different periods in the history of salvation. These different historical times give greater flexibility to the concept of nature. Bernard Häring emphasized the concept of *kairos*—the special moment in history which involves an existential call for the Christian believer. Both these authors insist on a true Christian situation ethics which gives more importance to the historical, the temporal, and the individual aspects of Christian existence. Unfortunately, the manuals of theology were based on the human essence or nature which is common to all but failed to recognize this more dynamic, personal element. Häring and others insisted on the fact that all Christians were called to perfection. Thus a more dynamic and personalist moral theology was taking shape.

The moral theology written in Europe in the 1950s also attempted to broaden the sources on which moral theology is based. Most agreed on the need to give greater significance to the Scriptures, for Sacred Scripture must be the soul of all theology. Häring also insisted on the significant connection between liturgy and moral theology. The sacramental encounter symbolizes the personal encounter of God and human beings—the gift of God and the loving response of creatures. In addition, Häring introduced a different philosophical perspective of personalism and value theory. All of these changes have become even more significant in the ensuing years.

These newer developments with their acceptance of historicity set the stage for a more critical approach in moral theology. In the area of Scripture, the acceptance of historicity raised the heremeneutical question. The Scriptures are historically and culturally conditioned. What meaning do they have in a different historical and cultural setting? Once one applies hermeneutic principles to the Scriptures it follows that the teachings of the hierarchical magisterium must be subject to the same type of analysis. Only a few years ago a need for such an interpretation was not acknowledged. Since moral theology deals with anthropology and claims to be based on human nature, the acceptance of historicity calls for an evolving and changing understanding of human existence. All of these factors play an important part in contemporary moral theology.

Yes there are important differences (as well as significant continuity) between the manuals of moral theology and contemporary moral theology. However, the developments in contemporary moral theology were seminally present especially in European moral theology in the 1950s. Unfortunately, in the United States many people were not familiar with these developments although later many of these works were translated into English. American- and English-speaking theologians as well as many people in the Church were therefore caught by surprise when new developments became even more apparent in Catholic moral theology.

Fortunately, in the last few years moral theologians in the United States have been very much aware of and contributing to the ongoing development of moral theology. O'Connell's book is indicative of the work being done in moral theology in general and in the United States. His express aim is to write a textbook in contemporary fundamental moral theology, and he has succeeded admirably. The author recognizes that he is dependent on the recent developments in moral theology, but perhaps he is too modest in assessing his own contribution. Now for the first time there exists a text written in the United States which systematically and coherently brings together the developments in moral theology. O'Connell combines the strength of the manualist tradition—clarity, order, and precision—with the content of the new approaches. Many moral theologians (myself included) will disagree with particular aspects or emphases in this book. However, college students, seminarians, and all engaged in pastoral ministry will profit from this clear and systematic presentation of contemporary moral theology.

CHARLES E. CURRAN
Professor of Moral Theology
Catholic University of America

PREFACE

In the autumn of 1973 I began to teach a course in principles of Catholic morality. And as I began to develop this course, I soon became aware of a major obstacle: the lack of appropriate resources.

It was not that I had no idea of what I wanted to do. Having previously studied the development of one of the major moral theologians of our time, I was conscious of the basic shape of moral theology today. On certain ideas that remain controversial, I had been following and participating in the dialogue in the theological community. And it was certainly not that there was no literature available. If anything, recent years have witnessed a superabundance of writing on the issues in this field. So if one wanted simply to distribute articles to students, there were plenty of articles to choose from.

But articles do not necessarily make an appropriate resource, and that was the problem. The writing that was available to me was episodic and incoherent. On some topics it was extremely repetitive while on others it left many questions unanswered. Different authors used different vocabularies to say the same thing and similar terms with different meanings. In a word, it was the sort of literature that is both interesting and useful *after* one has a general understanding, but is a poor tool for the achievement of that understanding.

What I was looking for was a statement of Christian moral principles that would have three qualities. It would be moderately resonant with contemporary human experience, speaking to the real lives of Christians today and making sense to them. It would be internally consistent, not contradicting itself or presenting its various ideas in a disintegrated way. It would at least attempt to be comprehensive, trying to ask all the important questions and to formulate all the necessary answers. That is what I was looking for. And it did not exist.

This book was conceived, therefore, in the autumn of 1973. As I have continued to teach the course on principles of morality, as I have developed my own ideas on the various topics, and as I have shared my conclusions and dialogued about them with audiences of clergy and laity,

Catholics and Protestants, teachers and college students, as all this has taken place, this book has moved slowly toward birth. It has now arrived, and a few introductory comments are in order.

First of all, while the book clearly exists within the context of contemporary Catholic moral theology, it is a personal synthesis. It is true that many of the insights developed here are derivative, and I have tried to give credit to all those thinkers on whom I depend. But at the same time, the structure and organization of the synthesis as well as a number of the assertions are purely my own. They must therefore stand or fall on their own merits.

Secondly, and following from the above, as a personal synthesis the book tries to blend the worlds of ordinary living and scholarly reflection. It is forthrightly scholarly in the sense that it attempts to deal with and make use of the best work being done today in the science of moral theology. But at the same time, it also attempts to speak plainly and directly about a topic which is, after all, our own lives as we live them. So for the most part, the intramural debates of scholars are relegated to the footnotes. The text itself simply takes a position and seeks to present it clearly and meaningfully.

Thirdly, this direct style is intended to make the book useful to a relatively wide audience. Its ideas are addressed not only to students of theology or to clergy, but also to anyone interested in understanding the living of the Christian life. Just as the ideas of this book have already been presented to widely divergent audiences and have been found helpful, so I hope that offering them in written form will also provide a service.

Fourthly, while it is hoped that this book is an appropriate resource for the academic study of moral theology, it cannot pretend to be an exhaustive resource. Much has been written on the various questions that challenge moral theology today, and many worthwhile and enriching nuances have been developed by various authors. Within the limits of this book it has been impossible to give extended attention to all of these. So again I have had to settle for the modest indications that can be given in footnotes. Many of the notes function as doorways to further study, indicating some of the more important available resources which the reader may wish to investigate, some of the participants in and locations of the ongoing discussions of the various issues we will consider.

Finally, the book deals with principles of *Catholic* morality. And that needs a bit of explaining. I do not mean to adopt a sectarian stance that would make the discussion meaningful only to Catholics. Quite the contrary, when I have shared these ideas with those who are not Catholic, they have found them helpful. I hope that the book will have some ecumenical import, too. But at the same time, we all think about life in ways that are influenced by our traditions, by the perspectives we habitually adopt, by the questions we have learned to deem most important. So it seems only fair to acknowledge that in the case of this book the fundamental commitments that color the way our topic is handled are those of a Roman Catholic. This may mean that some issues are pursued which are of little interest to non-Catholic readers, but it should also mean that such a reader has here an opportunity to discover the style and content of Catholic moral theology today.

Among the many debts I hold for the development of this book, at least a few must be enumerated. First in importance and in appreciation are my colleagues on the faculty of St. Mary of the Lake Seminary. Their vision of the intimate link between theology and ministry, and of the accountability of each to the other, has permanently shaped the perspective out of which I work. Of those colleagues, Rev. Michael Place has earned my particular gratitude for his support, challenge, and continuing theological dialogue. I am grateful, too, to my students, who endured reading earlier drafts of most of these chapters, whose suggestions were always helpful, and whose occasional frank admissions of total confusion sent me back to the typewriter anew. My thanks to Mr. Michael Leach and Mr. Frank Oveis of The Seabury Press, who have been both conscientious and kind in facilitating the publication of this book. Finally, I am indebted to Mrs. Dorothy Hatton, whose skillful and efficient secretarial assistance greatly expedited this project.

PART I

INTRODUCTORY ESSAYS

1

THE MEANING OF
MORAL THEOLOGY

A s the title of this book indicates, our topic is Catholic morality. And
since the reflections which we shall pursue will seek to be systematic
and intelligent, we will actually be involved in moral philosophy; or, since
they will be the reflections of believers based on a fundamental religious
commitment, in moral theology.

But to call this project a presentation of moral theology perhaps raises
more questions than it answers. For both theology in general and moral
theology in particular are understood in many different ways today. By
some people they are not understood at all. So the starting point of this
book must include some account of what we mean, and do not mean, by
these terms. This, in turn, will lead to a clearer definition of the project of
this book.

Theology's Task
This is certainly not the place for a full-scale treatise on the science of
theology. Whole books have been written on the subject.[1] But perhaps a
few brief remarks will be helpful.

Jean Daniélou has observed that Christians often confuse the two terms
"religion" and "revelation."[2] Religion is the term we use to denote all those
efforts of human beings to touch the transcendent, to contact and appease
the divinity. Revelation, on the other hand, indicates divine initiative, the
actions of God by which he approaches and touches us. Thus understood,
says Daniélou, Christianity is not so much a religion as a revelation. It
proclaims not human searching but divine salvation, not human effort but
divine gift. And it celebrates that ongoing revelation-presence of God
himself.

But if Christianity is essentially revelation, God's action and not ours, that does not eliminate the need for human involvement. Quite the contrary, inasmuch as revelation was humanly articulated from the beginning, and inasmuch as it must be humanly transmitted as time goes on, the human contribution is utterly essential.

First, it was humanly articulated from the beginning. If we understand the primeval revelation of the Father to be Jesus himself, then we must take seriously the fact that he came among us humanly. That means concretely, specifically, with all the particularities of time, place, and situation. Jesus was not "man" in some general and undifferentiated sense. Indeed, to give him only this vague and unspecified sort of humanity is to deny him any humanity at all. The flesh of human living exists only in concreteness and particularity; it exists only here or there, now or then, in this way or in that. Thus, if we are truly to understand the Jesus of revelation, we must pursue the human task of understanding, in all its specificity, the cultural and personal situation in which he lived. If we understand revelation to be the words of Scripture, then it is even more apparent that a human, cultural task of understanding will be required. Indeed, the whole science of biblical exegesis is premised on the fact that we can only understand the texts of Scripture if we understand the language in which they were written, the cultural and historical context, the philosophical and religious presuppositions of their human authors, the current literary conventions, the prevailing metaphors and symbol systems, and so on. If the Scriptures are God's revelation, still they are that revelation as humanly articulated. And thus the human task of discernment cannot be avoided.

Secondly, a human contribution is demanded by the need to humanly transmit revelation as time goes on. In either of the conceptions of revelation mentioned above, Jesus himself or the Scriptures, it is clear that we are dealing with a culture different from our own. And just as Jesus could not be "man" in some general and undifferentiated sense, just as the words of Scripture could not speak their truth in some uncultured and universal language, so also we cannot share the Good News of revelation with our time and our place in that vague form. Rather we must deal with the concreteness of the present as well as the concreteness of the past. Thus the believing human community stands forever charged with the duty of translating the truth of revelation into new languages, new symbol systems, images, and metaphors.

This task of translation, of reconstituting the inner meaning of revelation for successive audiences, belongs to theology. In fact, theology can be defined as the science which seeks to understand and forever to rearticulate the life-giving Good News of God in Christ Jesus. That is the definition that will be presupposed in this book. But if we accept that definition, several things follow.

Consequences

First, it is obvious that theology is an essential function within the Church. For the Church to fulfill its mandate to "proclaim the good news to all creation" (Mk 16:15), it must continually restate that Good News. That is, it must "do" theology. Therefore, the ministry of theology and of the theologian is a service the Church cannot do without. St. Paul declared that "God has set up in the church first apostles, second prophets, third teachers . . . " (1 Cor 12:28). And history has borne him out. The pastoral leadership in the Church, the pope and the college of bishops, comes first. But that is not sufficient. There is need also for those especially trained in the human understanding and translation of the Good News. There is need for teachers, for theologians, to serve the Church.[3]

Second, it follows from our definition of theology that all Christian believers are theologians. Inasmuch as all the members of the Church must, of human necessity, express to themselves the meaning of their inner experience of faith, they are involved in the theological enterprise. One sometimes hears a dichotomized description of Christian experience: that theology is somehow peripheral and that "we will avoid theology and simply speak the truths of revelation." But of course that cannot be. To "speak" revelation is to "do" theology; that is, it is to make use of language, cultural vision, and so on. Therefore, all the words of faith that are spoken within the Church are theological words. The difference between the ordinary member of the Church and the theologian, then, is a difference in degree and not in kind. It is a matter of scientific sophistication and not of fundamentally different tasks.

Third, our definition makes clear that theology is a sort of bridge between revelation and culture. In pursuing its objective of translation, then, theology must constantly seek to be faithful to both, to remain fully established on both shores. To lose touch with the ground of revelation experienced in faith is to have nothing to say, or even worse, to misguide the listener with that which is false. Equally true, to lose touch with the canons of the culture is not to be heard, or even worse, to be misunderstood. The challenge of theology, therefore, and of all Christians insofar as they "speak" theology, is to speak both from deep faith and from broad cultural sensitivity.[4]

Fourth, defining theology as the science of understanding and rearticulating makes clear that there is no such thing as a "perennial theology." To be sure, the central faith-insights which theology seeks to express are perennial. But inasmuch as theological expressions are culturally derived and directed, they are subject to all the laws of life and death which are the fate of human cultures. Theologies, like societies, are born, they live, and they die. As people change, so theology must change. Thus, what is perennial about theology is not its formulations, but rather its critically important task.

Finally, and following from all that has been said thus far, our definition suggests that the real goal of theology, its objective in all that it does, is not truth but meaning. It is not truth as if truth could be achieved once and for all, as if truth could be grasped and articulated in a way that transcends all the limitations of time and culture. Rather it is meaning, truth as understood, truth as effectively communicated, truth not only as sincerely given but also as successfully received. The goal of theology is meaning. Not some cheap relevance that is achieved at the price of falsehood, of course, but that real meaning which is the appropriate incarnation of the perennial inner truth of faith in the passing flesh of particular cultures.

Theology's Divisions

As theology has pursued this task over the centuries, however, it has demonstrated a perduring concern with two different agendas. On the one hand, it has attempted to discern the meaning of the gift of God which is the Good News of revelation. And on the other hand, it has sought to discover what this gift means for the conduct of our daily lives. To put this another way, theology has reflected on revelation both as a gift to and a challenge for the human person.

This double understanding of revelation is not surprising. Even human experiences of self-revelation always include these two moments. On the one hand, an offer of the self to another. And on the other hand, an implicit call for response, for acceptance and appreciation and reciprocity. So if it is true that the God of revelation is also the God who created this human world, it is not surprising that a similar dialectic should be discerned in divine revelation as well.

Be that as it may, it is a fact that theology has always had this twin focus. It has even structured itself along these lines, dividing into dogmatic theology and moral theology, or systematic theology and Christian ethics.[5] These two subsciences have related in different ways at different times, as we shall see in the next chapter. But they have always existed in some form or other, and they have always related in some fashion or other.[6]

Moral Theology

Moral theology, then, is that portion of the theological enterprise which attempts to discern the implications of revelation for human behavior, to answer the question: "How ought we, who have been gifted by God, to live?" In answering this question, moral theology has itself discovered a

double focus. On the one hand, there are questions about the general shape
of the Christian life. What does it mean to live as a Christian? How shall
we understand all the moral terms we use: right and wrong, good and evil,
sin and virtue? What is an appropriate strategy for responding to the
divine challenge? And on the other hand, there are any number of questions about specific areas of living. What is appropriate behavior for the
Christian in such areas as justice, respect for life, truth-telling, property
rights, sexuality?

From the beginning, then, moral theology has included concerns both
general and concrete. Indeed, in the course of Catholic tradition, these
eventually evolved into two treatises, General Moral Theology (*De principiis*) and Special Moral Theology (*De preceptis*). And while these two need
to be continually and carefully related, they are at least logically distinct.
This present volume will concern itself only with the first of these. That is,
it will be concerned with the principles of Christian morality.

But even General Moral Theology implicitly contains two different
agendas. And it is important to note these since they will dictate the shape
and order of the chapters which will follow.

In seeking to understand the basic shape of the Christian moral life, one
can direct one's attention either inward or outward. One can ask questions
about the moral agent or about moral action. On the one hand, one can
inquire about who we are when we seek to respond to the Good News.
What really constitutes that authentic response? What is the significance of
human knowledge and freedom? How do we go about choosing our response? How does the reality of conscience fit into all this? What is the real
meaning of sin and virtue? In a word, who is the moral person? And on the
other hand, one can investigate the outer world of moral behavior with an
eye to discerning its general characteristics and dynamics. What makes an
action right or wrong? What is the place of law in a Christian ethic? What
of moral values and norms? Are they real? Objective? Unchanging? What
of all the human laws that confront us? In a word, what is the moral
world?

Resources

These are the two agendas that will occupy our attention in these pages.
And as we deal with each in turn, we shall make use of a number of
resources.

To be sure, our immediate sources in many cases will be the insights of
the community of contemporary theologians into the nature of the moral
person and the moral world. But their insights do not carry some arbitrary
weight of authority; they are only as strong as their arguments. So, really,
our major source will be human wisdom itself. Whatever meaning can be
found in the thoughts of those theologians, and of this present writer, will

be exploited and synthesized. An attempt will be made to integrate these ideas, to produce a coherent whole that at the same time speaks to the contemporary experience of responding to the Lord.

Equally important as a resource will be the insights of scholars in other fields of study. At times, for example, we will be interested in the data of the social sciences. For if the resonance of our synthesis with the experience of people will be a benchmark of our success, so also the shape of their experience will be a guide for our reflections. Interpretations of experience by theoretical social scientists and philosophers will also play a significant role. For they will reveal to us the self-understanding of contemporary humankind, an understanding which cannot just be uncritically accepted, but which cannot be ignored either. Finally, even the data and theories of the physical sciences will occasionally be of use.

But wisdom and insight are by no means the sole possession of our age. So, as we proceed, we shall also give considerable attention to our past as a Christian community. As was noted in the Preface, we hope to avoid a narrowly sectarian outlook in these pages. Much wisdom is to be found in the past and present of all the Christian communions, and we will try to make use of it all. We will try to listen to the convictions and values of past ages of disciples of the Lord, to discern their significance for our time and to incorporate them into a contemporary statement. In so doing, we will try to accept the warning that those who do not learn from history are doomed to repeat it. And, of course, given the perspective of our study, we will particularly be concerned to listen to the statements of the Roman Catholic magisterium and of that Church's theologians through the centuries.

A fourth resource for our project will be the Scriptures. The Bible is the charter document of the Church, after all. As inspired, it is a sort of privileged theology which puts us in especially close contact with the truth of revelation. So we shall be quite concerned to listen to its moral proclamations, to try to understand them, and to translate them for our time.

Finally, moral theology always remains rooted in dogmatic theology. Just as our vision of revelation made clear that the task is always grounded in the gift, so these two branches of theology must always be related. While the limits of this current project will not allow the development of a comprehensive dogmatic theory, we will draw on dogmatics as we pursue our own objectives.

Structure of the Book
On the basis of everything said thus far, we can now state clearly the way in which the principles for a Catholic morality will be developed.

The three last-named resources, history, Scripture, and dogmatics, will play a role throughout these pages. But they surely deserve more than passing attention. What is more, their contribution to our project is not only in terms of content but also of context. So the remainder of Part I will look to each of these in turn. What can they tell us that will help to specify our task and guide the direction of our reflections?

In Part II we shall give our concentrated attention to the moral person. And in Part III we shall turn outward to consider the shape and dynamics of the moral world. Finally, a number of conclusions will be offered in Part IV.

As we pursue each of these topics, we shall have in mind that the goal and criterion of theology is meaning. Indeed, if meaning is central to theology in general, it is even more so in the case of moral theology. For in talking about the moral person we are talking about ourselves; in seeking to understand the moral world, we are attending to our world. So, surely, the ultimate test of our discussions will be whether they are meaningful, in the best sense of the word. Do they seem faithful to our experience of revelation, of God gifting and challenging us in our lives? Do they speak in terms which resonate with our human experience, with our own particular cultural presuppositions and perspectives?

This book is ultimately about us. Thus, only if these questions can be answered in the affirmative will we really have achieved principles for a Catholic morality.

2

The History of Moral Theology

Children have always asked the question: "Where did I come from?" As they have begun to experience themselves as persons, they have realized that their roots are part of their identity. Of course, the issue of one's roots can be addressed at various levels and in various ways; a child's question is quite different from an adult's. But one way or another, to one degree or another, the question always seems to present itself.

The question of one's history is also relevant to the transpersonal world of ideas and cultures and institutions. Where did we come from? Where did these ways of understanding, of living and functioning, come from? Why are we the way we are today? And just as the personal question cannot be avoided, neither can this corporate questioning.

At least it can be avoided only at high cost. For to the extent that we do not understand our past, we really do not understand our present, and we are less prepared to intelligently construct our future. So the purpose of this chapter is to sketch the broad outlines of our ethical history. We want to try to understand the historical reasons for the way Catholic moral theology has developed and for the way it expresses itself today. We want to see, at least in a general way, the path by which we have come to the present. We want to recognize that foundation on which, of necessity, our future must somehow be constructed.[1]

Patristic Era

The writing on moral topics in the first 500 years of the Church's history is fascinating, both because it represents the initial understandings of Christian theology and because it bears so many similarities to the reflections of our own time. From the very beginning a concern with the behavioral implications of the Gospel proclamation manifested itself. The *Didache* (c. A. D. 75) begins with a portrayal of the "two ways," the way of virtue and the way of evil, and challenges the listener to a deep conversion. But this ethical concern did not result in any comprehensive moral systems, let alone any single, universally accepted system. Rather, the writing of the period was characterized by a desire to respond to the concrete needs of the community in a way that is still authentic to the core of the Christian faith.

This dialectic of faith and experience was differently handled by various authors. Clement of Alexandria (d. 216) exhibited a rather optimistic vision of life, a willingness to integrate the Gospel truth with the insights of the pagan world. He viewed pagan wisdom as "so many seeds strewn by the Logos,"[2] and thus expected a fundamental continuity between experience and revelation. Clement was not above dealing with concrete issues; at one point he described in detail the typical day of the Christian with its various ethical challenges. But even in such discussions he revealed a humanistic and optimistic perspective.

In contrast, Origen (d. 253) was much more negative. It is true that he was an educated man, in touch with pagan knowledge and willing to make use of it. Indeed, it was Origen who first used the classic concept of the cardinal virtues in Christian theology. But even so, one discerns in his discussions of sin, of human freedom, and of the meaning of salvation a relatively pessimistic view of human life. As a representative in theology of the burgeoning monastic movement, of the concern for "white martyrdom," Origen was much more inclined to dichotomize the life of Christian faith and the life of the world.[3]

A century later a landmark book was written by Ambrose, the Bishop of Milan (d. 397). His *De officiis* followed the lead of Cicero in both title and area of concern. While contextualizing his reflections with the vision of Christian faith and doctrine, Ambrose addressed himself to the myriad "duties" of the believer. And he sought to articulate these moral responsibilities in a concrete way that presaged the works of casuistry that would flourish 1300 years later. Perhaps we might call Ambrose the first of the Christian casuists.

Most notable of the patristic figures, however, is Ambrose's disciple, Augustine of Hippo (d. 430). Augustine is a compelling, and at the same time rather confusing, representative of the early Church. Some have called him one of the greatest moral theologians of all time.[4] Others note the negative influence of his rigorist, perhaps subtly Manichean perspective on later Church teaching.[5] All this is debated despite the fact that he never attempted to develop a coherent and inclusive system of moral theory. Instead, Augustine's style (and it is a characteristic of the era) was to range far and wide across the spectrum of theological concepts and human concerns. He sketched his personal theological vision in his *Confessions*, he developed his understanding of the world in *City of God*, and he wrote shorter works on such diverse ethical topics as lying, widowhood, and especially sexual ethics.

If Augustine does not demand our attention because of his systematic approach, he does because of the shape of his thought. He addressed himself to the perennial underlying issues of ethics: the relationship of faith and works, of grace and freedom, of sin and virtue. He focused on the centrality of love in the Christian life. He utilized a rather psychological, introspective, and inductive approach to the development of ethical insight. And in all these ways he revealed himself as a fundamentally modern Christian thinker.[6]

Sixth Century

In the history of Christian theology the sixth century marks an important watershed. The Christian faith had emerged from its minority status and had become the commitment of the masses. It had become the officially espoused religion of the state, and its theological vision and pastoral approach had to be appropriately adjusted.

One of the more significant elements of that adjustment was the change in practice as regards the Sacrament of Reconciliation. During the Patristic era this sacrament had been relatively rare. Its use was limited to the confession of truly major sins, lengthy penances were required before absolution, and the penitent was not allowed to return to the sacrament with any frequency. During the sixth century, however, this practice changed. Particularly in Ireland and through the ministry of the Celtic monks, the confession of sin became more private and more frequent, a much more comprehensive variety of sins were submitted to the confessor, and penances began to be fulfilled after absolution. In a word, then, the Sacrament of Reconciliation became much more an ongoing component of the Christian life.

This, however, had immediate implications for moral theology. For it was presumed that the penances should fit the particularities of the sins confessed. Therefore, some systematic reflection on the nature of sin, its varieties, and on the demands of retributive justice was required. Moreover, at this time the level of clerical education was notably low, with the result that priests could not generally be trusted to make unguided judgments in these matters. As a result, there emerged at this time a series of compendiums known as Penitential Books.

These were not really works of theology. Even less were they descriptions of the ideals to be sought in the Christian life. Rather they were simply lists of typical sins along with an indication of the appropriate penance in each case. But despite their modest intent, these books exercised a far-reaching influence on the future of moral theology.

For one thing, the Penitential Books were addressed to priest-confessors.

Thus began the rather unhealthy identification of moral theology both with the Sacrament of Penance and with priests. This presumption that moral theology is primarily for priests has survived to our own time, and only recently has it been challenged. Secondly, the very specific purpose of these books inevitably led to the association of moral theology with Christian minimalism. That is, the very existence of lists such as those in the Penitential Books tempted the Christian world to conclude that virtuous and faithful living consisted in the *avoidance* of the sins mentioned therein and that successful avoidance of these sins justified *confidence* in one's moral righteousness. There was, or appeared to be, no reason to "walk the extra mile." Thirdly, the specific association of penance with sin encouraged an approach to Christian forgiveness that emphasized not mercy but justice. Absolution became more a matter of retribution. And thus the focus on the loving kindness of God, while never lost, was quite overshadowed. Finally, the Penitential Books contributed to an emphasis on the importance of the individual act, an emphasis that remains today. We shall consider this emphasis in great detail in this book, and we shall attempt to downplay it by locating the act in its broader context. But before any of that, it is important to note how this act orientation, the urge to fragment the Christian life into its smallest possible components, developed. And the Penitential Books played a significant role in that development.

Tenth to Twelfth Centuries

Shortly after the passing of the first millenium, the character of European culture underwent a significant change, and that change had considerable influence on the progress of moral theology. This was the era of the rise of the great European universities. Centers of learning proliferated and the quality of education greatly improved. It was still Catholic Europe of course, and thus theology held a central place in these new universities. But if theology influenced the academic scene, it is also true that the academic world influenced theology.

Systematic thought was the order of the day; the urge was to integrate, summarize, and logically articulate. This approach became the approach of theology as well. It was the era of the Summas, those great constructs of systematic theology, those attempts to proclaim the Gospel in a philosophically consistent and logically compelling manner. And among those who contributed to this development, two in particular deserve our attention.

One was the Franciscan, Bonaventure (d. 1274). His fundamental commitment was still to the Platonic tradition which had prevailed in the centuries before, and out of that perspective he developed a brilliant synthesis of Christian theology and morality. For Bonaventure, the central characteristic of people was their will, their power to decide and to act.

The intellect, while extremely important, was in the order of means, a tool to be used for action. Indeed, Bonaventure declared that the purpose of all theology was "not merely to serve contemplation, but also to make us holy. In fact its first purpose is to make us holy."[7] And even in his discussion of the intellect he emphasized the "practical intellect" as our highest achievement.

Bonaventure had no separate presentation of moral theology; that was not the style in the age of the Summas. But for the reasons mentioned above, his theological synthesis was an amiable contribution to later reflections on that reality.

The other figure was Thomas Aquinas (d. 1274). Aquinas, the Dominican, holds unparalleled fame in Catholic theology, and for many wise reasons. In his time the writings of Aristotle were being rediscovered; and it was Aquinas who especially demonstrated the aptness of that philosophy for the articulation of Christian theology. For Aquinas, as for Aristotle, humans were preeminently intellectual beings, rational animals. And their highest achievement was precisely that contemplation which Bonaventure played down. Theology was for understanding; it was a pure science in the service of pure truth. It is clear, then, that Aquinas would have no place for a separate science of moral theology. The isolation of behavior from truth was precisely what he opposed. But to say this is not to say that he was disinterested in ethical questions. By no means.

On the one hand, the method espoused by Aquinas led surely to an attempt to understand the Christian life; our understanding of ourselves and of our behavior was an important component of our attempt to understand God. And on the other hand, once the Gospel was heard and understood, it was clear that a responsive life-style was demanded. So Aquinas was quite willing to discuss the specifics of that life-style. Indeed, the whole *Pars Secunda* of his *Summa Theologiae* is a sort of treatise on moral theology, dealing first with general concepts (I-II) and then with specific ethical topics (II-II). But for our purposes the important point is that these ethical discussions were incorporated into the overall synthesis of Christian theology and not isolated in any way.

To a certain extent this integration of dogmatics and ethics characteristic of both Aquinas and Bonaventure is also characteristic of the whole of the High Middle Ages. There was no compartmentalizing of theological components, no isolating of faith and action, no dichotomizing of grace and nature. Reality was viewed holistically, theology was developed holistically. And in writings such as the Summas, this integrating perspective yielded a rich and clearly contextualized moral theology.

Fourteenth to Sixteenth Centuries
Shortly after the deaths of Aquinas and Bonaventure, there began a process of change and development which can hardly be overestimated in its

influence on moral theology. The first step in the process was marked by two highly significant changes in the theological situation.

On the one hand, the philosophical context shifted radically. The high Scholasticism of the thirteenth century devolved, in the fourteenth, into a nominalistic vision of reality. The conviction that the human person was capable of distilling concepts, universal notions that capture and represent the real essence of things, was replaced by a skepticism in this regard. Philosophers such as Ockham (d. 1349) became convinced that there were no such essences, that the human person did not achieve universal concepts. Rather it was the uniqueness of each existing thing that was the object of human intellectual attention. The only way in which one could move beyond the unique existent was by a somewhat arbitrary process of "collection." Nominalists willingly conceded that it was common practice to grant various groupings of objects a general and inclusive name. But in their judgment these names were simply that and nothing more. There is no essence or nature "tree." We simply group various unique existing things and *call* them "trees." For nominalists, reality is fundamentally discontinuous.

This philosophical development was ethically important because it rendered useless the attempt to discuss the nature of the Christian life and to predict intrinsically good or intrinsically bad acts. Where there is utter uniqueness there is no tool of predictability. And where that tool is lacking, there can ultimately be no useful objective component to ethical decision-making. In fact, the consequence of a nominalist epistemology is complete ethical individualism. My situation is utterly unique, and I am an utterly unique person. Hence, only I can judge what I must do; and even I can only judge in the midst of the experience. If society finds itself threatened by this individualism, it has only one alternative: the arbitrary imposition of law. Society cannot attempt to impose demonstrably rational guides for action. For these presume the existence of universals and essences. So it can only have recourse to power, to the naked demand for conformity. Thus, if the immediate consequence of nominalism is individualism, its eventual consequence is legalism.[8]

The other highly significant change in the theological situation of the time was economic. This was the period in which medieval feudalism was giving way to an emerging structure of middle-class commerce. The exchange of goods and services greatly increased, individual mobility became more common, and thus a quantity and variety of relationships among strangers became necessary. In this situation, it was no longer sufficient to appeal to the duties of fraternity to justify correct behavior. Instead, it became necessary to articulate the precise demands of justice, to specify with great accuracy what one is due. As a result, traditional Christian virtues such as love, fidelity, and piety came to be neglected as justice and equity were emphasized. And a certain moral minimalism was inevitable.

These two developments, the philosophical and the commercial, combined to give fifteenth-century morality a peculiar flavor. Law was celebrated as central to moral thinking and living, and was seen as a tool for expressing the necessary minimum, for establishing rights and duties in such a way as to regulate the rapidly multiplying relationships within the European community. There was a pragmatic and utilitarian tone that, while somehow surprising, is in retrospect completely understandable.

Into this situation, then, came one of the most influential figures in the history of Christendom: Martin Luther (1483–1546). Luther the monk, Luther the Christian tortured by personal feelings of inadequacy and sinfulness, Luther the student of St. Paul. This Martin Luther entered a Christian situation that was far removed from the Gospel ideal. The situation emphasized justice, and Luther was convinced that no one is just. The situation emphasized the law, and Luther shared Paul's distrust of law. The situation focused on minimums, and Luther felt driven to perfection. The situation cherished good works, and Luther placed his trust in faith.

We are, of course, sketching with a broad brush events that included innumerable subtleties. But for our purposes it may suffice to become conscious of the polarities. For they indicate the shape of the response to Luther. When the Church finally formulated its Counter-Reformation in the Council of Trent, it was faced with a full-scale rebellion. Much of Europe had been lost to the Church, and the first priority was to establish the lines of demarcation with clarity. The placement of those lines has influenced moral theology down to our own times.

In a situation of such total conflict the council, and the Church, may be forgiven for an overwhelming emphasis upon the practicalities of behavior. This was not the time for leisurely theological or philosophical discussions; like any time of war, it left little time for speculation. Action was required; unanimity and uniformity were necessities. Thus the response of the council had those characteristics.

For one thing seminaries were established. For the first time in the history of the Church a clear and formal system for the education of clergy was developed. Clergy were to be isolated from the crises and turbulence of the day. They were to be provided with clear and concise directions for their ministry. They were to be inculcated with loyalty and a willingness to obey.

For another thing, the kind of education provided seminarians was to emphasize the *behavior* necessary for the Catholic. It was important to know what to do, and those areas of theology which indicated the proper action were to be highlighted. And thus, again for the first time in the history of the Church, the separate science of moral theology emerged. No longer was it merely a matter of reflecting on the truths of the faith and, in the course of this, taking note of their behavioral implications. Now it was a matter of directly and extensively specifying the requirements of the Christian life.

For a third thing, when this separate moral theology emerged, it took on a specific character. It, too, was expected to emphasize the concrete, the objective, the necessary and required. And thus, as moral theology became separated from its roots in dogmatic theology, it became affiliated with that other science dedicated to these qualities, namely canon law. It was the law that indicated most clearly what one must do; and so it was completely reasonable to graft moral theology onto law, to give them the intimacy of sister sciences. This integration was done so completely and so successfully that, even to our day, textbooks of Christian ethics have borne the title *Theologia moralis ad normam juris canonici* (Moral theology according to the norm of canon law).[9]

Seventeenth and Eighteenth Centuries

The consolidation of the post-Reformation period did not, of course, bring to an end the questioning that has always characterized moral theology. But it did establish the terms in which that questioning took place. Throughout the centuries after Luther, the issue was predominantly one of the precise meaning of the law. What, exactly, is the right thing to do? What is the minimum expected of the Catholic Christian? How can one permit a certain amount of legitimate Christian freedom while at the same time protecting the supremacy of objective moral demand? What is the proper response to a situation in which the demands of the law are in doubt?

Questions such as these were hotly debated by moralists. At the one extreme a Jansenist rigorism was proposed; at the other (and partly in reaction to Jansenism), a laxist preoccupation with freedom. And all these debates eventually led to the development of a variety of moral systems for the responsible resolution of ethical doubts. Of these systems, perhaps the best known today is "probabilism," the system which held that when there is a genuine division of expert opinion on a specific moral issue—and therefore two probable (reasonable) opinions—one may feel free to follow the more lenient opinion. And this even if the lenient opinion is held only by a minority of the experts.

One of the major figures in the debates of the time was Alphonsus Liguori (1696–1787). Alphonsus is notable in the history of moral theology not precisely because he was creative or innovative, but rather because he was a prudent man, able to formulate balanced, reasonable, and humane opinions. In the midst of a morass of disagreements, with zealots on all questions, Alphonsus was a beacon of reason, of common sense, in the eighteenth century. Although he actually supported "equiprobabilism," a slightly more strict alternative to probabilism, his commitment to prudent moderation made him a model for moral theology up until the very recent past.

Alphonsus is also significant because his moral method, noting the various opinions and then seeking to walk a prudent middle course, modeled an ethical style that has perdured. That style is exemplified in the "manuals," textbooks which summarize the prudent and reasonable position on the various issues of the time. Manuals were largely designed for the use of seminarians, and they were clearly oriented toward the application of moral theology in the confessional. But while they were in some ways conservative documents, greatly dependent upon arguments from authority, they were also somehow pastoral. For given the legalistic premise that prevailed, there was a great tendency to multiply laws to the point of completely eliminating the reality of Christian freedom. In this context, manuals often functioned as voices of reason, guiding the confessor away from the extremes and toward the moderate position. They prevented the priests of the day from arbitrarily imposing unreasonable demands on their people and instead protected a certain gentle and patient spirit in moral theology.

Still, one could hardly celebrate the manuals as paradigms of profound moral theology. They were simply too much creatures of their own philosophical, theological, and cultural milieu for that. And so eventually a move away from the manuals was to be expected, a fundamental renewal of moral theology was required.

Nineteenth and Twentieth Centuries
When that renewal of moral theology began, it had its start at the University of Tübingen, in Germany. Perhaps the first significant figure in the renewal was John Michael Sailer, Bishop of Ratisbon (1750–1832). He was soon followed by John Baptist Hirscher (1788–1865). These two figures, and the school they represented, were greatly influenced by the revival of scriptural studies in Germany. And in light of those new scriptural insights they began to question not specific moral teachings, but rather the whole style of moral theology. They issued a call for a more kerygmatic moral teaching, with emphasis upon the inner realities of conversion and discipleship. They pointed out the essential link between Christian morality and Christian spirituality. They participated in the revival of interest in the Fathers of the Church, and particularly Augustine. Noticing patristic themes that resonated with the science of psychology developing in northern Europe, they called for increased psychological sensitivity in moral theology. Finally, and perhaps most importantly, they demanded a reunification of moral theology and dogmatic theology; they sought to reestablish the truly theological roots of Christian ethics.

This renewal did not achieve hegemony with any speed. Such political realities as the First Vatican Council, the Syllabus of Errors, and the mood of suspicion that separated Italians and Germans made this impossible. But it did continue, and at a slow and painful rate it developed. In the early years of this century theologians continued to develop their ideas of moral theology. Such individuals as Joseph Mausbach (1861–1931) and Th. Steinbüchel (1888–1949) made significant contributions. And when German theologians Bernard Häring (1912–) and Josef Fuchs (1912–) assumed their posts at two Roman universities (the Alphonsianum and the Gregorian, respectively) the widespread dissemination of these ideas was assured.

Conclusion

To say this, however, is not to say that the renewal of moral theology has been completed. Quite the contrary. If anything, it has just begun. Perhaps it is because institutions are, by instinct, more conservative about behavior than about intellectual doctrines. Or maybe it is because a renewed moral theology must depend upon (and await) renewals in scriptural and dogmatic studies. But the fact is that Christian ethics continues to lag behind the other theological disciplines in renewal and renovation.

In large part, the fundamental renewal of scriptural sciences took place in the early part of this century. Even the development of dogmatic theology was well advanced before the Second Vatican Council. Indeed, in many ways the Council was the ratification and implementation of that development in terms of the theology of revelation, Church, culture, and liturgy. But in the area of moral theology this is not the case. The council said very little about moral theology; and when it did speak, its words had much more the tone of a call for renewal to come than of a ratification of tasks completed. Consider these words which, significantly, appear in the *Decree on Priestly Formation:*

> Special attention needs to be given to the development of moral theology. Its scientific exposition should be more thoroughly nourished by scriptural teaching. It should show the nobility of the Christian vocation of the faithful, and their obligation to bring forth fruit in charity for the life of the world. (art. 16)

Hence the moment at which we find ourselves in moral theology is a moment of beginning. It is not the time for complete new systems. Even less is it a time for the repetition of old formulas. It is a time to mine the past for useful and helpful insights. And it is a time to begin to reformulate and rearticulate the perennial truths of the Christian life. It is a time to ask hard questions, and it is a time to attempt tentative but internally coherent answers to those questions.

And that, of course, is the goal of this book.

3

ELEMENTS OF
A BIBLICAL MORALITY

At various points in this book we shall take the time to look into Scripture and to investigate the biblical testimony on specific topics. But before we even begin to do that, a more general task demands our attention. What sort of an ethical *flavor* does the Bible present? What sort of approach to ethical issues does it dictate? These are the questions which concern us here.

They are not easy questions to answer, however. For one thing, it is axiomatic that the Bible does not provide us with any one ethical system. The ethical ideas to be found in Sacred Scripture are not comprehensive and integral as those of a philosophical system might be. Nor are they even consistent. One might possibly be able to speak of the "ethics of" Hosea or Jeremiah, Luke or Paul. But as soon as one moves beyond generalities it is clear that one cannot speak of the "ethics of" the Bible.

Another reason, related to the first, why our questions will not be easy to answer is the sheer quantity of biblical materials. Questions of behavior, and the issues of ethical and religious vision that underlie them, arise continually in the pages of Scripture. Volumes have been written analyzing this material, and thus any attempt at exhaustive treatment here is doomed to failure.

We will therefore set ourselves a modest goal. Selecting our materials in an almost arbitrary way, we shall try to gain an appreciation of at least some of the themes and perspectives of the biblical authors. We shall try to develop a *sense* of their approach to the personal and perennial challenges of the ethical life. Thus we shall hope to achieve, to some useful degree, a frame of reference for our own ethical reflections.[1]

Covenant

In some ways, the axis for the entire story of ancient Israel was the notion, and the reality, of "covenant." From the first bond between Yahweh and Abraham (Gn 15:18) through the time of Moses and the Sinai experience (Ex 34:10) and on into the era of the prophets, the mystery of covenant was a recurring theme. Not some cold-blooded contract, but an intimate and very personal reality. For the Israelite, to covenant with another party was, in some ways, to join families. Indeed, one's obligations to a covenant partner were second only to the responsibilities of immediate family life. Covenant did not mean that one agreed to do this *thing* for or with another; it meant that one agreed to be responsible for the person himself or herself in this and any other context.

All of this is exemplified in one of the classic formulations of the Israelite covenant with Yahweh: "They shall be my people and I will be their God" (Jer 24:7; Ez 11:20; cf., also, Jer 7:23, 11:4; Ez 14:11; Hos 2:25). Scholars tell us that this formulation was nothing more than an adaptation of a common text of the marriage vow: "She is my wife and I am her husband this day and forever." The reality of this covenant was that Yahweh was marrying his people, assuming that kind of responsibility for them and expecting that kind of fidelity in return. It was not a relationship of convenience or efficiency; it was a relationship of intimate and genuine love.

Indeed, the emphasis on intimacy and inner authenticity grew in the writings of the prophets. Jeremiah declared: "The days are coming . . . when I will make a new covenant. . . . I will place my law within them, and write it upon their hearts; I will be their God, and they shall be my people" (Jer 31:31ff). And Ezekiel proclaimed: "I will give you a new heart . . . taking from your bodies your stony hearts and giving you natural hearts. . . . You shall live in the land I gave your fathers; you shall be my people, and I will be your God" (Ez 36:26ff).

And finally we should note that the idea of covenant continued to be important in much of the New Testament writing. All four of the Last Supper narratives, though they varied in other ways, were one in pointing out the function of "new covenant" (Mt 26; Mk 14; Lk 22; 1 Cor 11), while John seems to have "rescheduled" his passion narrative to make the death of Jesus coincide with the moment of the Passover covenant sacrifices.[2]

Kingdom

Jesus, for his part, does not seem to have laid primary emphasis on the idea of covenant. Instead, as Rudolph Schnackenburg points out, the central focus of Jesus' preaching seems to have been the "kingdom."[3] Indeed, inasmuch as this term is very common in the Synoptics and yet is quite rare in the other books of the New Testament, there can be little doubt that it goes back to Jesus himself. And so as we move out of a predominantly Old Testament context and begin to focus our attention upon the moral themes of the New Testament, perhaps we should begin with this idea.

But we must be clear about the meaning of the term. The Greek word is *basileia*, which is better translated as "reign." The emphasis is not upon a place, like the "kingdom of England." Rather the term speaks of a situation, a state of being where the Lord rules and with his loving power holds sway. And this nuance makes important differences in a number of familiar texts. For example, the Lord's prayer: "Our Father, who art in heaven . . . may your reign come!" (cf. Mt 6:9). Or the request of the good thief: "Remember me when you come in your kingly power" (Lk 23:42 RSV). Or again, the powerful words of Jesus: "You cannot tell by careful watching when the reign of God will come. . . . The reign of God is already in your midst" (Lk 17:20f). God does not primarily rule with signs of outward power. His power is the power of love; it rules through and in the hearts of human persons.

But if the idea of kingdom, of the reign of God, is central to Jesus, still it is not alone. There are a number of other themes connected to the idea of kingdom which are also prominent. And they have high relevance to our search for Christian ethics.

Repentance

First there is what may be called the "prerequisite for the kingdom." At the very beginning of the Synoptics there appears the call of John the Baptist challenging his listeners to repentance. He describes the baptism to which he invites them as a "baptism of repentance" (Mt 3:2–11; Mk 1:4–6; Lk 3:1–14). And this for a very special reason: the kingdom. "When John the Baptizer made his appearance as a preacher in the desert of Judea, this was his theme: 'Reform your lives! The reign of God is at hand' " (Mt 3:1–2).

But what is this repentance? It is not merely a change of behavior. Indeed, the Greek (*metanoia*) actually means "change of mind." It suggests a total reversal of life-style, a turning round of one's whole being, a personal moral revolution.[4] Jesus himself compared it to becoming like a little child (Mt 18:3). Paul described it as putting on "the new man," as dying to sin (Rom 6:11). And Nicodemus was warned: "No one can see the reign of God unless he is begotten from above" (Jn 3:3). (It is interesting that since John's Gospel was addressed to believers, he never actually used the word "repentance.")

This focus upon repentance is no small thing. It was not a new concept in Israel; the prophets had repeatedly issued the same call. But Jesus and John the Baptist did not live in the age of the prophets. And the Jewish leaders may well have considered themselves and their people as much better than their ancestors who were the objects of the prophetic condemnation. So when John the Baptist, and then Jesus, spoke in these terms, they were making a highly volatile political statement. Their listeners knew the word, knew its association with an unfaithful Israel. There must have been a stinging, humiliating pain in having those words addressed to them.

But addressed they were. And inasmuch as this theme of repentance is much more prominent in the Synoptic Gospels than in the other books of the New Testament, there is a strong likelihood that it really belongs to the message preached by Jesus himself.

Discipleship

A number of other themes are associated with the idea of repentance in one way or another. Among these are faith, baptism, and the good works that should exemplify the new life now lived. But perhaps the most powerful of these themes is that of discipleship. If repentance is the prerequisite for the kingdom, then discipleship represents "membership in the kingdom."

It was not uncommon in Israel for rabbis to gather around themselves a body of disciples. They were to be learners (*matheiteis*), followers ready and willing to learn from the teacher. They were to follow him, remain with him, become loyal to him. And since this practice was somewhat common, it is not surprising that Jesus acquired and encouraged disciples also. But in his case, the notion of discipleship took on several interesting nuances.

First of all, it meant the simple fact of following after the Lord. One statement, at least part of which appears in each of the Synoptics, proclaimed:

> If anyone comes to me without turning his back on his father and mother, his wife and his children, his brothers and sisters, indeed his very self, he cannot be my follower. Anyone who does not take up his cross and follow me cannot be my disciple. (Lk 14:26f; cf. Mt 10:37f and Mk 8:34)

Or again, Jesus advised the rich young man: "There is one thing more you must do. Go and sell what you have and give to the poor; you will then have treasure in heaven. After that, come and follow me" (Mk 10:21). Indeed, this quotation is representative of the total commitment which Jesus demanded of his disciples. To follow after him meant leaving everything else behind (Lk 5:11), giving up family (Lk 14:26), money and wealth (Mk 10:21), former occupations (Mk 2:14), and, indeed, all economic security (Lk 9:58).

This notion of following after Jesus, demanding though it was, still remained within the Jewish tradition. What was much less traditional was a second meaning that discipleship had for Jesus: the idea that the disciple was to replace Jesus, act on his behalf, take on a mission for the sake of the Lord. Indeed, the entire "apostolic discourse" in Matthew's Gospel (chap. 10) was premised on this idea. To be a disciple of Jesus was, sooner or later, to be *sent*. It did not involve remaining forever at the side of the rabbi; on the contrary, it involved going forth to do his work. "To another he said, 'Come after me.' The man replied, 'Let me bury my father first.' Jesus said to him, 'Let the dead bury their dead; come away and proclaim the kingdom of God'" (Lk 9:59f; note the connection to kingdom).

Finally, discipleship to Jesus even went beyond this call to mission. To follow the Lord ultimately meant to share in his very destiny. "No pupil outranks his teacher, no slave his master. The pupil should be glad to become like his teacher, the slave like his master" (Mt 10:24f). "If anyone would serve me, let him follow me; where I am, there will my servant be" (Jn 12:26). Indeed this participation would include the specific rhythms of Jesus' life. There would be the victimhood of suffering:

> If a man wishes to come after me, he must deny his very self, take up his cross, and follow in my steps. Whoever would preserve his life will lose it, but whoever loses his life for my sake and the gospel's will preserve it. (Mk 8:34f)

And there would also be the gift of ultimate victory:

> You are the ones who have stood loyally by me in my temptations. I for my part assign to you the dominion my father has assigned to me. . . . You will sit on thrones judging the twelve tribes of Israel. (Lk 22:28ff)

Law

The theme of discipleship reveals that membership in the kingdom of Jesus was a rigorous and demanding thing. It included obligations, or at least the reality of being obligated. This aspect of obligation we may consider under the rubric of law, the "rule of the kingdom." However, since we shall return to the topic of law in Chapter Twelve, and examine it in detail, only some brief comments will be included here.

Law, of course, was a concept with a powerful and pivotal history in Israel. And as we shall see, at least part of Jesus' mission was to free his followers from its curse. But that call to freedom did not mean there were no expectations placed upon them. Quite the contrary. "Let the dead bury their dead; come away and proclaim the kingdom of God. . . . Whoever puts his hand to the plow but keeps looking back is unfit for the reign of God" (Lk 9:60, 62). No, the kingdom to which Jesus dedicated himself required a singlemindedness. It demanded fidelity and commitment of a very personal, authentic sort. "What emerges from within a man, that and nothing else is what makes him impure. . . . All these evils come from within and render a man impure" (Mk 7:20, 23). It demanded a position of priority in one's life, and a willingness to trust the Lord. "Stop worrying, then, over questions like, 'What are we to eat?'. . . . Your heavenly Father knows all that you need. Seek first his kingship over you, his way of holiness, and all these things will be given you besides" (Mt 6:31ff).

So if anything, the "law" of Jesus was more demanding than the law of Israel's history. But it also was more discriminating. In the matter of ritual and ceremonial laws, Jesus appears to have felt quite free. He was quick to reject that sort of "legalism" which would use the law as an excuse. He would cure whether it was the Sabbath or not (e.g. Lk 14:1–6). He was undisturbed that his disciples should pick grain to eat on the Sabbath (Mt 12:1–8). But at the same time, where the law expressed the requirements of genuine and generous living he could be amazingly rigorous. "Anyone who looks lustfully at a woman has already committed adultery with her in his thoughts" (Mt 5:28). And his expectations of marital fidelity went beyond those of the Mosaic tradition (Mt 5:31f).

As Rudolph Bultmann declares, for Jesus

> One decisive demand shines out. The good that it is a question of doing must be done totally. Anyone who does it a little lazily, with reservations, just so that at a pinch the outward precept is fulfilled, has not really done it at all.[5]

Thus, if law is understood as demand, it is a concept very central to the message of Jesus. But the demand had a very different flavor. With the proclamation of law by Jesus there was a distinct and decisive shift to the interior. The reality of surface appearance was relativized, while the reality of inner authenticity was absolutized. It is the quality of one's heart, the mystery of intention, that is truly central.

Love

This increasing emphasis upon interiority is nowhere more manifest than in the New Testament considerations of the theme of love.[6] We will postpone consideration of one aspect of this theme, the two great commandments of love, until Chapter Twelve. But several other aspects demand immediate attention. So we move now to reflect on love, the "life of the kingdom."

But what do we mean by love? Psychologists sometimes say that only one who has been loved is capable of love. If this is true, then love can be defined simply by looking to its source. And in this respect the New Testament offers a very special insight. "I give you a new commandment:

Love one another. Such as my love has been for you, so must your love be for each other" (Jn 13:34). "This is my commandment: Love one another as I have loved you" (Jn 15:12). "Love, then, consists in this: not that we have loved God, but that he has loved us and has sent his Son as an offering for our sins" (1 Jn 4:10).

So the school of love, especially as this is envisioned by John, is God himself, and that Jesus whom he has sent. The starting point for the ethic of love is not the Golden Rule of self-love but the astonishing faith-truth of God's love for us. In this love we are taught love, and according to its measure is our own love to take shape. And as that love of ours takes shape, it points in two different directions.

First there is the love of *koinonia* (community, fellowship). This theme is developed particularly by John. Indeed, some scholars accuse John of a dualism by which the love command is restricted to within the community. They argue that John is concerned *only* that Christians love "one another" (see the quotations above), and not that they strive to love the more general "neighbor."[7] Be that as it may, there is no doubt that the love of fellowship is a theme dear to the Johannine vision. Jesus proclaims it at length in his final discourse. He exemplifies it in the powerful symbol of washing his disciples' feet. And he lives it in his own self-sacrifice: "The way we came to understand love was that he laid down his life for us; we too must lay down our lives for our brothers" (1 Jn 3:16). It is total love, therefore, that ought to characterize the Christian community, a love that is willing to sacrifice to the point of death. "If God has loved us so, we must have the same love for one another" (1 Jn 4:11).

There is also another kind of love, however, the love of *diakonia* (service). There is the charity that reaches out to all people in need to care for them and raise them up. As we suggested above, the degree to which John envisioned this love of general service is debated by scholars. But there is no doubt that Paul is concerned about it (as well as about the love of fellowship).

> Owe no debt to anyone except the debt that binds us to love one another. He who loves his neighbor has fulfilled the law. The commandments, "You shall not commit adultery" . . . and any other commandment there may be are all summed up in this, "You shall love your neighbor as yourself." Love never wrongs the neighbor, hence love is the fulfillment of the law. (Rom 13:8ff)

And this love has several specific characteristics. It is universal in its scope; we are expected to show love "for all" (1 Thes 3:12; cf. 1 Thes 5:15). It calls for humility and a spirit of self-sacrifice that are rooted in Christ, "Though he was in the form of God, he did not deem equality with God something to be grasped at. Rather, he emptied himself and took the form of a slave, being born in the likeness of men" (Phil 2:6–7; cf. 2 Cor 8:8f). It constitutes the sum and substance of all Christian moral demands. For love "binds the rest together and makes them perfect" (Col 3:12–14). It is therefore by love that we "fulfill the law of Christ" (Gal 6:2).

All of this is gloriously summarized in Paul's great hymn to love (1 Cor 13). He begins by stipulating the absolute necessity of love (If I "do not have love, I am a noisy gong . . ."). Then he goes on to be thoroughly concrete about the love he has in mind. Not some vague feeling of affection. No, the love of concrete service, the very mundane struggle to be "patient . . . kind . . . not jealous . . . not snobbish. . . ." And he concludes by proclaiming the permanence of love's centrality: "Love never fails. . . . My knowledge is imperfect now; then I shall know even as I am known. There are in the end three things that last: faith, hope, and love, and the greatest of these is love" (1 Cor 13:8, 12f).

Beatitudes

We conclude this series of scriptural reflections with some comments on the Beatitudes. For if repentance is the prerequisite for the kingdom, if discipleship represents membership in the kingdom, if law speaks the rule of the kingdom, and if love is the life of the kingdom, the Beatitudes can with justice be described as the "charter of the kingdom."

To say this may seem strange. The Beatitudes are more commonly viewed as new and challenging requirements, as part of the "law of the kingdom." But that is a misunderstanding. Note that the text in both Matthew (5:3–12) and Luke (6:20–23) is not a series of imperatives; it is a series of indicatives. It makes statements, it proclaims facts. The significance of the Beatitudes is not that they announce something to be done; no, they announce something that *is*. In the kingdom, life is ordered differently than it is in the world of men. The priorities of men—money, power, comfort, joviality—do not pertain. In the kingdom the priority is love.

Thus Jesus announced with great solemnity: even if you are poor, nonetheless in the kingdom you will be happy (blessed). Even if you suffer or hunger, nonetheless God's gift of joy will be yours. There is no doubt that these experiences are evil. No one seeks suffering or persecution or the pain of death's separation. But they will nonetheless come. When they do, you must not despair. Their supremacy is not final. Do not grieve if you appear to be a loser in the categories of the world. In the kingdom those categories will be toppled. Naïvely immediate human values will be disposed of; they will be supplanted by the inner values of the Lord. So all people, no matter what their human situation, if they share in the kingdom of the Lord, have good reason to rejoice and forever to be glad.

The Beatitudes can thus be called a charter. They are Good News. They are an instrument of liberation and exaltation. They are Gospel in the fullest and richest of senses.

Conclusion

This, then, leads us to a conclusion which is significant for our purposes. We have been considering themes that are morally relevant, that define the shape of Christian morality. We have seen that the Christian life is not a matter of conforming to abstract ethical principles. It is a matter of responding with fidelity to the God of the Covenant. We have seen that the Christian life is a wholly new life, a life of the kingdom where the Lord reigns supreme. It is a life turned completely around by repentance and focused on the Lord in discipleship. It is a life which accepts the new law of total, demanding commitment. And it is a life generated from and expressed in love.

But as these themes are morally relevant, so are the "indicatives" of the Beatitudes. But the moral relevance of *this* theme lies precisely in its relativizing of the entire moral enterprise. Morality, whether viewed as an intellectual science or as the practice of personal living, is not of preeminent importance. What is most significant, in the end, is in no way the mundane facts of our decisions and actions. What is most significant is the transcending fact of God's decisions and actions.

We speak of Christianity as a "religion." The word is very significant. It comes from the Latin, *religare,* which means "to bind together." The axis around which all of Christian living and all of Christian teaching revolve is this mystery of being bound together with and in the Lord. And this binding, we know, is not something we do at all; it is something God does. That is what the Beatitudes represent: the final, irrevocable, infinitely loving act of God.

Only in the context of an awareness of that divine initiative can any consideration of morality be worthy. Only after one has acknowledged the fact that human actions are not initiatives but responses to the call of the Lord, only then can one truly understand the reality of Christian ethics. And only when one has grasped the peculiar quality of the divine initiative, that it is an inner reality, a matter of the heart, only then can one comfortably accept and confidently live the fact that even morality is primarily a matter of interiority. It is not appearances, not even the shape of our behavior, that ultimately count. It is the mystery of intention. And this because that mystery somehow participates in the primeval interior intention of God himself.

This balance between exterior and interior, between human and divine, is well captured in the words of Schnackenburg. And even though many other biblical themes that have relevance to the enterprise of moral theology might still be developed, we will conclude our reflections by quoting them.

> Jesus' preaching was both a proclamation and a warning, an announcement of a divine act and a demand for a response to it from mankind. Everywhere in the New Testament we find that the acts of God are a call to men; the summons arises from the message. The sequence is invariable too. God acts first, and his act lays responsibility on men. Nowhere in the New Testament do we find a mere morality, a mere ethical system, but neither do we find a piety that imposes no obligations and is divorced from moral behaviour.[8]

4

CHRIST AND
MORAL THEOLOGY

We have established the basic understanding of theology that will ground this book. We have recapitulated the history of moral theology and taken note of the ethical tone of Sacred Scripture. Before we begin our methodical reflections on the nature and content of Christian ethics, moral theology, one further task remains. That is to indicate the way in which moral theology is rooted in the theology, and reality, of Christ.

> We conclude our remarks on Paul's ethical teaching in general by insisting on its Christocentrism. As Christ was the "image of God," so man in his earthly existence is to be the "image of the heavenly man." It is growth in Christ that Paul recommends to his readers, contemporary and modern. In this way the Christian lives his life "for God."[1]

These words of Joseph Fitzmyer indicate one of the reasons for this chapter. As our own investigations in scriptural ethics revealed, looking for Christian morality in the Bible inevitably leads us to meditation on the person of Jesus himself. Discipleship is an ethical dictate, but discipleship requires that we know well the teacher.

There is another reason for this chapter. Contemporary theology has become increasingly conscious of the central role in *all* theology that is held by Christ. Christ is not *one* of the important aspects of Christian belief; he is not *one* of the truths espoused by Christian faith; he is not *one* of the realities proclaimed in Christian revelation. No, Christ is the summary of all those things. He is *the* way, truth and life. He is *the* revelation of God to mankind. When Edward Schillebeeckx wishes to develop the theology of the seven sacraments, he begins by asserting that his study is really an aspect of Christology. Indeed, Christ is *the* "sacrament of the encounter with God."[2] All grace is grace of Christ; the only Church worthy of the name is the Church of Christ; the kingdom to come is the kingdom of Christ. When Jesus says that "he who sees me sees the Father," he is not merely making *a* statement. He is making *the* statement, summarizing all that he was to say and do in his earthly life. And so we are Christians in a most profound sense. We are Christ-people. We pray to the Father only "through Christ our Lord."

Therefore, to establish the ideas that will certify this book as "Christian ethics," as moral *theology*, we must root them in Christ himself. And on the other hand, as we shall see, to root our ideas in the person and mission of Christ is to begin to discover the particular shape which that ethics must take in our time. It is to discover that moral theology is a very particular thing, a discipline which possesses very particular characteristics.

The prolegomenon to our Christian ethics, then, is a series of reflections on the mystery of Christ, an explicit consideration of the relationship of Christ and morality.

One further note. It must not be forgotten that theology is in pursuit of meanings, not proofs. In this discussion, therefore, we will not be attempting to prove anything. We will not justify our assertions on the ground that they are irrefutable. Rather we will present an understanding of Christ which is common in contemporary theology, which is rich in meaning and implication, and which resonates with common experience. The test of these reflections, then, will not be their syllogistic logic. Rather the test will be their internal coherence and their external adequacy. The test will be the fact that they make sense and nourish our Christian lives.[3]

Christ and Creation

"In the beginning was the Word." These words open the Gospel of John (1:1). And they open our reflections as well. Indeed, as we proceed, we shall repeatedly return to John's proclamation for insight and support. But we begin with this very simple statement. Jesus the Christ is the Logos, the Word of God. But if this is so, if we know this about Jesus, then we know much more as well. For we know about "words." They are part of our experience, of our everyday lives. That experience may help us to grasp the mystery that is Jesus Christ.

Words. Tools of communication. Means of human interchange. Very common things: intuitive, immediate, universal. But at the same time very specific, particular things. Human communication has quite particular characteristics; and these are worth noting here.

First of all, where there is communication there are always two persons. There is a speaker and a listener. These two persons are united by means of a word, a symbol of some sort. And this word is what causes the communication to take place. What is more, for real communication not just any word will do. On the one hand, it is not possible to achieve communication unless the word really represents the person who speaks it. It must manifest his mind, his judgment, his question. On the other hand, the word must be aptly proportioned to the listener. That is, it must be in a language he understands, and it must use images and concepts with which he is familiar. Thus the essence of communication, in our human experience, is two persons sharing a word that is representative of the speaker and proportioned to the listener.

If this is true of human experience, however, and if St. John is correct in saying "In the beginning was the Word," then we can expect to find in God's actions some of these same characteristics.

We have a speaker, the Father himself. Indeed, the Father *is* a speaker, a producer of words, a creative, fruitful, fertile being. That is what follows from John's simple assertion. God is not some static and sterile being. He is a font of energy, dynamic and, quite literally, expressive. The Nicene Creed asserts that God is "creator of heaven and earth." But now, reflecting on John's words, we realize that God the Father is much more. He is creator of this world because he is a creative being. Indeed, an infinitely creative being. Should not such a being also be creative within himself, be the producer of the infinite Word? Or, to say this another way: Would the Father even be able to create those finite words that comprise our world if he were not also and preeminently the source of his internal and infinite Word, if he were not by nature creative and fertile and dynamic? These are mere speculations, of course. We cannot presume to dictate what God can or cannot do. But they are reasonable speculations. If it is not logically compelling, it is nonetheless quite plausible to hold with Karl Rahner that "the immanent self-utterance of God in his eternal fullness [the Word] is the condition of the self-utterance of God outside himself [human persons and their world]."[4]

All of this is supported elsewhere by St. John when he proclaims that "God is love" (1 Jn 4:8). Love, that most fertile, most unitive and creative of realities! God not only *has* love, he *is* love. He is fertility, energy, creativity itself. So we are very close to the mystery of God himself when we notice (without really understanding, to be sure) that God is a speaker, a producer and proclaimer of words.

"In the beginning was the Word." John invites us to set up the analogue to the human experience of communication. We do so, and we discover that with God, as with that human experience, we have a speaker. We also have listeners. We have the human community, those whom Jesus was to save, those whom God loves. We have the person who "hears my words and puts them into practice" (Mt 7:24). And, of course, we have the Word itself.

This Word, moreover, is representative of the speaker. As we have already intimated, it is an infinite Word. As it comes from an infinite speaker, unlimited in creativity, so it is infinite and unlimited. This Word does not have only that "representative" existence of our human communications. It does not merely point to the existence of the speaker. It participates in that existence. The Word is so representative of the speaker that it shares his life. It is a person as he is a person; it is eternal as he is eternal. This Word is consubstantial with the Father. It has real existence. It shares in the very Godhead of the speaker. And thus we are not at all surprised when John goes on to declare that "the Word was in God's presence and the Word was God" (Jn 1:1).

This Word is proportioned to the listeners, too. Here is a point that we often overlook. God is a speaker interested in genuine, successful communication. And so his Word is adjusted to the capacities of his listeners. "The Word was made flesh, he lived among us." That is what John says (1:14). The Word took on human proportions, became humanly present, became palpable and thus able to be humanly experienced. And thus communication of a most important sort took place.

Revelation occurred, and revelation's name was Jesus, the Christ, the Word of God. This, of course, we know not *a priori* but *a posteriori*. We know it not because some logic drives us to it; we know it because it happened. As Christians we believe that the Father revealed himself in Christ. We believe that revelation took place, and was incarnated in Jesus. And thus we conclude, on the basis of the historical evidence which we choose to believe, that the Word of God is both representative of the speaker and proportioned to the listeners.

"All things were made through him, and without him was made nothing that has been made." These words of John (1:3) give us another angle. They make us reconsider the above argument, at least in one particular. For we realize that divine communication is not, after all, exactly like human communication. In God there is a power that is beyond time, that somehow stands outside of time and makes time be. God is not only the Speaker of Words, he is also the creator of the world, of the listeners. In God, the Word preexists the listeners; it is an eternal Word bestowed on temporal, finite listeners. So in this case, it is simply impossible to proportion the Word to the listener. In this unique, divine case, the listener must be proportioned to the Word.

"All things were made through him" because all things were made for him. The world was created, was shaped, as a readiness for God's Word, as a place apt to receive the Word which he would share. It was, quite literally, proportioned to the Word. We are, in Karl Rahner's phrase, "hearers of the Word." Hearing the Word of God is not just something we can do and may do. It is something we are created in order to do. Under the light of faith we discover that the very essence of humankind is this capacity to receive the Word of God, to give it flesh and make it present.

In scholastic terminology, Christ was the exemplary cause of creation. He is the model, the pattern according to which we and our world were created. He is the paradigm in terms of which creation was accomplished. Thus, when in due time the Word does become flesh in Jesus Christ, it can honestly be said that "he came unto his own." The entry of the Word into creation is not some frightful coincidence of opposites. It is not the magic of God making the impossible happen. It is not, if you will forgive the metaphor, like a dozen circus clowns somehow fitting into a tiny automobile. Quite the contrary. When the Word becomes flesh, humanity fits him like a glove. Humanity was made to order for this event, it was shaped as a ready receptacle for divinity. In Rahner's terms, humanity is "that which ensues when God's self-utterance, his Word, is given out lovingly into the void of god-less nothing."[5]

Christ is the exemplary cause of creation. Creation is shaped in terms of the Word of God, is proportioned to that Word. And the result of this is that incarnation is able to occur. Communication is able to take place. God the speaker is able to share his life with us the listeners. He is able to communicate his Word. And the act in which this communication preeminently, irrevocably, takes place is the Incarnation. In Jesus of Nazareth the "Word became flesh and dwelt among us."

Implications

Now, from this understanding of Christ in relationship to creation, a number of important implications may be drawn.

First of all, it follows from what has been said thus far that Christ is the forethought of the Father's creative action, not its afterthought. So often Christians seem to assert that creation and incarnation bear no relationship to each other, that the world was created as it was for no particular reason and that the idea of incarnation came to God "late in the game." We're speaking anthropomorphically, of course; Christian theology cannot altogether avoid doing so. But at least we should take care that our anthropomorphisms are attuned to the truths of our faith. In this case we have an anthropomorphism that utterly betrays our faith.

To assert, then, that the very idea of incarnation, the possibility of that joining of God and humankind, enters into our salvation history only after creation is complete, and in a way that is irrelevant to creation itself, is to distort the Christian faith. It is to divide the God of creation from the God of redemption in a most unacceptable way. And most certainly it is to stand apart from the brilliant insight of St. John. No, the God of redemption *is* the God of creation. This world is created *in view of* the incarnation. Even if we do not wish to hold that the Father *committed* himself to incarnation in creating this world, still we must hold that he *permitted* it. If the human race was not shaped as it was in view of a *necessary* self-utterance of God in incarnation, still it was so shaped in view of a *possible* self-utterance. Thus, in some sense the incarnation stands at the head of creation, as its presupposition and guiding principle. The incarnation, at least as a possibility, is the blueprint for *all* that God does in our regard.

It follows from this, in the second place, that the incarnation of God's Word in Jesus Christ makes sense with or without the reality of original sin. Once again, we have here the response to a common misunderstanding of our faith. There is no doubt that the reality of sinful alienation is present when the incarnation takes place. It is also true that the life, death, and resurrection of Jesus succeed in overcoming that reality and reuniting us with God. But it does not follow from this that original sin is the necessary prerequisite for incarnation, that apart from original sin incarnation would be meaningless and absurd.

It is debated in theology whether incarnation *would* have taken place apart from the "mystery of iniquity." Both those who say yes and those who say no are well within the bounds of Christian orthodoxy. What must not be debated is the fact that incarnation *could* have taken place apart from original sin. Inasmuch as this world was created as a potential receptacle for the divinity of God's Word, incarnation was possible from the first moment of creation. Therefore, even if the *function* of incarnation was (at least in part) the rectification of the evil situation of mankind, such was not the *essence* of incarnation. No, the essence of incarnation was simply the self-gift of God to his people, the union of God, through his Word, with that good world which had come from his creative hand. If the function of the incarnation was to transform the world from evil to good, still the essence of incarnation involved an affirmation of the preexisting goodness of the world that was entered. Or to put this one last way, the most fundamental premise of incarnation was not, as is often implied, the evilness of the world, but rather its goodness. If sin makes incarnation necessary, virtue yet makes it possible.

Consequently, and in the third place, the entrance of God's Word into this world is not to be likened to the surreptitious entry of a guerilla warrior into enemy territory. It is not to be described as the entrance of an envoy from the kingdom of heaven into the midst of the kingdom of the demon. Indeed, if one speaks in this way (and people do speak in this way, in Christian preaching if not Christian theology), one espouses a profoundly un-Christian dualism. No, St. John says that the Word "came unto his own," and he means precisely that. God is "at home" in this world; this world is *his* kingdom. In some very real sense (and in view of God's preparation in the act of creation), the incarnation represents the "coming home" of God's Word to this world. It is a matter of the word finally taking possession of the "kingdom prepared for you since the foundation of the world" (Mt 25:34), as Scripture says in another context.

Thus, if the incarnation in some way constitutes the first act of redemption (as it surely does), nonetheless it also constitutes the "eighth day of creation." It is the completion of creation, the fulfillment of the promise that lies within the very fiber of creation itself. There is, then, a sense in which creation itself is not complete until the moment of incarnation. Even if the Father was not compelled to complete his creation in the gift of incarnation, still, since he chose to do so, we ought to be conscious of the "rightness" of the act. It did, indeed, complete the process of communication that began at the first moment of creation. It brought to magnificent fullness the ancient promise that "I will be your God and you will be my people."

Finally, this understanding of Christ and creation makes us appreciate with unparalleled richness the potential of this human world. It is a world filled with hints of the incarnation for which it is prepared. It is modeled on the Word, it is designed as his potential receptacle. It possesses the Word already before the act of incarnation as its exemplary cause. Thus this world is always and everywhere a certain revelation of God the Father.

How often people will exclaim that a particular human experience makes them feel very close to God. It may be the beauty of nature, the wonders of technology, the excitements of art and music, the intimacy of another human person. Whatever it may be, it gifts the recipient with an experience of closeness to God. We see now that this is no accident; it is not an illusion. All of creation contains hints of God. All of it speaks of God the way clothes speak of their wearer, the way a room speaks of its inhabitant, the way these pages speak of their author's beliefs. Everything in our experience is revelation; everything is words of God, words modeled on the Word. The fertility of God is thus expressed and communicated in the fertility of creation. All that is is a vehicle of God, able to transmit his love. All that is, all that we encounter in the process of human life, is a matter of whispers preparing for the great shout of God's Word. And that shout, that final, irrevocable, unsurpassable shout, is incarnation.

Christian ethics must therefore take this world seriously. It is God's world—and God's words. It is a gift from God to us, and it is part of our way to God. It holds a wonderful place in the process of God's self-revelation to his creation. It must also hold a prominent place in our efforts to respond to that revelation by Christian living. Christian ethics is humanistic ethics, and for deeply theological reasons.

Christ and Redemption

We have referred in the preceding pages to the redemptive function of the incarnation. We have acknowledged that function, but we have not emphasized it. Now we must give it our direct attention.

Given the fact that God's Word entered this world in Jesus Christ, what was he up to? What did he do in this world? It is the common conviction of Christians (and a central tenet of their faith) that he saved humankind. He overcame the alienation of sin, he reunited us with God, and he established the new covenant in his blood by which we are all made one.

This is true. Indeed, it is more than true. Not only did Jesus bring about this union, not only did he effect it, he also constituted it. Jesus Christ *was* (and is) the union of God and humanity. Throughout the early centuries of the Church great battles were fought over various ways of understanding the person of Jesus. And in spite of various heretical adversaries, the Church always remained faithful to its central conviction: Jesus is God and man made one. Right in his very personhood is the reunion of humanity with God accomplished. If Jesus is the Redeemer, he is all the more redemption itself. If he is the Savior, yet he is more profoundly salvation itself. The deeds of Jesus are important primarily because they express and manifest his personhood. They are the *result* of what occurs when the promised reunion comes to pass. The Christian Church throughout its history, therefore, celebrates the personhood, the salvific and redemptive personhood, of that Jesus who is the Christ.

Still, to say all this is not to say that the deeds of Jesus were unimportant. Quite the contrary. To the extent that we discover how the Word-made-flesh comported himself in this world, to that extent we have the possibility of discovering how we should live as well. So it is worth taking note of what the New Testament reveals about the life-style of Jesus Christ.

The first thing to be noticed in pursuing this investigation is the strong emphasis on the humanity of Jesus. Unlike some of the apocryphal writings of early Christianity, the Gospels present us less with a divine wonder-worker and more with a preeminently human person. We notice his solicitude at the marriage at Cana. We are repeatedly reminded of his need for solitude and reflection. We are allowed to view his tears before the grave of Lazarus. And, although we tend to take the force out of the words, we are clearly informed that his ministry began and ended with "temptations." He loudly proclaimed that "as often as you did it for one of my least brothers, you did it for me" (Mt 25:40), and he lived that style himself. He fed the hungry, gave sight to the blind, cured the sick.

He worked miracles, so we are told, out of solicitude for the people and that faith might be strengthened. But as best we can tell from the scriptural testimony, Jesus never worked a miracle for himself. Indeed, he refused to do so. "Do you not suppose I can call on my Father to provide at a moment's notice more than twelve legions of angels?" (Mt 26:53). Do you not know that I can appeal beyond this human world, can claim power and privilege that is far above human rights? But I will not do so. God has become human, and he will be faithful to that humanity.

That is the essence of what Jesus did: he was human. He lived the human life that he had embraced. And he lived it faithfully, unstintingly, and without exception. Indeed, he lived it to the end. Sometimes one has the impression that Christians believe that Jesus came only to die, that it was his death alone that gave us the gift of salvation. But that seems to us a distortion. Better to say that life, authentic and faithful human life, was his purpose. And inasmuch as that life leads to death, for him as for us all, the death of Jesus was the *outcome*, the inevitable completion of his commitment to human life. Christ "humbled himself," humbled himself to his heavenly Father but also to his human vocation, "obediently accepting even death, death on a cross." Therefore, because of that fidelity and love "God highly exalted him" (Ph 2:8f).

This then is the redemptive mystery espoused by the Christian faith. The incarnation is the embrace of humanity by God; in that embrace is its fulfillment and salvation. God becomes human, and in so doing he divinizes humanity. It is the personhood of Jesus Christ, both God and human, that unites God and all of us in a finally salvific way. And precisely because of this salvation in his person, Jesus lives his human life; he lives it completely, in love and fidelity and generosity. He lives it even when it leads to the ignominy of murder at the hand of his Father's creatures.

Implications

This doctrinal statement, then, also leads us to a number of implications. And these have great import for the task of moral theology.

First of all, it is clear from all of the above that this human world is not only fertile with hints of God (as we saw before), it is also truly salvific. It is precisely the place where salvation takes place. It is where God meets humankind, and where he transforms it into a community of his sons and daughters. As we might express it colloquially, God does his saving thing "on our turf." God's commitment to the reality of communication, his desire to proportion himself to his listeners, is so deep that we can declare quite literally that salvation is a *human* event. Thus the dignity of this world, which we perceived in the previous section of this chapter, is now seen to be totally beyond what we might have imagined.

It follows from this, in the second place, that we human persons are not only *permitted* to appreciate this world, we are *commanded* to do so. For this world is where God is to be found.

For thousands of years our religious instincts have led us to desire union with God. This desire has, in turn, led to religious behavior. A common characteristic of that behavior has been to set aside some quantity of "sacred space," some place within this world which is viewed as "outside" this world, a bit of heaven on earth. As religious people, then, we become one with God by leaving "this world," by going to that place where God is. We find God "on God's turf," or we do not find him at all.

The Christian faith, we now see, is quite otherwise. If we leave "this world," go beyond the world in the search for God, we will miss him. For God is here. To attempt to enter the domain of God is not only ludicrous; for the Christian it is also futile. We will simply pass God on the way. And it is also unnecessary. God is to be found in the fabric of human life, in the midst of those tasks and projects that constitute the human experience. God does his saving thing "on our turf." It is here that we encounter God; it is here that we receive his redemptive gift.

This insight has, of course, all sorts of consequences for Christian theology. It explains why the Church (*ekklesia*) is not really a place, a building, or an institution. It is the community itself. For it is in the Church, in the community, that God is found. It explains why Christians do not really have "sacred space," in the theological sense. We do not have temples, necessary for the encounter with God. We have gathering places for the community Church, nothing more.[6] This insight also explains the high importance of sacraments. We do not apologize for the apparent outrage of saying that God can be encountered and experienced in oil and water, bread and wine. Indeed, God can be met in all of creation. But his presence is particularly promised in these peak moments of the human experience.

Finally, this insight explains why the Church-as-institution is both the minister of God's gifts *and* a merely human reality. Perhaps of all Christians, Catholics are particularly tempted to expect of the Church a wisdom and virtue that are superhuman. They can be angered by the frailty of the Church, by its failures, its errors, its infidelities. But to expect more than this of the Church is unfair. The Church is human, no less and no more. And it is precisely by struggling with this humanness that the Church succeeds in proclaiming the Gospel and sharing the gift of salvation. As we shall repeatedly see in the pages of this book, the human vocation of the Church, grounded in the human vocation of God's Word in Jesus, is a privilege and a burden. But in any case, we must be careful to ask no more than the Church can give. As Jesus refused for himself those legions of angels, so he refuses them for his Church. And that is the mystery of our faith.

All of this leads to the third implication. Namely, that the fundamental ethical command imposed on the Christian is precisely to be what he or she is. "Be human." That is what God asks of us, no more and no less. Imitate Christ, and do this by seeking to be as faithful to the human vocation as he was. Love your neighbor as yourself. Do unto others as you would have them do unto you. Christian ethics is human ethics, no more and no less.

This is a most important point. There is, often enough, an implicit gnosticism in the way people talk about the ethical life of Christians. One has the impression that they view moral theology as some sort of arcane science, some body of wisdom from another world. In principle, though, Christian ethics knows nothing that all people do not know. It reflects upon human experience, it searches for the human good. It attempts to articulate, in a way that is helpful, the demands of human living. For right human living is precisely what is demanded of the Christian.

Or again, some people will describe Christian moral demands as if they were constituted by a body of arbitrary and extrinsic divine commands. It is as if one thought God had created an intrinsically amoral world and then, after the fact, added a few rules. It is as if one believed God to have said: "My people, there's really nothing wrong with murder. But I do want to test you. So as one of my regulations I insist that you refrain from murder. It is only my command that makes murder wrong."

What a travesty this sort of legalism is! And yet it is not uncommon. It can be heard regularly in the pulpits of Christian churches. Perhaps it is not expressed so clearly, but it is there. "God's law," the "will of God," "it is wrong *because* it violates the Ten Commandments." Phrases like these are heard often. As we can see, they are insidious. Christian ethics is not arbitrary, it is not a form of religious legalism. It is the faithful articulation of the meaning of Jesus' call that we should "be what we are." And if there is a place for moral laws (as there surely is), that place can be justified only by the fact that the laws helpfully express what it means to live the human life with fidelity and generosity. Christian ethics is human ethics. Christians are unconditionally humanists; that is our pride and our privileged vocation.

A fourth and final implication follows from this line of thought. By reflecting on the way of life which Jesus shared we are eventually led to a quite particular strategy for Christian ethics. And that strategy will comprise our methodology in the remainder of this book.

Christian ethics, like all of the Christian faith, is essentially and profoundly human. It is a human task seeking human wisdom about the human conduct of human affairs. It is therefore not an isolated enterprise. It does not possess any secret sources of information, and it does not lead to any "mysterious" conclusions. Thus, in a certain sense, moral theology is not theology at all. It is moral philosophy, pursued by persons who are believers. Moral theology is a science that seeks to benefit from all the sources of wisdom within our world. It listens respectfully to all philosophies, and uses them. It accepts and cherishes the evidence and conclusions of the social sciences. It tests its own conclusions against the experience of mankind, not only that of members of the Church. It speaks in the midst of the human community and attempts to speak for and to that whole community.

Thus, among all the potential criticisms which may be leveled against the chapters which will follow in this book, one must be rejected at the outset: He seems to be merely talking philosophy. Quite true! And quite intentional! For all the reasons that have been developed in this chapter, for all the reasons that comprise the warp and woof of the Christian faith, for all those profoundly theological reasons, we shall talk philosophy in this discussion of Christian ethics.

Of course, this does not mean that we shall go to the other extreme, adopting an utterly secular approach to the ethical process. Quite the contrary. We shall be pursuing moral theology. But by that term we mean something quite specific.

We mean, first of all, that these will be the reflections of believers, developed in the midst of the Christian community. Indeed, as we shall see, it is an important premise of our approach that ethics is always an intrinsically communal product. Since our ethics will be the sort generated within the Christian community, we will be proud to call it moral theology. Secondly, we use this term because, as believers, we shall confidently expect to find applicable and valuable insights in our tradition. We have already given our attention to the resources of Scripture, dogmatic tradition, and theological reflection, and we shall continue to do so. These resources will, it is true, have to be tested against our personal and communal experience; that is what it means to say that our ethics is human. But they will nonetheless be highly useful. Thirdly, our enterprise deserves the name of moral theology because our very starting point, indicated to some extent in this chapter, is a fundamentally Christian vision of human beings and their world. This is our perspective. And as it is unique, so the resulting ethic will in some ways be unique.

Conclusion

St. Paul called Christ "the Image of the Invisible God, the first-born of all creatures. In him everything in heaven and on earth was created . . . ; all were created through him and for him. He is before all else that is. In him everything continues in being" (Col 1:15–17). This is a description of cosmic Christology, of the relationship of Christ and creation. And in essence it proclaims to us that we *may* be human. It is permitted to be human, Christ himself permits it. And Paul continues that Christ is "the first-born of the dead, so that primacy may be his in everything . . . and, by means of him, to reconcile everything in his person . . . making peace through the blood of his cross" (Col 1:18–20). In these words he summarizes historical Christology, the relationship of Christ and redemption. In this we discover that we *must* be human.[7]

Be human! No more and no less! Christ permits it, and Christ demands it. That is the central conviction of the Christian faith. And it is the fundamental premise of the following principles of Christian ethics.

PART II

THE MORAL PERSON

5

HUMAN ACTION

" **W**e are not just animals. We may share much with the animal kingdom; our prehistoric roots may be theirs. But we are more." Words like these represent the common-sense wisdom of most human beings. More than that, they represent the conclusion reached by most serious thinkers through the centuries. Of course, to accurately understand ourselves as human beings it is necessary to take seriously our connections with the animal world. But it is equally necessary to notice and take into account those things that make us different. To neglect either of these emphases is to distort the reality that we find ourselves to be.

It is true that during the past century human distinctiveness has come under attack from several quarters. It has been suggested that human persons are not really *free*. Rather they are determined by biological drives (psychoanalytic psychology) and cultural influences (behavioristic psychology). What is more, said some, the human ability to find and know the *truth* is largely self-deception (Marx). Persons do not see reality as it is, but as they would like it to be. Consequently, one should not speak of knowledge at all, but rather of self-serving ideology.

These critiques of human distinctiveness have much to commend them. Past theories may well have been characterized by a naïve humanism which failed to take into account the myriad sources of and influences upon human behavior. As we continue with this study, we shall often have occasion to utilize the insights of these recent thinkers. But we will not adopt their conclusions uncritically; nor, in the end, will we accept the fundamental perspective of their thought. And this for a number of reasons.

For one thing, the thoroughgoing affirmation of a deterministic and ideological vision leads one to the strange contradiction that even this affirmation is intrinsically unreliable. Indeed, the only really consistent response to this antihuman vision is silence, no response at all. For another thing, a number of thinkers, even in the fields of psychology and sociology, no longer give complete allegiance to the vision we have described. In addition to the perspectives of psychoanalysis and behaviorism, one also finds psychologists today proposing a number of theories which take far more seriously the distinctively human characteristics of persons: existentialism, transactional analysis, and reality therapy, to name just a few. Similarly, the Marxist theory of ideology has, in recent decades, been nuanced by the still developing field of the sociology of knowledge.[1]

In the next two chapters, then, we will attempt to sketch out an understanding of human persons that takes due account of both what unites them to and what differentiates them from the animal kingdom. We will do this by utilizing and uniting three distinctive sources of insight. For one thing, we will employ a number of categories from the heritage of Roman Catholic moral theology. For another, we will introduce various insights from contemporary thought. And third, we will test all of these ideas against the benchmark of our own human experience. For in the last analysis, to describe the human person is to describe ourselves. And thus we have the right to expect from any theoretical analysis a synthesis that is true to our own experience and that contributes to our own self-understanding.

To begin, the present chapter will establish a basis for our synthesis by presenting a number of assertions from traditional moral theology.

The Human Act

Scholastic manuals of moral theology often begin their discussion of human beings and their behavior by introducing a fundamental distinction between an "act of man" and a "human act." Indeed, it is not unusual for this distinction to be employed as the starting point for the entire discussion of moral theology.[2] And this with good reason, since the distinction is truly fundamental.

A human act (*actus humanus*) describes an action performed by a human being and, what is more, performed in a truly human way. That is, a human act is an action done with at least a modicum of awareness and free choice. The act of reading this book, or of choosing to read it, the planning of a day's activity, the purchase of a new set of clothes, the pursuit of a pleasant conversation, all these are human acts. They are actions done by us as human persons, and they are actions done through and with the human capacities for knowledge and freedom.

An act of man (*actus hominis*), on the other hand, describes a piece of behavior arising through human agency, but without that same knowledge or freedom. I am driving my car when suddenly one of the tires goes flat. I lose control of the car, swerve across the road, and collide with another car, injuring its driver. I may grieve over this event, I may feel tremendous sorrow because of the harm that has been done. Very likely I will even feel an obligation to make some recompense for the evil that has befallen my fellow man. But I will not judge myself to be guilty of any moral fault, any true irresponsibility or sin, in this situation. The "accident" (the term itself is significant) is not something that I did; it is something that happened to me. It was not truly a human act, but rather an act of man. Indeed our daily lives are full of acts of man, and examples could be multiplied. Sleepwalking, actions following unintentional intoxication, the reflex response of a person being attacked: all of these take place in the human world. But they are no more than acts of man.[3]

So, some actions are merely acts of man while other actions are genuinely human acts. And it is human acts which are the focus of attention in moral theology. For one can only be morally responsible when one has knowledge and freedom, when one is truly in control of the events that transpire.

This traditional distinction, then, commends itself in that it resonates with our common experience. But in that it does not *fully* resonate with that experience, some additional nuancing remains necessary. For the fact of the matter is that only rarely does a human action fall clearly and completely into one category or the other. Behavior grounded in comprehensive awareness and thoroughgoing freedom is really uncommon in our daily lives. So upon further reflection, it becomes clear that the categories of human act and act of man represent not so much two mutually exclusive alternatives as rather two extremes on a continuum of human experience. Most of our behavior falls somewhere between those extremes, being neither totally unfree nor totally free, being neither totally ignorant nor totally aware. Most of our human actions do not deserve the title of human act in any full and unequivocal sense. Rather they can only be accurately described as limited, partial, incomplete examples of the reality denoted by the traditional term.

Impediments

In the manuals of moral theology, the notion of "impediments" embraces those factors which limit and inhibit the humanity of human acts. Far from being rejected today, this notion has become more prominent. For, as was intimated above, the insights of the social sciences have lately made us more and more aware of the numerous factors which can oppose and inhibit truly human behavior. Consequently, even though we shall need to return to the notion of impediments and to consider it far more deeply later on, it may still be helpful to discuss it briefly now. For a standard scholastic list of common impediments to human acts, summarizing our ordinary experience as it does, can serve to illuminate that sense of inner unfreedom that we have.

Ignorance is a very common impediment. Indeed as was already suggested, total ignorance has the effect of completely "dehumanizing" a human act. But a much more common experience is that of partial ignorance, the situation where I know what I am doing, but do not *fully* appreciate the implications and consequences of my actions. Consider our previous example of an automobile accident, and now add the factor that I was driving in excess of the posted speed limit. I knew that I was taking a risk, but to the best of my knowledge it was a calculated risk. I was late and trying to make up time. Inasmuch as I was not driving in a completely responsible manner, I consider myself to be a real cause of that accident and to be morally responsible for it. But inasmuch as I did not know about the road hazard that caused my flat tire and, in fact, did not even consider the possibility of that happening, I consider myself much more a victim of fate than a creator of my own destiny. Ignorance did not completely eliminate my personal responsibility. For in the last analysis I probably should have considered all those possible factors. But it did function as at least a partial impediment, blocking the full expression of a truly human act.

Another impediment is passion. Indeed, to be an adult is to be aware of the extent to which anger, envy, sexual desire, and other emotions can limit one's freedom of choice.[4] Is a person completely absolved of responsibility for actions that follow upon these emotions? Very likely not. But by the same token he or she is not completely responsible either. Such actions fall in the grey area between acts of man and human acts; that is our experience. And the traditional moral theology simply ratifies that experience in its analysis of the moral life.

A third impediment found in traditional lists is fear. In this case the older wisdom is even more strongly urged today as a result of the input of the social sciences. Psychologist Abraham H. Maslow distinguishes people motivated by a desire to eliminate "deficiencies" in their life situation from persons generally motivated by an open-ended desire for a fuller experience of "being" (D-people and B-people).[5] In Maslow's perspective, the latter goals, though ideal, cannot be pursued until the former have been duly addressed. For the anxiety generated by deficiencies in one's life makes decision for fuller being difficult, if not impossible. Other psychologists may analyze the situation a bit differently, but their ultimate conclusion is remarkably similar. Fear and anxiety are the enemies of full human life and genuinely human decision. They are, in the traditional terminology, impediments to human acts.

Finally, the presence of violent force, or the threat of such force, stands in obvious opposition to the exercise of the human act. Whether the case be that of a "shotgun wedding," the dire threats of a rapist, or the more subtle pressures of the corporate supervisor against a needy employee, the underlying reality is the same. The presence of force (and the fear it engenders) inhibits and at least partially prevents the clear thinking and free choosing that comprise a really human act.

Now one might argue that these factors do not really prevent moral choice, but are the very objects of that choice. To be moral is to withstand temptation in spite of fear or force. This understanding of impediments, therefore, really constitutes a rationalization of moral irresponsibility. The response to this objection is very simple. If the facts of the case are as the objection suggests, if I really have the power within me to withstand this pressure and don't use it, then of course I am morally responsible. But is it not possible that the facts are otherwise? Is it not possible that these pressures truly have robbed me of the power to resist? And if that is so, then the reduced responsibility suggested by this theory of impediments cannot help but make sense. In other words, the notion of impediments is not intended to prejudge the facts of the case. It is only intended to explain what may very well be the facts of the case. As always, the objective data of our personal experience are the benchmark against which moral theory must be measured.

The four types of impediments mentioned above share one thing in common: they all tend to be associated with particular actions or moments. They tend to be passing things, more associated with the situation than with the person. Because of this connection with particular acts, such impediments have traditionally been known as "actual." In contrast with these, there is another sort of impediment that is more intrinsic to the person. It constitutes an aspect of a particular person's individuality and is carried from situation to situation. This type of impediment, because of its continuous aspect, is termed "habitual." A few examples of habitual impediments may be helpful to our reflections.

The first and most obvious habitual impediment is the simple fact of the individual person's personality structure. It is a commonplace of experience that some people are "morning persons" while other people are "night persons." Whether an individual is one or the other is beyond free choice. It just happens to be so. But it still has very real implications for the exercise of human life. When am I most able to make really human decisions: To think clearly? To decide freely? It may be early in the day or it may be toward evening. But in any case it is not always the same. At some time or other in my day, the very structure of my personality stands as an impediment to the exercise of fully human acts.

And not only my personality. Habits, particular ways of doing things that have, over time, become relatively automatic, can also serve as impediments. They were not always so, of course. For habits are, by definition, aspects of the human person that have been developed over a period of time. Nor are habits necessarily bad. No human person could sustain the tension of making new and conscious decisions about every detail of everyday life. It may very well be in a person's best interest that his procedure for washing and dressing in the morning, the route by which he drives to work, the choice of a time to eat should remain on the level of an act of man. All we are saying is that at the present moment such automatic ways of operating are, in fact, habits, and that such habits eliminate from activity the freedom required for a fully human act.

A third habitual impediment is particularly relevant in contemporary society. Traditionally it went by the name of "false opinion." But for our purposes it can be well understood as prejudice. Prejudice distorts the way people see things. It blinds them to certain facts and encourages them to see what is not there. It consequently results in ignorance—and a particularly pernicious sort of ignorance at that. Inasmuch as prejudice is an habitual and perduring sort of ignorance, it is especially difficult to remedy. Prejudice is not the simple fact of ignorance in an individual and unique situation. Rather it is a way of "mis-seeing" a whole range of experiences of a particular person's life. In any case, prejudice has the effect of generating actions which lack either the knowledge or the freedom to be considered really human.

The way a racially prejudiced person, for example, behaves is surely evil. But objective evil and moral fault are not at all the same, as we shall have occasion to see in great depth later in this book. A fervent desire to remedy the objective injustices caused by a prejudiced person should not blind us to those factors that really render him or her unfree. Good people, with good intentions, often do evil deeds. And the habitual impediment of prejudice is one reason why.

Finally, mental illness can also function as an habitual impediment. It is clear that the psychotic, during the periods when his psychosis is active, is so lacking in awareness and freedom that his behavior can only be termed acts of man. What is not always so clear, but what is surely true, is that neurotic anxieties, obsessions, and feelings of guilt can also have somewhat the same effect. A housewife knows she ought to forego her cleaning regimen and care for her sick neighbor. But she "cannot stand" a dirty house. A Roman Catholic may have a perfectly good excuse for not attending Sunday Mass, but "just wouldn't feel right" about it. Despite repeated attempts to change, a businessman besieged by his own insecurity continues to indulge in harmful gossip about his coworkers. In many ways (and psychology is making us aware just how many), the neuroses that affect us all inhibit the freedom necessary for a fully human act. A desire to change may be morally demanded. A willingness to accept help may be expected. But for the present, the simple fact is that such neuroses place many human actions in the grey world between the act of man and the human act.

The twin categories of actual and habitual impediments, with the various subdivisions within each, all serve to articulate a very simple insight. There are moments in human life when a person is totally ignorant or totally unfree; there are such things as acts of man. There also are, or seem to be, moments in life when one substantially succeeds in mobilizing one's capabilities for human acts. But the vast majority of life lies somewhere between. We are somewhat aware, somewhat free, somewhat human. And moral theology must take account of that fact.

Freedom and Knowledge

In our initial discussion of human acts, it was stated that such acts are characterized by freedom and awareness. We then proceeded to consider in detail these impediments which stand in the way of either freedom or awareness. It now remains to go into greater depth regarding those two central ideas. What does it mean to be free? To be aware? What sort of liberty and knowledge is required? These are the questions we must now consider. We will discuss freedom first.

What do we really mean when we say that freedom is a prerequisite for a human act? Isn't it true that in a very common-sense sort of way we mean that the agent has some choices available, some options at his or her disposal? A common characteristic of several of the impediments we considered above was that they robbed the agent of options. They certainly limited and inhibited the options available, and in some cases they totally eliminated all the options but one. So to be free, in the sense in which it is being used here, means to have options, to have choices. In some deeper philosophical sense, freedom may be a separate reality, a capacity of humans, a general state of being. But in any ordinary sense of the word, freedom must be more than this. It must be a *concrete* state of being, a state of being-in-this-situation. This freedom, then, is what St. Augustine meant by his term *liberum arbitrium*. Indeed, that phrase is accurately translated as "freedom of choice." And it designates the sort of freedom that exists where an agent has more than one alternative: the alternative of doing this or that, the alternative of doing or not doing a particular action. In any case the agent is in a situation of alternatives that are really there and really available to him or her.

What of knowledge? Is there anything to be said about the *kind* of knowledge necessary for a really human act? Indeed there is, and it is very important. To state the point very baldly (before developing it in detail), many psychologists as well as theologians today distinguish between quite different ways of knowing. There is what may be called "speculative knowledge." On the other hand there is "evaluative knowledge." And in the last analysis, only evaluative knowledge can serve as the required prerequisite for a genuinely human act.[6] But before we can see why this is so, we must develop a much fuller understanding of these two sorts of knowledge. We begin with a sketch of speculative knowledge.

In a very gross sense, speculative knowledge can be viewed as the knowledge of science, whereas evaluative knowledge is the knowledge of art. This is not altogether accurate, as we shall see. But it does give us a place to start. Speculative knowledge is intellectual knowledge, as we ordinarily speak of it. It has a certain objectivity, a certain independence from the knower. The fact that two plus two is four is not particularly associated with me as knower. Rather it stands apart from me. It is something I just happen to know. What is more, precisely because of this objectivity, speculative knowledge is easily communicable. It can be passed from person to person, it can easily be shared. It is universal in its character, prescinding from individual circumstances and differences. Speculative knowledge is, therefore, in a certain sense essential knowledge. It deals with the essence of things, that which both is and must be. Or at least it deals with that which happens to be and has the potential for *always* happening to be.

Speculative knowledge is fact-oriented. Because speculative knowledge has this factual, objective, essentialistic character, the knowledge of the physical scientist can, as we suggested, be taken as a prime example. Similarly, the scientific method can be viewed as a paradigm for dealing with all speculative knowledge. Just as we expect experimental scientists to maintain a certain disinterest in their research, a distance from their materials which allows them to search for the truth and not for their own desires, so all speculative knowledge has the characteristic of disinterestedness. Speculative knowledge, like scientific knowledge, is proveable. And what is more, it ought to be proved. We do not admire people who quote facts to us without any attempt to prove or ground or justify those facts. We want to know why something is so. Or at least how the speaker knows it to be so. Speculative knowledge can be taught, because it is objective and independent. But if we are willing to be taught, we also expect to be responsibly taught. Thus the demand for proof is considered thoroughly appropriate in the case of speculative knowledge.

Finally speculative knowledge is, in a certain sense, subservient to the knower. We use such knowledge. After a period of serious study, we are proud that we have "mastered the facts." While we feel obligated to have respect for the truth, in the case of speculative knowledge that respect is grounded in our own needs, and not in the reality of the facts. In other words, we respect the facts, because we need the facts in order to achieve *our* goals. We respect the facts the way a carpenter respects his tools, as the means that are necessary and thus must be carefully used.

Evaluative knowledge is quite otherwise. It has to do with quality rather than quantity. It deals with the goodness or beauty of a thing, with its value. And inasmuch as value does not exist "out in space," by itself, evaluative knowledge is not universal, but intensely concrete. Evaluative knowledge is a particular way of knowing the individual existing thing. It deals, therefore, not with essences but with existence. We stand before a particular thing, a particular experience, and interact with it. We find it to be good or bad, beautiful or ugly, and we appreciate it (*ad pretium* = toward value). In the case of evaluative knowledge we "understand" (stand under) it. We go out of ourselves and attach ourselves to the value that we find in the object. Indeed, in an ultimate experience of evaluative knowledge, we may achieve a sort of ecstasy (*ekstasis* = standing outside).

Evaluative knowledge, then, is in a certain sense not subservient to the knower, but rather superior to him or her. The knower serves this knowledge, going out to embrace and accept and appreciate the value that he finds. The knower finds the self confronted by a beautiful sunset, a magnificent piece of music, an awe-inspiring work of technology, the mystery of a human person. He or she cannot remain disinterested in the face of this knowledge. Rather it calls for, it demands, commitment. Evaluative knowledge is involving knowledge. It is knowledge that is at the same time a command. Consequently, evaluative knowledge is intensely personal. It is not subjective in the sense of being fabricated by the knower. Quite the contrary, it is in a certain sense the most objective of all knowledge. For in evaluative knowledge the knower is presented with something that transcends the self, something he or she didn't ask for, may not even have wanted, but something that is there and must be accepted. At the same time, though, evaluative knowledge is deeply personal. It results from the unique interaction of a unique subject and a unique object. And thus it cannot be shared, at least in its entirety.

I can try to tell you of the beauty I found in the Grand Canyon. I may even succeed in sharing a partial understanding of that experience. But I can never fully express or communicate the knowledge that is mine as a result of that experience. Similarly, precisely because evaluative knowledge is so personal, it cannot really be taught. Rather, the process of sharing evaluative knowledge, to the extent that this can occur at all, is a process of education (*e-ducere* = to draw out), where a similar experience is occasioned and encouraged in another person, where the knowledge is quite literally drawn out of the other. For example, the briefest presentation of definitions would have been sufficient to give the reader of this chapter a speculative knowledge of the difference between speculative and evaluative knowledge. But we are hoping for more. Through this long discussion of the two sorts of knowing, through the use of many evocative words and images, through the introduction of a number of examples, our hope is to call forth from the reader a genuine appreciation of that differ-ence. We hope, quite literally, to evoke an evaluative knowledge of evalua-tive knowledge.

Two further points need to be made on this topic. The first is to nuance our opening statement regarding the relationship of speculative and evaluative knowledge, pairing the two with science and art, respectively. We said at the beginning that this was imprecise, and we can now see why. The two terms, speculative and evaluative, refer not to two different *objects* of knowledge but rather to two different *ways* of knowing. Indeed, it is more than likely that a person dedicating his or her life to the pursuit of science does so precisely because of a deep *evaluative* knowledge of the wonders of the natural universe; and contrariwise, who has not been bored by an academic course in art, where all that was shared was the most *speculative* and technical explanation of the artistic medium? So anything in the world can be known both speculatively and evaluatively. What makes the difference is the *way* it is experienced by the knower.

The second point has to do with the importance of this distinction. Insofar as contemporary culture is highly technological in character, em-phasizing scientific objectivity, efficiency, a "businesslike" approach, we are confronted with a certain bias in favor of speculative knowledge. In-deed, one can often find discussions of evaluative knowledge in which the propriety of the term "knowledge" is itself denied. Such people prefer to view evaluative knowledge as intuition or feeling, taken in a pejorative way. The real knowledge, they say, is the knowledge of the disinterested scientist. The knowledge of the poet, of the artist, of the lover is not knowledge at all. Such an approach, however, has the effect of greatly cheapening human life. And in some cases it can be positively destructive.

Two young newlyweds, for example, may boldly proclaim their confi-dence in each other's love. And they are right; they know their love with-out proof or technical analysis. But as time passes, that confidence may pass as well. Under the pressure of the American technological bias (as well as their own insecurity), they may attempt to *prove* their love. Indeed, like good scientists, they may demand such proof. So signs of love are tendered by the other party. Gifts are given. But do they constitute the required proof? Of course not. Each gift can be variously interpreted; it could be sincere or it could be a lie. Professions of love are distrusted, gestures of love are overlooked, and the uncertainty does nothing but grow. Why? The answer lies in the difference between speculative and evaluative knowledge. The knowledge of love cannot be proved, for it is not grounded in quantifiable facts but in qualitative realities that must be directly perceived. The nervous lover has attempted the impossible. He or she has attempted to make evaluative knowledge follow the rules of speculative knowledge. And what is really insidious is that the lover has been encouraged to do precisely this by the technological, speculative bias of our culture. The lover is told in a thousand different ways that what is not proveable is not real, that objective is best. And thus he or she attempts to make the experience of personal love fit that model.

It cannot be done. What is more, with a reasonable understanding of the unique differences between speculative and evaluative knowledge, it need not be done. As many contemporary Americans are realizing, both sorts of knowledge are needed and both sorts of knowledge are valuable. But each must be allowed to follow its own laws. There is a place for mysticism, for poetry, for the beauty of a simpler life style, for rich and varied human relationships, for meditation and quiet reflection. And our culture must make room for these as much as for the knowledge of science and industry.

Conclusion

The distinction between speculative and evaluative knowledge is, finally, of pivotal importance for the understanding of the human act, and therefore for moral theology. As human persons we cannot build a life or make a real decision on the basis of some bare fact flatly transmitted in a didactic and noninvolving way. When the exercise of *liberum arbitrium* brings us to the moment of decision, we are not deciding among facts. We are deciding among values. We are choosing good over bad, or good over less good, trying to respond to reality as *we* find it. Therefore, the only kind of knowledge that can genuinely fund and prompt the decision of a human act is truly evaluative knowledge.

The implications of this insight for moral theology are many. They can only be alluded to at this point. For one thing, an appreciation of evaluative knowledge would seem to demand considerable revision in the style of moral education for children. It is not sufficient to pass on to the next generation the objective facts of what we find to be good and bad. Much more is required by way of occasioning and encouraging in the children a growing *appreciation* of those values. For only in this way can children be provided with the data on which to base concrete behavioral decisions. Another implication of this analysis of evaluative knowledge pertains to the communication of moral values among adults. Just as a speculative style of teaching will not satisfy the needs of children, neither will it satisfy the needs of adults. Church leaders or ethical teachers cannot acquit themselves of their duties by edict. Education, in the fullest sense of that word, is what is required. A third implication, which we will have occasion to discuss again, has to do with the function of moral norms and rules. All too often such norms have been analyzed and used as "fact-purveyors." In many cases, however, moral norms function preeminently (and importantly) as evokers of value-appreciation. And that is quite a different thing.

Other implications may become clear as this study continues. For the present, this discussion of evaluative knowledge must be allowed to conclude our consideration of the human act. We must go deeper now, and consider the place where the human act resides: the human person.

6

THE HUMAN PERSON

In the previous chapter, we attempted to understand ourselves. We took as our starting point the idea with which the Scholastic manuals of moral theology ordinarily begin: the human act. Then, finding that bare concept somewhat inadequate, we began a process of nuancing. We enriched our reflections by adding a strong emphasis upon the impediments to full human action. We clarified our understanding by bringing the concepts of knowledge and freedom into clearer focus. As a result, we achieved a fair approximation of our own experience. The description of the human act distilled from the tradition of Catholic theology and elaborated in the light of the contemporary social sciences eventually found a strong resonance with life as we live it every day.

Still it was only an approximation. It did not fully coincide with experience. Why was that? The answer can be found in the notion of permanence. Starting with the idea of the human act, as the manuals of moral theology did, has many advantages. But it also has one disadvantage, one deficiency, that must now be remedied. Human acts are, by definition, passing things. They happen, and once they have happened they are gone. But human beings are not passing things. They continue. They change. They grow or deteriorate, but they continue nonetheless. And the Scholastic understanding, beginning with the human act, failed to take due note of that perduring aspect. So it is interesting that the flaw in the previous presentation, the inadequacy which we sense, was not the result of some middle step in our reasoning. Nor was it the result of some factor accidentally excluded from our calculus. Rather it was the result of the starting point itself. What was said in the previous chapter needed to be said; but now we must say more. Without denying the truth found in our reflections on the human act, we must now consider the continuing, perduring reality of the human person.

What do we mean by human person? That question is not as easy to answer as it would seem. For in fact we never see "person" in its bare reality. What we see, what we experience in ourselves and in others, is person-clothed-in-action. Or more precisely, we experience actions which, we realize, do not stand by themselves, but rather reveal and manifest and express a person that lies beneath. Let us consider our own experience.

I am a person: I find myself to be a person. Why is that? First of all, I assert my own personhood because I experience myself as being more than my actions. I am never apart from action, of course. I am never "doing nothing." The "being" and the "doing" of my life are never separated, but rather always coexist. Still I sense that to view myself as nothing more than the sum total of my activities is to reduce myself, cheapen myself, make myself less than I really am. "People are known by their actions." That is true, but it is not altogether true. If you could make a comprehensive list of all the things I do, all the deeds I perform, all the thoughts I think, all the feelings I possess, you would still not have captured the being that I am. Or so my experience tells me. There is a "moreness" to life, something that is not adequately accounted for in the passing reality of events and actions and experiences. To account for that moreness, we must posit another reality beyond the human act. And that reality is the human person.

But there is another reason for asserting the notion of person. Namely, it is personhood that gives actions their human importance. When I make the statement, "I am cold," I am really asserting two things. First, I am asserting the experience of coldness. But I am also asserting the presence of person. Coldness in itself is unimportant; what is important is that it is *mine*. It is the localization, the grounding, the rootedness of the experience or the event that ultimately gives it its value. How different it is to say, "A man died" and, on the other hand, "I killed a man." But what is the difference? The difference is personhood. Killing didn't just happen, it was not merely a human act that came and went. Rather it was the action of a person, of a reality that remained. In fact, just as a garden plant can live only because its roots lie deep in the soil, so these human acts have life only in and because of the person in whom they are rooted.

A third reason for our assertion of human personhood follows from what has been said. If moral theology means anything, it means that human beings are responsible for their behavior. But whence comes that responsibility? It comes from personhood. We are not merely the sum total of an infinity of actions laid end to end, so to speak. And we do not totally change from moment to moment, moving from identity to identity as we move from place to place. If we were thus, we could not be held responsible for our actions. "That was yesterday's human act," we would say. "Today I am someone different." But we reject that. The actions pass, but the agent remains. And thus we are responsible, whether we admit it or not. In the last analysis, then, human beings are morally responsible precisely because (and only inasmuch as) they are persons.

The vision presented by the previous chapter, then, must be complemented by this new insight. The people we met in the previous chapter, we might say, were two-dimensional. They had length and width. They had various different actions, various different experiences. They moved from place to place, from event to event, from feeling to thought to conviction. But there was a flatness to them; they were no more than two-dimensional. Now, however, the people we see are three-dimensional. They still have those two dimensions of the previous chapter, but more than that, they have a certain depth. And that depth is personhood. Beneath and within human actions, the depth of person resides. And it is that third dimension that ultimately grounds and generates action, gives action its importance, and continues to survive when the action passes.

In an appropriate if homely image, then, people might be compared to onions. Like onions, they are comprised of myriad layers beginning at the surface and moving to the center. None of these layers can stand by itself, and yet each has its own identity. At the outermost layer, as it were, we find their environment, their world, the things they own. Moving inward we find their actions, their behavior, the things they do. And then the body, that which is the "belonging" of a person and yet also *is* the person. Going deeper we discover moods, emotions, feelings. Deeper still are the convictions by which they define themselves. And at the very center, in that dimensionless pinpoint around which everything else revolves, is the person himself or herself—the I.

This, then, is the understanding of that person we most centrally are. But there is one paradox to this understanding, and we must now highlight it. Although we are driven to assert the existence of the human person within activity for all the reasons that have already been adduced, nonetheless it remains true that personhood is the one thing about human beings which we cannot actually see. In a process of reflection I seek to discover myself. I hold up to the eye of my mind the experiences that I have. But who looks at those experiences? I do, the person that I am. So I look deeper, at my emotions, my feelings, my attitudes. I reflect upon those things that characterize the way I live. But who does the looking? I do, the person that I am. I go deeper, ever deeper, lifting up from within myself my most central convictions, my deepest identity. Repeatedly I attempt to gaze upon the very center of myself. But I always fail. For the real person that I am always remains the viewer, and can never become the viewed. As a person I am a subject. And I cannot become an object, even to myself.

So I do not assert my personhood, and the personhood of all human beings, because I can see that personhood. No, that personhood is subject, not object to be seen. Rather I assert the existence of personhood because I am *aware* that it is the subject implied by and experienced in the contemplation of all objects. In the terminology of Karl Rahner, personhood is not something we consider; rather it is the "condition of the possibility" of all things that we consider. And thus we can see why, even in the process of introducing and analyzing the nature of the human person, we did not reject or deny anything that had already been said about the nature of the human act. For to do this would not only be to give personhood more credit than it deserves, it would also be to destroy the very reality that reveals personhood to us.

Person and Agent

With all of these nuances, distinctions, and warnings said, we can now proceed to clarify the differences between the human person and the human act. Or more precisely, we can highlight the various characteristics of these two aspects of that being we find ourselves to be. We can be viewed as agents, as doers of human acts. But we can also be viewed as persons, as beings who precede, ground, and transcend those actions. We can be viewed on the surface of our day-to-day lives or, through more subtle considerations, we can be viewed in the depths of our own reality. The listing, then, of a number of these characteristics should serve to clarify what has already been said.

First of all, humans-as-agent, human beings as they were especially viewed by the Scholastics, are objects. Humans-as-person, on the contrary, are subjects. And it is precisely this nonobjective status that makes human persons unique in the world. It follows from this, in the second place, that humans-as-agent are able to be analyzed. In fact, inasmuch as they are objects, they are the perfect focus for human knowing. Not so with humans-as-person. Persons are simply there, self-aware and implied in activity. But as subjects, they are never the direct object of knowledge. Thirdly, agents, by definition, are changeable beings. As actions change, so the doers of actions change. Persons, however, perdure beyond the life-span of any individual action. It follows from this, then, that agents are preeminently "do-ers," while persons are more clearly understood as "be-ers." Human beings, inasmuch as they are agents, exercise their existence through action. But humans-as-person exercise their reality precisely by being. Another way to say the same thing is to assert that inasmuch as human beings are agents, they are little more than particular instances of "humanity." I can make a particular decision, perform a particular deed. But you are capable of making the same decision, performing the same deed. We are both agents, and both of our actions, as actions, can be really the same. But humans-as-person are far more than mere instances of human nature. They are also unique. The "being" that comprises them as persons is at least partly unique being, never before real and never to be reduplicated.

But if all the above characteristics differentiate humans-as-person from humans-as-agent, by far the clearest way of distinguishing them is through the realities of knowledge and freedom. We considered these two realities in the last chapter, in the context of our overall discussion of the human act. But now we must reconsider them, adding the new, deeper vision of the human person which we have achieved.

Inasmuch as we are human agents, performers of human acts, we exercise a very real sort of knowledge. What sort of knowledge? Our response was: evaluative knowledge. Without denying that, we must now add a new term and a new understanding. The sort of knowledge involved in human acts is "reflex knowledge." What does that mean? When you and I say that we know something, we are really saying two things. First of all, we are saying that we know the object of our attention. We know that the house is green, that the plain is vast, that murder is wrong. But we also know that very knowledge of ours. As the Scholastics said, we "know that we know." We are able to hold the very knowledge that we have up to the eye of our mind. We are able to make *it* the object of our attention. We are able to reflect, as in a mirror, upon the knowledge that is ours. Thus we can term our original knowledge of the house, the plain, the act of murder reflex knowledge. It is knowledge that is or can be the object of its own reflection within our minds.

But when, in this chapter, we considered ourselves under the aspect of our personhood, we came upon a different sort of knowledge. We discovered that our personhood could not be "reflected upon." It could not be the direct object of our attention. Person could not be held up to the mirror of the mind for the very simple reason that person (as subject) would always be viewing that mirror image. We do have a certain awareness of ourselves. We have a sense of our own identity. But that awareness, that sense, is not available as a direct object of reflection. Thus we find ourselves forced to assert a second sort of human knowledge, nonreflex knowledge. The knowledge of the human act is reflex knowledge. The knowledge of our core human person, however, is nonreflex.

And then there is freedom. Once again, in the previous chapter we discovered that freedom is an essential component of a genuinely human act. But what sort of freedom? Our answer, you will recall, was *liberum arbitrium*, freedom of choice. It was the freedom made possible by the presence of a number of options, multiple possibilities. And it was the freedom exercised in the selection among those options and possibilities. In our present context, however, let us pursue this a little more deeply. The freedom of the human act, of human-as-agent, is a dividing freedom. It is a freedom that takes the experience of life and separates it, divides it into alternatives. It organizes life into categories and then selects from among those categories. In a paradoxical way, the freedom of the human act is a limiting freedom, for it takes one from the situation in which all options are open to the situation in which all options but one are foreclosed. What is more, this selectivity of the freedom of the human act reveals itself from the very beginning. It is, no doubt, a human act to prepare the menu for a dinner. But to be involved in that human act precisely means that the agent is involved in no other act. To focus one's attention on, and to exercise one's freedom within, the category of food is to *not* do an infinite number of other possible things at this moment. Thus, because the freedom associated with the human act both operates in the context of categories and exercises itself by the selection of categories, that freedom can accurately be termed "categorical freedom."

The freedom of the human act is categorical, however, only because it is the freedom associated with "doing." At the deeper level of man's "being," his personhood, things are quite otherwise. We experience ourselves as men and women who are free, not only as agents but also as persons. But that does not mean that the freedom associated with these two levels of our reality is the same. No, the freedom associated with our core, our personhood, is a quite different sort. Only objects can be categorized, and my personhood is not an object. It is a subject. From the perspective of my central personhood, the focus for free decision is not one category of objects or another. Rather it is all objects taken together. Inasmuch as I am a "being," really the only free decision to be made is the decision "to be or not to be." It is the decision to accept or reject reality as I find it. The central core of myself, the "I" which is my personhood, is confronted with a reality that transcends all categories. It is confronted with the reality of my world, my situation, my body, my feelings, my attitudes and prejudices. In fact it is confronted even by the condition of the possibility of that reality: namely, God. And from the perspective of my own core, the subjectivity that I am, this cosmically inclusive objectivity presents itself for decision. A simple, singular decision: yes or no. The freedom of the human person, then, is not categorical freedom at all. Rather it is a freedom that transcends all categories, it is "transcendental freedom."

It is not a freedom that determines and limits my range of life. Rather it is a freedom that opens up life. For if through some perversity I were to respond to the cosmic choice presented to my core with the word "no," I would be saying no not only to my world, but also to myself. I would be rejecting my opportunities for action, the possibilities of my own being. I would, in a word, be denying and destroying myself. If, on the other hand, my response to this cosmic query is "yes," then I am in a very real sense bringing myself into being. I am freeing myself, liberating myself for action and for fuller reality. It is true that the decision of transcendental freedom, like the exercise of any freedom, defines me. But in the case of transcendental freedom I am doing a "de-fining" in the root sense of that word; I am de-limiting myself, going beyond my limits, making something exist which did not exist before.

So there are two sorts of freedoms. There is the categorical freedom of human-as-agent, the freedom associated with human action. And there is transcendental freedom, the freedom of human-as-person, the freedom associated with perduring being.

One thing remains to be said. And it is merely an extension of a point made previously. To assert the existence of human-as-person in addition to human-as-agent is not to assert that person ever exists apart from agency and action. I am never, quite literally, doing nothing. Rather, it is through and in my action that my personhood is expressed and realized. But if this is true of our basic understanding of person and action, it must also be true of the new understanding of knowledge and freedom we have just achieved. The self-awareness characteristic of human-as-person is an awareness that arises in the very midst of the actions with which we fill our day. And similarly the cosmic exercise of transcendental freedom occurs only in and through the exercises of categorical freedom with which we are so famliar.

If it could be determined that in the last twenty-four hours I have made one hundred categorical decisions, human acts, and if through some omniscience I were able also to clearly know and be certain that in that same period of time I have exercised my deep-down freedom to define and establish myself as person, how many decisions did I make? A hundred and one? No. Rather I made a hundred decisions, some one of which, in addition to being a decision about this or that action, also functioned as a decision about me myself. The exercise of transcendental freedom, then, does not stand apart from categorical freedom. The action by which I establish, create, and define myself does not stand apart from the actions by which I direct the events of my life. Rather, transcendental freedom— transcendental, self-defining decision—occurs within and through those day-to-day categorical choices.

As we have said several times before, the level of the human being which we have named "personal" is not asserted because we see it clearly or because it stands clearly apart. It is only asserted because if it were not, the reality that we find ourselves to be would be cheapened and aborted. And similarly, the realities of nonreflex knowledge and transcendental freedom are asserted not because they stand apart or by themselves, but rather because without them the reality of ourselves which we experience day in and day out would not be adequately accounted for.

Human Identity

If there is anything characteristic of adulthood, it is the fact of having a personal identity. Men and women are admired for being adults precisely because they have such an identity. They are not totally subject to the manipulations of the outer world or to the whims of their own desires. They do not live spineless, directionless lives. Rather they have taken charge of themselves. They stand in some particular way toward the world. Beneath all the actions that they do, and revealing itself through those actions, is a "fundamental stance." And it is that stance which gives their lives direction, significance, and definition. It is, in a very real sense, that fundamental stance which makes their lives human. For it affirms and expresses, as it also creates and effects, the person that they have chosen to be.

That fundamental stance, however, did not always exist. Just as such a stance is characteristic of adulthood, so the lack of it is characteristic of childhood. To be a child is to be subject to manipulation and whim. It is to be without particular direction. It is to be a being without a stance toward the world. But if that is true, then it follows that at some point or another we, as persons, assumed the stance that we now hold. There must, logically, have been a moment at which we chose that stance, a moment at which we exercised that transcending kind of freedom in order to define ourselves as persons. And if the stance we now possess is a fundamental stance, then we can appropriately term that moment of decision a "fundamental option."

This notion of fundamental option is, of course, a concept often discussed in contemporary theology.[1] So, having introduced the term here, it might be well to add a few comments immediately. First of all, it was most important that we approach the concept in this rather circuitous way. For the fact of the matter is that the fundamental option is only of secondary importance. What is really important is a person's fundamental stance. Fundamental option is nothing more than the name we give to the moment in which the stance is assumed or emphatically renewed. Fundamental option is the name for any exercise of transcendental freedom. Thus, just as all freedoms are subservient to the action or being they direct, so the fundamental option is subservient to the definition and identity it brings about: the fundamental stance.

Second of all, as is clear from the way we described it, a fundamental option does not exist all by itself. A fundamental option is not a particular decision standing next to all the other categorical decisions of life. Rather it is the deeper meaning and significance of some of the decisions of our lives. Indeed, like all the other aspects of human-as-person, the fundamental option is not something we can directly see or consciously analyze. At most, it is something of which we can be nonreflexly aware.[2]

Third of all, a fundamental option is not a once-and-for-all reality. True, it is a decision about the sort of person one chooses to be. It is an inner act of self-definition. But it is not irrevocable, not final or definitive. As one author expresses it, the fundamental option is a decision about the person *totus sed non totaliter* (as a whole person but not totally).[3] Our experience tells us that we retain the capacity to reverse even our basic approach to life, Indeed, even if we would like it otherwise, life periodically presents us with critical turning points, moments in which the making of a particular categorical behavioral choice also challenges us to elect once again the person we wish to be. The option may be a reaffirmation of a stance already adopted, or it may involve a reversal. But in either case it is a new, still not definitive but yet fundamental, election of the self.

Let us conclude. When we attempt to observe the life that we live, we discover that there are two distinct types of behavior. We have termed these types of behavior "act of man" and "human act." Upon further reflection, however, we have concluded that not all human acts are alike. Some are human acts pure and simple, focusing our attention in decision upon a particular categorical object. Others, however, are more than that. They are actions which arise from the very core of ourselves as persons. They are actions in which and through which we are not only choosing a particular categorical object, but are also choosing a transcendental subject for ourselves.

Within some of our human acts a human person is being born, or being recreated and reaffirmed. Not all our actions, to be sure; but some of them express and define us as persons. They are, in a very real sense, sacraments of the person that we are. These human acts are rich symbols of the person we are choosing to become, and like all sacraments they tend to effect that which they symbolize. Thus, in these most richly human acts, these acts that carry and include a fundamental option, we as beings of depth, as persons, create ourselves.

The human person that we sense ourselves to be does not stand apart from the actions we do. So also the nonreflex knowledge and the transcendental freedom that we find ourselves to have do not stand apart from the reflex knowledge and categorical freedom of our daily lives. The fundamental stance that gives us the identity we so highly treasure is not to be found in a vacuum but rather is to be found incarnated in the behavior by which we build our lives. And finally the fundamental option we have just been considering is not really something that we "do" at all, but is rather the term we use to describe what is "really going on" within the rich activity that we perform.

We are, then, three-dimensional beings. We are beings of depth. But this depth does not stand apart, it stands within. It is perceived, not next to the surface layers of human action but through those layers. Thus we should not be at all surprised if, like most realities perceived through covering veils, our understanding of our central personhood never ceases being somewhat opaque. It has often been said that the most important things in life are ultimately mysteries. Our analysis of the human person—of the being that constitutes our human acts, lies within those acts, and goes beyond those acts—does nothing to deny that thesis.[4]

7

MORALITY: SIN AND VIRTUE

Until now, our discussions have maintained a relatively neutral tone. It is true that we considered the mechanism by which we perceive and appreciate value. And our description of the "yes" and "no" that constitute fundamental option could certainly be taken to imply some sort of personal obligation. But inasmuch as we have consistently focused on human acts and the human person as facts, we have avoided any blatant value judgments of our own. That objectivity, that neutrality, now ends. To be human is to be responsible for oneself. And to be responsible is, in some sense, to be obligated. So, whereas we have thus far attempted to understand ourselves as beings who are free, we must now discuss ourselves as beings who are obligated.

But to talk about ourselves as obligated, whether to ourselves or to God, is to talk about morality. Indeed the term "morality" is nothing but a sort of shorthand by which we refer to the whole realm of obligation and human responsibility. To say that I am a moral being is to say nothing else than that I am a being responsible and accountable, and therefore obligated. But to discuss morality within a religious frame of reference is inevitably to introduce the notions of sin and virtue. Therefore, in this chapter our task will be to reconsider the human persons we have come to know and to attempt to analyze them precisely from the perspective of human and religious obligation, from the perspective of morality. In the process of doing this, we shall largely direct ourselves to the terms "sin" and "virtue" as they are currently understood. But as a sort of preamble to these systematic reflections, we shall begin with a consideration of the notion of sin as that reality is presented in the pages of Sacred Scripture.

Scriptural Sin

Throughout the pages of the Old and New Testament references to the reality of sin, and uses of the term itself, abound. Indeed, one could make a good case for the assertion that the entire Bible is "about" sin and what God has done about sin. There are, of course, a number of different nuances which the word takes in various contexts. In fact, the term itself has the relatively neutral meaning of "missing the mark." Still the fundamental meaning of sin in the pages of the Bible has a remarkable consistency.

Sin is, first and foremost, a *religious* reality. For biblical authors, sin makes no sense apart from the presence of God and our obligation to him. Why is that? The God of the Bible is the God of the Covenant, the God who has committed himself to us and who expects our commitment in return: "I will be your God, and you will be my people." This covenantal relationship, even when it is not the primary focus, stands as a perduring backdrop. Covenant is the horizon within which the biblical world is understood and the biblical life lived. Covenant is, therefore, also the context within which the biblical notion of sin makes itself evident. Sin is infidelity to that covenant, our refusal to live up to our part of the bargain.

Sin is our recurring refusal to accept the claims of the God of revelation upon ourselves. It is the substitution of some other reality for God, the placing of oneself or some created thing where God alone should stand. Thus, for biblical authors, the ultimate sin, the paradigmatic sin, is idolatry. Indeed, in the last analysis, all sin is but a form of idolatry. Sometimes the idolatry is blatant, as in the construction of the golden calf by the Israelite people at Sinai (Ex 32:1–6; Deut 9:7–21). At other times it is more subtle. In fact, one gets the impression that straightforward construction of worship objects is not, for the biblical authors, the most pernicious form of idolatry. Rather, idolatry at its worst is idolatry of self. Self-sufficiency is the greatest sin. From the story of Adam and Eve in Genesis to the era of the Prophets, the people are most forcefully condemned and most strongly rebuked for daring to "go it alone" (e.g. Deut 32:18; Is 10:13–19; Ez 28:2). It is their pride that Yahweh finds most offensive. They fail to love God, to serve God. They seek to make themselves God and to take his prerogatives to themselves. They are, therefore, "a people of unclean lips" (Is 6:5). They have sinned, and must repent (e.g. Hos 14:2–4).

This religious emphasis is so thoroughgoing that even offenses against the neighbor find their malice in the betrayal of God. We may say that David sinned against Bathsheba by his lust, or that he sinned against Uriah by sending him into the battlefront. But David says, "I have sinned against Yahweh" (2 Sam 12:13). It is true that one's love of God is to manifest itself in love of neighbor (e.g. Lev 19:9–18; Is 1:23–25). But the same logic led the scriptural authors to assert that the deepest malice of the offense against the neighbor is precisely that it implies a rejection of God (e.g. Ez 18:3–32).

In the Gospels, too, the religious dimension of social sin is emphasized. When the prodigal son finally repents and returns to his ancestral home, he confesses: "Father, I have sinned against God and against you" (Lk 15:21). Not one or the other; both have been offended by his action. And the two great commandments of love from the Old Testament, love for God (Deut 6:5) and love for neighbor (Lev 19:18) are expressed in a way that irrevocably unites them (Mt 22:34–40; Mk 12:28–31; Lk 10:25–37).[1]

In the biblical understanding, then, the reality of sin is not directly connected to any particular action in itself. Rather the focus of attention with regard to sin is the *meaning* of the action, the significance of the action for God and persons, and the effect of that action upon their relationship. Sin is the failure to love God and to serve him. No matter how it happens to manifest itself, its reality remains the same.

Moreover, inasmuch as the refusal to love can perdure and become a state of being, sin itself can be viewed also as a state. Sin is the state of alleged independence, of asserted self-sufficiency. Sin is that "hardness of heart" that lasts, the ears that will not hear and the eyes that will not see (Is 6:9). Sin is the situation of Israel, and humankind, when they refuse to acknowledge the claims and prerogatives of God. Indeed, it does not constitute an undue projection of our own perspectives upon the Bible to assert that "acts" of sin assume major significance only because of their effect upon the "state" of sin. Such typically biblical images as "stubbornness," "obstinacy," "refusal to listen and repent," as well as "divine readiness to forgive any number of offenses"—all this suggests as much (Is 65). And as time went on, the relationship between act and state became more pronounced. By the time of the composition of John's Gospel, indeed, this relationship had become so central that the Baptist says, "There is the lamb of God who takes away the sin of the world" (Jn 1:29). Sin in the singular, the state of sin. Not individual errors or acts of malice. Rather the cosmic situation of alienation, of fractured relationships between God and his people. It is this state of sin, this posture of proud self-sufficiency, that Jesus has come to change. And thus, for example, Jesus willingly associates with "sinners." It is only the proud ones, the arrogant ones, the Pharisees, that he continually condemns.

In the end, then, the *hamartia tou cosmou*, the sinful, fractured, alienated state of the whole world is what takes center stage. It becomes the symbol for all the individual sinful acts that we are wont to do. And it explains why these acts are, indeed, of ultimately religious and not merely ethical import.

These, then, are some aspects of the scriptural vision of sin. Much more could be said. We have, for example, emphasized the Old Testament roots of the understanding of sin. It would be interesting to indicate the developments to be found in the Synoptics and Paul. In fact, we shall return to some of these ideas later. But what has been presented is sufficient for our purposes here. Now we must go on. After all, even the most complete elucidation of a scriptural theology of sin would be insufficient for our time. We must expand our sights in order to develop an understanding attuned to our own culture, and our own needs. Using these scriptural themes as a backdrop, a benchmark against which to measure our own reflections, we must attempt to develop a contemporary theology of sin.

The Notion of Sin

At the conclusion of the last two chapters, we achieved a rather general statement describing ourselves as human beings. We asserted that human-as-person is more important than human-as-agent, that who we are is more important than what we do. We also asserted that the ongoing identity we possess is more important than the moment at which we assume that identity, that our stance is more important than the options by which we assume that stance. In the hierarchy of "importances," then, what comes first is our fundamental stance. After that come fundamental options. And in the third place come those actions, those exercises of human agency, by which we express or fail to express our inner personhood.

Now, if that analysis is true, and if it is also true that we are the responsible, accountable—and therefore moral—animal, it stands to reason that human morality will manifest itself most strongly in the area of fundamental stance. And that is precisely what we now wish to assert. Indeed, fundamental stance, looked at from the point of view of morality, is nothing else than the state of sin or virtue. Those terms are actually synonymous. St. John's Gospel made clear that sin and virtue are more profoundly viewed as states than acts. They are the states of alienation from and relationship to God, respectively. So also is our personhood more profoundly understood as a state of being, a fundamental stance. Just as Scripture strongly emphasizes the *religious* character of sin and virtue, so the theory of fundamental stance and fundamental option made clear that those realities always include a posture toward God. For from the core of the human person, the other to which a yes or a no is said is an undifferentiated and therefore all-inclusive other. It is impossible, within the understanding of fundamental option and fundamental stance which we have seen, for us to be positively related to ourselves and our world while yet alienated from our God. Our posture is either one of universal affirmation and openness or it is not. And whichever stance we assume and hold, it is a stance with an intrinsic and necessary reference to God. In this sense, then, (although this raises many other issues which cannot be pursued here) we are intrinsically and necessarily religious beings.

Another point. Thomas Aquinas states in his *Summa Theologiae* that it is only mortal sin that truly deserves the name "sin" (I-II, 88, 1). Any other event or reality which we may name sin deserves that name only in an analogous sense. This we can now very well understand, it is only another way of saying what was asserted in the last chapter. Namely, that we only become truly human by the exercise of basic, transcendental freedom, and not any other sort. It is only in the exercise of fundamental option, and in the assumption of fundamental stance, that we take ourselves in hand and "create ourselves." Sin and virtue are characteristically human realities. In their fullest, most correct sense, they only arise when we live our humanity in the fullest, most complete way. And that complete exercise of humanity only occurs in the fundamental stance arising through a fundamental option. Thus, to repeat, the reality we have previously termed fundamental stance is nothing but a philosophic synonym for the religious realities of sin and virtue, or, if you like, "the state of sin" and the "state of grace."

But there is also place for acts of sin and acts of virtue. For we also asserted in the last chapter that the concept of fundamental option, while not of primary importance, was still logically required. If to be adult means to hold a fundamental stance, to become adult means to assume that stance by means of a fundamental option. Similarly, to remain adult, and to exercise that adulthood, means to periodically review or change that fundamental stance by means of additional fundamental options. This series of ideas also, we now add, can be articulated in religious language. Mortal sin as an act is nothing else than a synonym for fundamental option. A mortal sin (or a mortal act of virtue—it is interesting that the Christian tradition has never generated a clear vocabulary for positive acts) is that act by which we substantially reject God and assume instead a posture apart from and in alienation from God. Mortal sin is the moment in which we deny the God who calls us through and in creation and thus, paradoxically, deny our own deepest selves. Mortal sin is the act of sin by which we take upon ourselves the state of sin.

But if mortal sin is nothing else than a negative fundamental option, it follows that, like that option, it is a transcendental act. That is, mortal sin is not precisely the doing of any particular categorical act. Rather it is the act of self-disposition occurring *through* and *in* that concrete categorical act. The "things" which in the past we had been inclined to call mortal sins are not precisely sin at all. Rather they are the symbols of sin, the sacraments of sin. In a very real sense those objective acts are "occasions of sin." But if all this is true, it is also true that, like the fundamental option, mortal sin never occurs *apart* from objective acts. Just as all transcendental acts occur in conjunction with (and are expressed through) categorical acts, so too mortal sin occurs in connection with the doing of specific deeds. Still, mortal sin and the deeds that we do are not precisely identical. And for reasons that will become apparent further on, that is a very important point to make. But before proceeding, certain implications of our identification of mortal sin and fundamental option must be highlighted.

First of all, it should be clear that according to this understanding mortal sin is a relatively rare phenomenon. We do not assert that mortal sin never occurs; far from it. But we do assert that it is a genuinely serious event. It is an event whose importance, moreover, is not the result of some extrinsic rule, but rather is intrinsic to the reality. The act by which we place ourselves in alienation from God, our world, and ourselves is not something that is done casually, flippantly, or in a moment of distraction. It most certainly is not something done by accident. Rather, as the most serious act that we can perform, mortal sin or mortal act of virtue (conversion) must be something that occurs relatively infrequently, in a sort of peak moment of human experience.

Secondly, it follows from our equation of mortal sin and fundamental option that we lack any clear reflex knowledge of our prevailing moral state. Because fundamental option occurs at the core of the person, where the person is totally subject and not at all object, we are intrinsically incapable of reflecting either upon that option or upon the state that it produces. In religious language we can therefore say that we are equally incapable of knowing, in a reflex way, whether a particular action truly involved a basic decision to reject world and self or not, whether we are truly in the state of grace or in the state of sin. We have a *nonreflex* awareness of our decisions and state, of course. Also, by honest observation of our categorical behavior, we are able to posit a reasonable conjecture about our situation. But we can never know in a definitive, irrefutable, proof-oriented way how we ultimately stand with God.

Given the understanding of sin that has often been taught to Christian people, and especially Catholics, this may seem a rather radical idea. But in point of fact it is a thoroughly traditional and orthodox Christian understanding. Consider, for example, these words of St. Paul in which he seems to be referring to this same sense of ultimate moral uncertainty:

> The first requirement of an administrator is that he prove trustworthy. It matters little to me whether you or any human court pass judgment on me. I do not even pass judgment on myself. Mind you, I have nothing on my conscience. But that does not mean that I am

declaring myself innocent. *The Lord is the one to judge me*, so stop passing judgment before the time of his return. He will bring to light what is hidden in darkness and manifest the intentions of hearts. (1 Cor 4:2f) (emphasis added)

What does it mean to say that the Lord will "bring to light what is hidden?" Does it mean that he will illuminate the state of *my* soul for you? At least that. But it can also mean that he will light up *for me* the secrets of my own heart. He will finally make me transparent to myself, finally remove the darkness that I find in the center of my own person. Thus when Paul insists that there should be no "premature judgment," he is referring not only to our penchant for judging others. He is also insisting that we must not pretend to be able to adequately and finally judge ourselves.

If this is what Paul is saying, it is also what theologians through the centuries have said. Even official Church teaching, in the Council of Trent, spoke to the issue of certitude when it declared:

Whoever reflects upon himself, his personal weakness, and his affective disposition may fear and tremble about his own grace, since no one can know with a certitude of faith which cannot admit any error, that he has obtained God's grace. (DS 1534)

Moreover, we may reflect that this sense of human unclarity about one's stance before God is the very reality to which the Christian virtue of hope responds. Hope, as distinguished from presumption on the one hand and despair on the other, prompts Christians to trust in God *despite their own lack of subjective certitude*. We have only a certain sense of our relatedness to God, we have only a nonreflex awareness. While our observations regarding our categorical behavior may generate a certain prudent confidence, we are nonetheless aware of our own capacity for self-deception. Therefore, there is truly no alternative for the Christian except to hope; there is no place for "premature judgment."[2]

Our identification of mortal sin with fundamental option, finally, yields one additional implication. Namely, it reminds us that acts of sin and virtue can occur in a person who has *already* assumed the stance against or for God, as the case may be. That is, the fundamental acts of sin and virtue do not only occur in the moment when we reverse the stance of our lives; they can also occur in the moment in which we ratify and reassert that stance. Sinners are capable of redeclaring the choice for alienation in a new fundamental option (that is, a new mortal sin). Similarly persons of virtue are capable of deepening their positive fundamental stance by means of a new act of virtue, a new positive fundamental option. Sin and conversion, then, are seen to be complex terms, referring as they do both to the moment of reversal in life and to the moment of ratification.[3]

Impediments Revisited

Everything that has been said thus far in this chapter may serve to explain the religious notion of mortal sin in a helpful way. But it does not succeed in totally explaining our experience. For the fact of the matter is that, in our everyday experience, we often choose to do things that are wrong without thereby redefining ourselves as total persons. In the vocabulary of the last chapter, we find ourselves performing human acts which are merely that, and nothing more. Acts which are not "fully human" in the way that fundamental options are. And of course our attempt to find a parallel in the language of religion for this natural experience is not difficult. Catholic theology has for centuries spoken of venial sin. But before we can establish the identity between venial sin and "merely human acts," we must answer a prior question. How is such a merely human act possible at all for the human person? Why does not every decision of the human person constitute a self-definition from the core of that person? Or to put this another way, why is not every human act a fundamental option?

The answer to this question lies in a deeper and fuller consideration of the reality called "impediments." We have already discussed impediments in the context of distinguishing human acts from acts of man. In that context we defined them as realities which affect either the knowledge or the freedom necessary to a human act, and thereby rob that act of at least some of the human force it should contain. But now we are in a position to broaden and deepen that definition.

As we saw two chapters ago, our experience reveals that our categorical acts, our decisions to do this or that concrete deed, are often flawed by the presence of impediments. We may lack the proper knowledge or the totality of categorical freedom necessary for a genuinely human act. And thus we saw that the actions in which we are really involved in our day-to-day lives lie somewhere on the continuum between human acts and acts of man. But since we articulated the reality of impediments in that way, we have come to appreciate the deeper dimensions of human beings. We have come to see that we are not merely our actions, nor are we merely agents. We now understand that we are more deeply persons, and that we are characterized by transcendental levels of being. With that new knowledge, then, we can return to our experience. And what do we find? We find that the forces of division, of disunity, of disintegration run deeper than we had ever expected. In addition to the flaws within our activity at the categorical level, there are deep flaws that mar the connection between the categorical and transcendental levels of human beings.

How do we know this? The answer is very simple; we
our categorical behavior is a strange and contradictory c
good things, and we do bad. That is clearly our experienc
this experience mean? If I hold a fundamental stance, ai
which I perform at the categorical level are symbols and saci
stance, then it should follow that there is in my behavior a cc
continuity that are symptomatic of that stance. There shoulu ue a pattern
to my everyday behavior, and more than a pattern. There should be an
absolute homogeneity; everything that I do should be good or bad. And this
is clearly not the case. The fact of the matter is that my life-style is a
combination of good and bad, of virtue and vice. Indeed, it is that very
ambiguity lying within my behavior that makes it impossible for me to
draw sure conclusions regarding my fundamental stance.

But if there is that ambiguity, that lack of consistency, in my behavior,
then it follows that at least some of that behavior must be at variance with
my fundamental stance. Perhaps I am fundamentally an evil and self-
seeking person, and my occasional acts of kindness, of generosity, of honor,
do not truly represent the person that I have chosen to be. Or perhaps the
opposite is the case; that I am in fact a person of love, and that this love
somehow strangely coexists with selfish and unloving acts. But no matter
which of these two alternatives is the case, the central fact remains Some
of my behavior does not coincide with the basic self-identity that I have
assumed. Some of my actions, it is true, are symbols and sacraments of my
fundamental stance. But by the same token, some of my actions are veils of
that stance. They hide my stance both from others and from myself.

How can this be? Only one answer is possible. This type of contradiction is possible only on condition that we suffer from a strange sort of
disunity within ourselves. The connections that link our inner core with
the more superficial levels of our behavior are fragile connections. They
are connections that are sometimes broken, sometimes missing. If, as we
have suggested, the human person can be imaged as an onion, then we are
now suggesting that certain intermediate layers of that onion are flawed.
We are not, after all, thoroughly integral persons. Quite the contrary, we
are "untogether."

What shall we say of this lack of inner integration? The Christian religious tradition has a term to describe it: original sin. Or more precisely,
the effects of original sin. In traditional Catholic theology it was said that
original sin, that primeval action by which our forebears chose to stand
apart from God and to be alienated from him, had produced certain effects
in the human world and the human person. Chief among these effects was
"darkening of the intellect" and "concupiscence." But what are these effects if not the very things which we called impediments two chapters ago?

So it is because of these effects of original sin, to speak in religious language, that we find it so difficult to perform a genuinely human act even on the categorical level.

In contemporary theology, with its enriched understanding of the depth of the human person, this same concept has been expanded. Any negative fundamental option is a negation not only of God and the world, but also, in some mysterious sense, of the self. It is an act of self-destruction. We ought not to be surprised, then, that with the very first rejections of God and world and self by our primeval ancestors, we should lose that integration, that wholeness and consistency, which would ideally characterize our persons. There are, indeed, effects of original sin (however one understands the sin itself). And those effects make us beings who are out of sorts, beings working somehow at cross-purposes with ourselves, beings divided and divided again. So, just as traditional Catholic theology asserted that even with the "remission" of original sin the effects remain, we assert the same. No matter that individual human persons have opted in a fundamentally positive way for God and the world and themselves. No matter that their stance in life is virtuous. The integration which ought ideally to be theirs is not forthcoming. We are not transparent; we are not consistent. Our behavior can reveal our inner stance, but it can also hide that stance. Similarly, no matter how sincere the stance that a person has adopted, the integration of the whole manifold of categorical behavior in that stance, the rendering of behavior consistent with that stance, remains a long and arduous task, a project yet to be completed.[4]

To say this, of course, is to do nothing more than describe our experience. What is often overlooked, however, is the fact that this insight has long been part of the Christian experience as well. As just one example, consider these powerful words of St. Paul:

> We know that the law is spiritual, whereas I am weak flesh sold into the slavery of sin. I cannot even understand my own actions. I do not do what I want to do but what I hate . . . the desire to do right is there but not the power. What happens is that I do, not the good I will to do, but the evil I do not intend. But if I do what is against my will, it is not I who do it, but sin which dwells in me. (Rom 7:14, 18–20)

The "sin which dwells in" Paul is original sin. It is that fact of sin, that situation of alienation and brokenness which is at present a part of the human condition. As that sin lived in Paul, so it lives in us all, with the result that our fundamental stance never succeeds in fully and unequivocally expressing itself in behavior.

Venial Sin

Now, at last, we are in a position to understand the reality of venial sin. Venial sin (or virtue) is purely and simply a human act which is not fully so, which does not come from the core of the human person and which does not involve a fundamental option. It is, we say, a human act. It does involve freedom and knowledge. But it is not a fully human act, a fundamental option. It does not engage the transcendental freedom of our deepest level. In venial sin there is a genuine decision to do this or that action. But there is no decision to become this or that sort of person.

The difference between venial and mortal sin, then, is nothing other than the degree of personal penetration, personal involvement in the act. In the former there is no deep core involvement, while in the latter there is. In the case of mortal sin the person, deciding to do this deed, is also deciding to be a particular sort of person, to reject God and world and, paradoxically, self. In the case of venial sin, however, this is not the case. The person is rather choosing to do this deed while also more deeply choosing to be the sort of person who stands opposed to this deed. In every act of venial sin, then, there is an inner contradiction. And such an act would be simply impossible for us were it not for the inner divisions which separate us from ourselves. Or to put this another way, venial sin would be impossible were it not for impediments, the effects of original sin.

But problems yet remain. To explain in a theoretical way the intrinsic difference between venial and mortal sin is not to explain how we can concretely identify these two, how we can knowingly distinguish them from each other in real life. Two possible answers to this problem immediately suggest themselves, although both must be ultimately rejected.

First of all, it was often suggested in the past that one could distinguish venial sin from mortal sin by the "gravity of the matter." That is, one could simply consider the deed that had been done, evaluate its objective and intrinsic significance, and conclude that if it was a seriously evil act, then a serious and central decision must have been made. In other words, the older view suggested that every commission of a seriously wrong act involved a fundamental option. The insights of modern psychology, however, force us to reject this position. It is clear that for a variety of reasons (impediments, once again) we do things that are seriously wrong without in fact making such a personal decision. And we know this because of the rapidity with which we do such deeds and repent of them. It is inconceivable that a person could define himself or herself, repudiate that definition, and then reassert it in a matter of hours or days.[5] Indeed, to suggest that this could happen is to undermine our very dignity and to cheapen us as persons. So while lists of objectively grave matter may serve a useful function (as we shall see), they do not provide us with an infallible list by which to judge whether a particular action involved venial or mortal sin.

A second alternative suggests itself. We could simply invite agents to look within, to reflect upon their motivations and desires. And we could ask them to tell us if, by this action, they intended to define themselves as persons. However, this, too, will not do. For as we have repeatedly seen, the self-awareness characteristic of our core being is a nonreflexive awareness. We simply do not have that sort of clarity about ourselves and our own identity. We cannot hold our innermost being up to the mirror of our mind; we cannot make our subjectivity into objectivity. Thus we cannot establish with absolute certitude the depth from which our moral decision came.

We are forced back, then, to a conclusion we saw earlier, a painful but realistic conclusion. Just as we cannot be certain of what our fundamental stance is in life, whether we are in the state of sin or the state of grace, so we cannot be certain about the import of our individual actions. We can have in this case, as in the other, a conjectural certitude, an awareness or sense of the truth. But we cannot establish unequivocally and certainly that a particular deed was or was not a fundamental option. Therefore, we are forced to locate the line between venial sin and mortal sin in the mystery that is the human person. That both sorts of sin are real is a datum of experience. That both sorts of sin have occurred in our experience is a greater or lesser possibility. But that any particular act was one or the other is a question mark.

Once again we are driven to the virtue of hope as the only reasonable (and Christian) way to deal with ourselves. Just as God is ultimately a mystery, impervious to our rational efforts, so God's creation, the human person, is a mystery. And there is no avoiding that fact.

The Tradition

We can conclude this chapter by isolating two elements of traditional moral theology, two ways of speaking that are very common in the Catholic world. This we ought to do in order to make perfectly clear that we no longer support these particular formulations, at least as commonly understood.

The first formulation has to do with the so-called "fonts of morality." Briefly, it asserts that there are three elements of a moral act, all of which must be considered in order to accurately judge that act. First of all there is the deed itself, what is to be done. Secondly there are a variety of circumstances which can alter or modify the value of that deed. For example, if I tell you that I gave my neighbor a ride in my automobile, but fail to mention that I did so at gunpoint, I have clearly ignored an important element of the situation. And thirdly there is the motive for the deed. The reason I forced my neighbor into the car was that he was gravely injured and, in his hysteria, was refusing treatment.

Now, it is clear that this principle, focusing upon the action itself as it does, is primarily concerned with objective morality. And as such, it more directly pertains to the considerations that will comprise the second half of this book. We shall discuss this principle again in Chapter Sixteen, but inasmuch as the principle includes the notion of motive, some comments will be useful now. For "motive" is really a term describing the *meaning* that an action has for its agent. And as such, it is a term that summarizes everything that we have been discussing in the last several chapters. It is very much part of the vision of subjective morality that we have been pursuing and, indeed, stands as a sort of symbol of that vision.

And here, precisely, is the problem. By grouping together deed, circumstance, and motive, the three-font principle brings together both subjective and objective morality. It unites these two, which is admirable since they are existentially united in the lives we lead. But it also confuses the two, which is something we must avoid in the extreme. How is there confusion?

In manuals of moral theology the question was often raised as to which of the three fonts was the primary determinant of the morality of any particular action. And the usual response was that it was the deed itself that made an act moral or immoral. But is that the case? If by "moral" one means to refer to *objective* morality, to the actual goodness or badness of the action, then the statement is somewhat true. (It is not altogether accurate, as we shall see in Chapter Sixteen.) But by the same token, if one is discussing objective morality, then motive is not at all germane. For actions, as such, do not have motives; they only have ends or results. Agents have motives; human persons, human subjects, have motives.

Thus, if one really wants to include the element of motive, then one must talk about subjective morality, about the sinfulness or virtuousness of an action. And once we assume this perspective, then it is clear that the motive is the primary determinant of the morality. Indeed, motive is the *only* determinant of the morality. For morality, in this subjective sense in which we have understood it in these pages, is not a quality of deeds but a quality of persons. It is a term that describes the sense of obligation, the accountability, which is characteristic of persons. To be moral, in this sense, then, is to be authentic, to be honest, to be *seeking* to do what is really good. And in the same way, to be immoral is to refuse to do so.

Thus, the three-font principle might best be altogether avoided. For in uniting the spheres of objective and subjective morality, it continually runs the high risk of confusing these two. And that confusion can have disastrous effects.

Indeed, these disastrous effects are clear in the second topic we must now consider. For based upon the assertion that the deed was the primary font of morality, the manuals of moral theology often asked a second question: What then distinguishes mortal from venial sin? And the only logically appropriate answer was given: the gravity of the deed or, as it was more often called, "the gravity of the matter." If the matter, the substantial reality of the deed, was the primary source of morality, then it must follow that the gravity of that matter would be the primary source of the grave moral act (that is, the mortal sin). Similarly where that gravity was lacking, the morality would be light (that is, venial sin). Indeed it was often said that for any sin there must be knowledge and freedom, and that for mortal sin there must be knowledge, freedom, and grave matter.

This, of course, we must altogether reject. It is not the gravity of the matter that makes a particular sin mortal, but rather the degree of personal involvement in the decision to act. And it is not the lightness of the matter that makes a sin venial, but rather the absence of such involvement. One is either involved in the decision in fact or one is not. Our transcendental freedom is either part of what we are doing or it is not. We are either choosing the sort of person we will be in this action or we are not. And if we are not, then the fact that the matter is in and of itself grave will change nothing. In that case we simply have a person who has committed a venial sin in the course of doing something which, objectively speaking, is gravely wrong. Indeed, as we suggested earlier in this chapter, that is precisely what happens in many cases.[6]

What then shall we say of all the lists of "mortal sins" and "venial sins" which have been developed over the years? Are they completely useless? No, indeed. It is not accurate to describe those lists precisely as mortal and venial *sins*, but it is certainly appropriate to formulate such lists of grave and light *matter*. Once this is done, such lists have several valid uses. For one thing, they are helpful information to those who are seeking to genuinely and objectively care for their neighbor. They instruct such persons as to what will or will not be truly in the best interests of their neighbor. Thus they have a noble role to fill in the task of moral catechesis.

In addition, such lists may, within limits, assist in the evaluation of one's past actions. We have repeatedly insisted that our transcendental level of being does not exist apart from our categorical level of action. We have warned that the link between these two levels is not perfect, due to the impediments, the effects of original sin. But by the same token we have been careful to deny that the two levels are totally separated. This being the case, it follows that individual human persons are much more *likely* to exercise their transcendental freedom, to perform fundamental options, and therefore to affect their fundamental stance in an action which is, in and of itself, grave matter. Thus there is a certain presumption, a prevailing likelihood, that a person who performs a deed that is gravely wrong of itself, and who does so with apparent freedom and awareness, will also have performed a fundamental option in that action. There is not, of course, absolute certitude. But there is genuine likelihood. Thus, given the mystery of human persons, to which we have alluded several times, it is more than appropriate that whatever wisdom we have regarding the objective value of acts be formulated into lists such as the moral manuals often possessed.

Again, such lists provide useful guidelines for the administration of the Sacrament of Penance. If it is true that we are and remain a mystery to ourselves, it is to be expected that the Sacrament of Penance, focusing on the encounter of human mystery with divine, will reveal a certain ambiguity. For one thing, penitents approaching the sacrament often have doubts as to the deep personal meaning of the actions they have performed. Was that really a moment of fundamental option against God? I am not sure. Indeed, there is no way to utterly eliminate that doubt. For another thing, it is often the case in practical experience that such people approach the sacrament precisely because of a feeling of repentance (that is to say, because they have already converted). But that means they have either made or reaffirmed a positive fundamental option. Therefore, even if the past action had the worst possible personal meaning, it is a distinct possibility that freedom, new grace, and conversion *precede* the moment of the sacramental act. But all of this does not eliminate the meaning of the sacrament, and here is where those lists serve their purpose.

Christians who truly believe, who hope, and who experience repentance will not be unduly concerned about isolating the moral significance of their past acts. Nor will they be turned away from the sacrament by the possibility that God's gift of grace has already been bestowed upon them. No, they will approach the sacrament in a simple and straightforward way, declaring the deed they have done and reaffirming their desire for the forgiving love of Christ. Were such a person a moral theologian (!), he or she might very well speak words somewhat like the following: "Father, this is what I have done. I don't know for sure if it was a fully human act, a fundamental option. I cannot even be certain that it was a human act, totally devoid of those impediments which affect the mind and will. But I know what I did, and I know that it was gravely harmful to my neighbor. I repent it. And I want the forgiveness of Christ, which may already have been given to me and which I may already have accepted, to be incarnated and renewed in this sacrament."[7]

Conclusion

Sin, then, is not only a religious concept. It is a deeply theological concept. As such it participates deeply in the mystery of God and man. But for all of that mysterious ambiguity, it cannot be ignored. Just as we assert the preeminence of the moral person over the moral act despite the fact that we cannot clearly articulate or see that person, so also we assert the preeminence of sin and virtue over the objective realities of value and disvalue. For in the last analysis, Christians who are called to covenantal relationship with their God live a life that cannot be measured by deeds. They live a life that can only be measured by love, the love that God puts in them, which is the love that is God himself.[8]

8

CONSCIENCE

There can be little doubt that any discussion of morality must include a major consideration of conscience. Indeed, in the popular mind, conscience is often taken to be a synonym for morality itself. The rights of conscience, the duty of conscience, what conscience demands or permits, all these are taken to be summaries of the human moral enterprise.

In point of fact, the matter is considerably more complicated than such colloquialisms might lead us to believe. But the popular understanding is at least correct inasmuch as it insists on a central role for the reality of conscience. Thus, having considered what it means to be a human agent and a human person, and having sought to analyze the moral implications of that agency and that personhood, we now turn to a particular aspect of the human person: conscience

In the course of this chapter we shall consider a number of separate though related topics. First will come a psychological discussion. Then we will summarize the scriptural input. Third, we shall present an overall understanding of conscience expressed in useful contemporary vocabulary. And fourth, we shall confront straight on the very real question of the relationship between the conscience and Church authority.

Guilt Feelings

In the course of this chapter we shall find that the term "conscience" has a number of legitimate meanings. But before we even begin to consider those meanings we must make clear one meaning that is not legitimate. And that is the understanding that equates conscience with subjective feelings of guilt. It may seem surprising that we should separate these two ideas, since they are ordinarily closely identified. We may say: "My conscience is bothering me." What do we mean if not that we "feel guilty"?

We are reporting our interior feelings and assuming that they are the voice of our authentic conscience. But that is a question.

One of the more significant contributions of contemporary psychology to the moral enterprise has been that discipline's emphasis upon the strange ways in which our feeling-systems operate. Feelings are very real, and it has been the desire of psychology to emphasize the importance of dealing with them. But in the process of calling for increased understanding of feelings and respect for them, psychology has also brought us to a greater appreciation of the nonrational and noncontrollable ways of feelings. What is the genesis of the feelings we have? Where do they come from? That question is, often enough, impossible to answer fully. But one thing is clear: they come from experiences and not from intellectual reflections.

Indeed, it is interesting to note that no matter how far various schools of psychology diverge from one another, on this point they share a common understanding. Freud speaks of the superego, that font of taboo and stricture, that policeman of the personal life, that agent of enforced socialization. And just as the id is prepersonal and prerational, the same is true for the superego. Indeed, it is precisely the function of the ego to mediate those prerational demands of the other two realities. Practioners of Transactional Analysis make statements that are analogous to those of Freud. They describe the "tape recordings" which every human person makes early in life and which continue to exercise influence into the adult years. In particular, they emphasize "Not OK Child" tapes, with their tendency to continue to generate feelings of guilt when guilt is no longer appropriate. And for behaviorists, guilt feelings, like *all* aspects of the human person, are not rationally generated, but rather are culturally conditioned.

The united voice of these diverse psychologists, then, is that feelings of guilt largely stand apart from human freedom and human rationality. If this is true, it must also be true that such feelings are morally neutral. It may happen that guilt feelings will call our attention to a situation or an action for which we are and ought to be truly guilty. But the exact opposite may equally be the case. For whatever reason, I may very well feel guilty about something which I should in no way repent. Consider the case of the compulsive housewife who leaves her home untidy in order to help a needy neighbor. Such a person, despite the realization that she has done the correct thing, is quite likely to feel guilty about the domestic disarray. Are such feelings an accurate barometer of her moral situation? By no means. They are purely and simply the result of some quirk of personality or accident of personal history. Nothing more. Thus, in and of themselves those feelings are morally neutral.

Opposite examples would be equally valid, and perhaps even more disturbing. The equanimity with which contemporary culture accepts the phenomenon of widespread nontherapeutic abortion suggests that many people feel no guilt whatsoever about a situation that is morally reprehensible. Once again feelings are seen to be an utterly undependable guide to moral value. If and when such feelings coincide with the actual moral facts of the case, that is purely an accident. It is just as likely that they will not.

Therefore, in the entire discussion of conscience which we shall pursue in this chapter, we will nowhere be talking about *feelings* of guilt. For they do not deserve the name of conscience. Rather we will be talking about a number of other realities which do deserve that term, and which, therefore, we need to understand much more fully.[1]

Conscience in Scripture

The idea, if not the term, of conscience receives generous attention in the pages of Sacred Scripture. And it will assist our subsequent reflections if we summarize now the data from that source.

The data from the Old Testament is both interesting and illuminating, for the Hebrew language simply has no word for conscience. Indeed, even in Greek and Latin the specific words for conscience (*syneidesis* and *conscientia*) are fairly late developments. But that fact is actually helpful to us. For research into Greek and Latin literature has discovered that prior to the emergence of the technical term those languages ordinarily expressed the *idea* of conscience by the word "heart" (*kardia* and *cor*). And even the most cursory look at Scripture makes clear that "heart" is a most common word. Indeed, there is even one case (Job 27:6) where the Septuagint translates the Hebrew "heart" (*lêb*) with the Greek "conscience" (*syneidesis*). So it will illuminate our understanding of conscience for our time if we search the Old Testament a bit for its major references to "heart."

The psalmist urges us: "O, that today you would hear his voice: harden not your hearts" (Ps 95:7f). Repeatedly we are told that "God probes the heart" (e.g. Jer 11:20, 17:10; Prov 21:2; Ps 26:2). Twice in the Book of Samuel, King David is described as a man whose "heart misgave him" (1 Sam 24:6; 2 Sam 24:10). The Book of Ecclesiastes (7:22) justifies an assertion by declaring that "you know in your heart." (This example is interesting because the Vulgate in this case renders *lêb* with the Latin word *conscientia*.) And Proverbs often urges us to "take it to heart" (eg. 2:1; 3:1; 4:10; 4:21; 7:3).

In the Book of Job, the beleaguered hero responds to his critics with the simple statement "My heart does not reproach me" (27:6). Indeed one could reasonably assert that fidelity to conscience, clearness of conscience, constitutes the very theme of the Book of Job. Similar calls for inner authenticity can also be found in the Prophets, particularly Ezekiel (11:14–21) and Jeremiah (31:31–34).

The New Testament also offers a number of interesting examples. Consider the Gospel of Matthew where Jesus condemns the righteous Pharisees by quoting Isaiah, "This people honors me with their lips, but their heart is far from me." Asked by his disciples for an explanation, Jesus proceeds to expand this critique by declaring:

> It is not what goes into a man's mouth that makes him impure; it is what comes out of his mouth. Do you not see that everything that enters the mouth passes into the stomach and is discharged into the latrine, but what comes out of the mouth originates in the mind? It is things like these that make a man impure. (Mt 15:11, 17f)

And this understanding of conscience/heart greatly illuminates the Beatitude: "Blest are the single-hearted for they shall see God" (Mt 5:8). Indeed, this example is particularly interesting inasmuch as the Lukan version of the Beatitudes, being more primitive and more socially oriented, lacks this Beatitude. It appears that Matthew represents a subsequent revision, a turning from the social to the personal level. We may be justified, then, in surmising that to the extent that Christianity emphasizes the inner realities of personal commitment, some reference to conscience is demanded.

And then there is a classic description of conscience (*kardia*) provided by John. He declares:

> This is our way of knowing we are committed to the truth and are at peace before him no matter what our consciences may charge us with; for God is greater than our hearts and all is known to him. Beloved, if our consciences have nothing to charge us with, we can be sure that God is with us. (1 John 3:19–21)

But it is to Paul that we must particularly direct our attention in this context. For on the topic of conscience Paul introduced something genuinely new, something truly creative in the history of Christian theology. The Greek word for conscience, *syneidesis*, was not in common use much before the time of Christ. Indeed, the Septuagint, the Greek translation of the Old Testament, used the word only twice. By contrast, Paul uses it thirty times in his letters and discourses in the Acts of the Apostles. As we shall see, he uses it in a number of different contexts which illuminate various meanings of the word. But before we spell out these details, we may appropriately ask why it is that Paul introduces this new emphasis. There appear to be a number of reasons.

First of all, the word *syneidesis* was common in the secular literature of Paul's time, and as we know, Paul was a well-educated man. He was an urban man, a cosmopolitan man. It is therefore to be expected that he was in touch with that literature. Indeed, as a child of the cosmopolitan city of

Tarsus, it is likely that Paul was part of the great philosophic discussions of his time. Secondly, we must be aware that Paul was often writing to educated people. In his letter to Rome he would have been conscious that those people were familiar with the writings of Cicero and Seneca, replete with their discussions of conscience. And the highly philosophic tone of the letters to Corinth makes clear that Paul was acutely aware of the educated status of his readers. So for these reasons, among others, it appears that Paul took a common secular term, united it with a traditional Old Testament notion, and forged a new and exciting insight for the Christian faith. He developed with considerable precision an aspect of the human person that had heretofore not been highlighted. But what was that insight? A consideration of a few selections from Paul's writings will answer that question.

"Gentiles . . . show that the demands of the law are written in their hearts [*kardias*]. Their conscience [*syneidesis*] bears witness together with that law" (Rom 2:15). Here we see Paul explicitly connecting the Old Testament notion of heart with his own understanding of conscience. Conscience is what bears witness to and illuminates; conscience judges that inner awareness, evaluating it in an impartial and unbiased way (cf. also Rom 9:1; 2 Cor 1:12f). But conscience is not an exterior judge; it is an aspect of the self. And thus understood, it can have several different qualities of its own.

It can be a bad conscience, denying the realities of the moral life. Thus the Christian is challenged to "draw near, . . . our hearts sprinkled clean from the evil which lay on our conscience" (Heb 10:22). Or conscience can be just the opposite. Paul declares that "I always strive to keep my conscience clear before God and man" (Acts 24:16). Secondly, conscience can function as an infallible guide to action. Paul commands his disciple Timothy to "fight the good fight and hold fast to faith and a good conscience. Some men, by rejecting the guidance of conscience, have made shipwreck of their faith" (1 Tim 1:19f). But in this case, too, the opposite is just as possible. Paul tells his disciples that it is perfectly acceptable to eat food sacrificed to idols. But then he warns them, "Not all, of course, possess this 'knowledge.' Because some . . . eat meat, fully aware that it has been sacrificed, and because their conscience is weak, it is defiled by the eating" (1 Cor 8:7). And this, says Paul, must moderate his disciples' behavior.

> If someone sees you, with your "knowledge," reclining at table in the temple of an idol, may not his conscience in its weak state be influenced to the point that he eats the idol-offering? . . . When you sin thus against your brothers and wound their weak consciences, you are sinning against Christ. (1 Cor 8:10–12)

So consciences can be weak; they can be erroneous. And to the extent that this is true, they demand the charity of the brethren, fraternal solicitude.

A number of these nuances are brought together in a classic statement on the topic of clean and unclean foods. Paul says this:

> "All things are lawful," but not all are advantageous . . . If an unbeliever invites you to his table and you want to go, eat whatever is placed before you, without raising any question of conscience. But if someone should say to you, "This was offered in idol worship," do not eat it, both for the sake of the one who called attention to it and on account of the conscience issue—not your own conscience but your neighbor's. (1 Cor 10:23, 27–29)

In all of these citations, then, we find a surprising variety of understandings of the word conscience. Conscience is infallible, yet it is fallible. Conscience is a value, a good thing, and yet it is also a bad thing. Conscience is dependable, and it is undependable. Conscience is a person's heart, and it is something that critiques that heart. Conscience is the person himself, and yet conscience is a subservient part of the person. All of these definitions find some support in the writings of Paul. And all resonate to some degree or other with our own experience. But how shall we put all this in order? The purpose of the next part of this chapter will be to organize these ideas and to develop an overall understanding of conscience.

An Understanding of Conscience

Traditional moral theology was in the habit of distinguishing three different meanings for the word conscience. And these it delineated by the use of three different terms: synderesis, moral science, and syneidesis.[2] Moreover, the tradition contended that the first and last of these terms, and the ideas they represented, were to be found in the twin fonts of Scripture and tradition. In our own presentation we will begin with a few brief remarks regarding that last assertion, the genesis of those two terms. After that we will proceed to a presentation that will not greatly diverge from that of traditional theology. But we will abstain from using any of the three terms. For in this writer's experience, those terms are never particularly helpful; and they often distract from the matter at hand. We will substitute for them, therefore, some terms of our own.

As we indicated, traditional moral theology distinguished between synderesis and syneidesis, and claimed that these two terms and ideas were to be found in Scripture itself. By synderesis they understood the habit of conscience, the basic sense of responsibility that characterizes the human person. And by syneidesis they understood the act of conscience, the judgment by which we evaluate a particular action. We have already seen that the term syneidesis is clearly present in Scripture. But what of synderesis? The simple and embarrassing fact is that this term does not appear in Scripture. Indeed, there is no such word in the Greek language. Rather, it appears that this entire theological tradition is the result of a massive error.

As near as we can tell, it was St. Jerome who first alleged the existence of these two different words for conscience. In preparing the first Latin text of the Bible, it seems that Jerome was working from a Greek manuscript which was not altogether legible. He had to deal with selections where the topic was clearly conscience, but where the word did not *appear* to be syneidesis. Rather the word in his text seemed to be "synderesis." Jerome studied the text, and thought he detected differing nuances when one or the other word was used. Thus he concluded that the latter term must simply be a Greek word with which he was unfamiliar, a word being used to make a very particular point. But, recent scholarship has made clear that Jerome was wrong. There are not two words in Greek for conscience, but only one. The distinction between the two *concepts* may very well be useful, and indeed we shall find it so. But in making that distinction, we must be clear that it is ours, not the Bible's.

What, then, can we say of conscience? We shall assert that the word "conscience," as it is generally used both in ordinary conversation and in theology, points at one or another of three quite different ideas. And for purposes of simplicity, we shall refer to these as conscience/1, conscience/2, and conscience/3.

To begin, we speak of conscience/1. And here we are referring to a general sense of value, an awareness of personal responsibility, which is utterly characteristic of the human person. Repeatedly through the chapters of this book, we have seen that to be human is to be accountable. It is to be a being in charge of one's life. This human capacity for *self*-direction equally implies a human responsibility for *good* direction. Indeed, so much is this true that we question the "humanity" of anyone who lacks an awareness of value. Psychologists speak of sociopaths and psychopaths, of people devoid of any sense of right and wrong. And they consider such people sick. The courts of law regularly ask the question: "Was this person aware of what he was doing, and of the wrongness of it?" If that question is answered negatively, the court will not bring such a person to trial. For he is in a very real sense not "human" and is not accountable at the bar of human law. But apart from such bizarre aberrations, all human persons share a sense of the goodness and badness of their deeds.

It is true, of course, that the contemporary period is replete with examples of moral disagreement. Lively moral debate is a sign of the times. What is more, there is tremendous disparity among various cultures in their judgment of what is good and what is bad. But far from refuting this first understanding of the word conscience, that debate and disagreement proves its existence. It is only because we agree that there is such a thing as good and bad, and that we ought to do the good and avoid the bad, that the conversation even begins. We can have varying opinions as to *what* is right or wrong only because we share the common realization that it makes a difference *whether* a thing is right or wrong. Thus every discussion of moral values, every consideration of moral questions, has as its presupposition the existence of conscience/1. The human person has such a conscience, and only because of that fact is the person genuinely and truly human.

But the existence of conscience/1 does not mean that we "rest on our laurels." Quite the contrary, conscience/1 forces individual human persons to search out the objective moral values of their situation. They feel obliged to analyze their behavior and their world, to seek to discover what is the really good thing and what is not. This search, this exercise of moral reasoning, can also be termed an act of conscience, conscience/2. "My conscience tells me it is wrong to take that money." Here we understand conscience/2. Conscience/2 deals with the specific perception of values, concrete individual values. And it emerges in the ongoing process of reflection, discussion, and analysis in which human beings have always engaged.

It is here, at the level of conscience/2, that we can differ and disagree. Some may find it right to withhold taxes used to wage war, while others will find it wrong. Some may condemn horse racing, while others will praise it. Some may judge our culture to be morally depraved, while others will consider it an advancement over previous ages. People disagree; and that is characteristic of conscience/2. Indeed, as we reflect on these examples and on many others which might come to mind, it becomes clear that conscience/2 permits not only disagreement but also error. We seek to find and understand the concrete moral values of our situation, but we may fail. We are capable of blindness as well as insight, of distraction as well as attention, of misunderstanding as well as understanding. In fact, whole societies can thus fail. Consider the nation of Germany in the 1930s. What shall we say of their moral sensitivity? Were they all sinners, refusing to do what they knew to be right? By no means. The worst that can be said (and it is a universal, often tragic human weakness) is that, by and large, the people of Germany were guilty of a moral blind spot, of an inability to see and appreciate the evil of their situation. One could well assert that our own culture is equally guilty of blindness in the areas of respect for human life and human sexuality.

So when we speak of conscience/2, we are speaking of a fragile reality. We are speaking of an aspect of humankind that needs all the help it can get. It needs to be educated. Individual persons are not always able to "see what's there." They need assistance. And if they are sincere persons, if they have accepted the fundamental responsibility implied by conscience/1, then they will seek that assistance. They will turn to their friends, their colleagues, their peers, and seek to benefit from their insights. They will listen to the larger culture, to the wisdom of previous generations, and they will listen to voices from other situations, more objective voices, as these help them to interpret their situation.

In a word, the sincere person will engage in the process known as "formation of conscience." For that, indeed, is a characteristic of conscience/2: it needs to be formed. It needs to be guided, directed, and illuminated. It needs to be assisted in a multitude of ways. Conscience/2, then, is quite different from conscience/1. It is not universal, at least in its conclusions and judgments. And it most certainly is not infallible. Quite the contrary, conscience/2 possesses a sort of humility, an emptiness that needs to be filled by the facts. Conscience/2 is not an arrogant thing, not proud. Rather we might say that it kneels before the truth. In the realm of conscience/2 truth is supreme; truth is the object which is sought. And conscience/2 sincerely and docilely undertakes the task of finding and respecting that truth.

It should be clear from what has been said that it is in the realm of conscience/2 that the Church has its greatest role. For the Church is, among other things, a teacher of moral values. Even viewed simply as a human institution, the Church deserves to be heard. And when one adds the belief of faith that the Holy Spirit somehow guides the Church, not protecting its every word from error but nonetheless providing it with some illumination and guidance, it stands to reason that the prudent person will listen to its declarations. But note that conscience/2 is not directly accountable to the Church. No, it is accountable to the truth and nothing else. In its search for truth, conscience/2 makes *use* of sources of wisdom wherever they may be found. And major among those sources is the Church, the religious community.

But we, as human persons, are not only thinkers, analyzers of facts. We are also doers of deeds. Indeed, it has been the wise insight of philosophy in our century that our highest achievement is not contemplation (as Aristotle said) but rather intelligent action. And so we may not settle at the level of conscience/2. We cannot be the perennial observer, commentators on the current scene. No, we must act. We must make a decision, we must judge our own behavior. At some point we must finally declare: "It is theoretically possible that I may be wrong, but it seems to me that I ought to do *this*." And that we proceed to do. This final declaration, this judgment, this commitment, likewise deserves the name conscience: conscience/3.

Conscience/3 is consummately concrete, for it is the concrete judgment of specific persons pertaining to their own immediate action. But for all that concreteness, the judgment of conscience/3 remains infallible. That is to say, it constitutes the final norm by which a person's action must be guided. Why is that? The answer lies in the unique conjunction of conscience/1 and conscience/2. It was conscience/2 that led us to analyze and understand our situation in a particular (fallible) way. But we also have conscience/1. And that aspect of conscience demands, insists, requires (infallibly) that we seek to do good and avoid evil. Thus, because the infallible obligation of conscience/1 permeates and fertilizes the fallible judgments of conscience/2, we find ourselves in the moment of action with a concrete yet infallible guide for our own actions. Is it possible that in following that conscience we may do that which is (objectively) wrong? Most certainly. Are we thus justified in saying that in doing so we have acted in a (morally) wrong way? By no means. It is the quintessence of human morality that we should do what we *believe* to be right, and avoid what we *believe* to be wrong. The fallibility of our objective judgment (conscience/2) in no way obviates that fundamental moral dictate.

Therefore, if it was accurate to say that conscience/2 kneels before the altar of truth, it is equally accurate to say that we kneel before the altar of conscience/3. If I genuinely *believe* that I should do something, it is not only accurate to say that I may do it. More than that, I should do it. Indeed, I *must* do it. And this for all the reasons that have been presented here.

A few additional comments about this presentation are now in order. First of all, it should be noted that this strong distinction between conscience/2 and conscience/3 would go a long way toward eliminating much contemporary confusion. Consider the endless debates over the maxim: "One must always follow one's conscience." It seems to us that arguments regarding the validity of this maxim result precisely from an unclarity about whether one means conscience/2 or conscience/3. One does not follow conscience/2; rather conscience/2 follows the truth—and, indeed, does not always do that very well. But one must surely follow conscience/3. For in the last analysis that is the only possible guide for action by a free and knowing human person. This is precisely what Bernard Häring means when he declares: "Everyone, of course, must ultimately follow his conscience; this means he must do right as he sees the right [conscience/3] with desire and effort to find and do what is right [conscience/2]."[3]

A second observation has to do with the "orthodoxy" of this presentation, and particularly of the notion of ultimately infallible conscience. It is no doubt true that in recent years many Catholics have been led to believe that conscience is the enemy of the true moral life. They have been told that in any situation of conflict between conscience and Church authority, they ought always to follow authority. We shall go into the role of Church authority in further detail shortly. But in the present context it still ought to be pointed out that this understanding is *not* the authentic tradition of the Catholic Church.

Even Thomas Aquinas strongly supported the rights of conscience:

> Anyone upon whom the ecclesiastical authority, in ignorance of the true facts, imposes a demand that offends against his clear conscience, should perish in excommunication rather than violate his conscience.[4]

The American bishops, in responding to the encyclical *Humanae Vitae*, make a similar point. It is, of course, the bishops' primary purpose to support the pope's teaching and to encourage Catholics to cooperatively accept it. And so they do not particularly *emphasize* the rights of conscience. But they do *affirm* those rights. For example, they assert that "we recognize the role of conscience as a 'practical dictate,' not a teacher of doctrine."[5] If that sentence had been phrased, "while we do not recognize conscience as a teacher of doctrine, we do recognize it as a practical dictate," the emphasis would have been quite different, but the basic affirmation would have been the same. And as if this were not enough, the bishops proceed to a lengthy quotation from Cardinal John Henry Newman:

> When I speak of conscience, I mean conscience truly so-called. . . . If in a particular case it is to be taken as a sacred and sovereign monitor, its dictates, in order to prevail against the voice of the Pope, must follow upon serious thought, prayer, and all available means of arriving at a right judgment on the matter in question. . . .[6]

To say this is simply to say that conscience/3, to deserve its name, can only follow upon the responsible exercise of conscience/2.

And one final quotation, this from contemporary moralist Josef Fuchs. For in this text he admirably unites the understandings of conscience/2 and conscience/3 that we have developed.

> The dictate of conscience [3] . . . enjoys absolute certainty. For it dictates that the person acting ought to act according to the personal judgment which he has concerning the act [conscience/2]. . . . In a word, the judgment [of conscience/3] . . . is not only infallibly true but is also absolutely certain.[7]

Conscience and Church Authority

Throughout this chapter we have made reference to the role of the Church as it relates to conscience and to the limits of that role. Before concluding, however, we should make explicit what has already been implied, and develop somewhat these reflections. But the reader should note that inasmuch as we have already indicated the unique personal character and inviolability of conscience/1 and conscience/3, we are here discussing the relationship between conscience/2 and the Church.

The first point to be made is very simple. It is that the Church, and particularly the hierarchical magisterium, has a very positive and very important role to play in the illumination of conscience. Why is this? There are a number of reasons.

First of all, there is the fact of human need. As we have seen, human persons, in the exercise of conscience/2, are not immediately in possession of the truth. And yet they must always seek the truth. The values for which they search are fragile and ambiguous values. Consequently they are genuinely needy, requiring all the assistance they can find. What is more, when we move beyond the individual case and view the culture as a whole, the same reality becomes evident. There is an overwhelming need for moral leadership in our world. Consequently, if the Church can fill that role, it will perform a genuinely valuable service.

A second reason why the Church should be viewed positively derives from its credentials in human history. There is no doubt that the Church has not always spoken unequivocally on behalf of moral values. There have been times when its behavior and its words betrayed those values. But the fact is that it often has been a force for the improvement of the human situation and for the protection of human dignity.[8] Perhaps this has been so precisely because of the shape of the Church. To the extent that it is a cross-cultural institution, it is perhaps more likely to overcome the biases and blindnesses that can afflict the consciences of people within a particular cultural context. To the extent that the Church is the beneficiary of centuries of tradition, of the accumulated wisdom that is part of its temporal longevity, it is perhaps in a specially good position to provide an objective evaluation of the trends and tastes of the moment.

Or at least this can be the case. And often enough, the human community finds it to be the case. When the delegates to the United Nations stand to applaud a small Italian man dressed in white as he enters the hall, it is not because they are members of the Catholic Church. It is not because they are believers, either. It is because they recognize in this man the symbol of an institution whose contribution to culture and civilization they admire. It is because they not only acknowledge the need for moral leadership in our time, but also celebrate the role the Church plays in providing that leadership. We, too, should celebrate that role.

A third reason why the Church should be viewed positively derives from Christian faith. For Catholics sincerely believe that the Holy Spirit inhabits the Church and, at least to some extent, guides and illuminates its actions. We do not arrogantly assert that the Church is identical with the kingdom of Christ; we are more than willing also to recognize the presence of the Spirit in other individuals and institutions (as the Second Vatican Council strongly affirmed). But we do assert that the Church is *part* of the kingdom, and that the Spirit is to be found here. Similarly, we do not profess that the Catholic Church is the "unblemished bride" of Christ. No, inasmuch as the Church is a human institution, composed of human sinful people, it may sometimes be more appropriately viewed as the "whore of Babylon." But ever since the prophet Hosea it has been part of the Judaeo-Christian tradition that God forgives the infidelities of his beloved, that he remains faithful even when we are unfaithful, and thus that his faithful presence is a permanent and irrevocable promise. It follows from this, then, that when conscience/2 sets out on its journey searching for the truth, it will take the time to respectfully listen to the insights of the Church. It will not listen in a way that makes it deaf to all other insights. But it will listen. And this because such listening is a dictate of common sense and a consequence of deeply held faith.[9]

But the other side of this coin is that there are distinct limits to the Church's role in moral reflection. And these ought also to be honestly acknowledged.

First of all, we should be cognizant of the fact that the Church never has spoken infallibly in moral questions. The First Vatican Council asserted the right of the pope (and by implication the Church) to so speak. But the fact is that that right has never been exercised. Therefore, all the existing moral teachings of the Church fall in the realm of "ordinary magisterium." That is, they are teachings which, although assisted by the Spirit, are nonetheless susceptible to error and therefore fallible. So the possibility of error constitutes one limit to the Church's role as that is ordinarily exercised.

The danger of incompleteness constitutes a second limit. Morality has to do with concrete life, with infinitely variable confluences of action and circumstance. In the traditional vocabulary, it has to do with contingent things, things liable to variety and to multiplicity. As a result, the Church in its teaching will never be able to speak to the totality of the concrete situation in which any person finds himself or herself. The most that the Church can hope to do is address particularly important values which are part of that situation. Thus the teaching of the Church in moral matters is liable to a certain incompleteness, a certain partiality. Individual moral agents will still be obligated to decide for themselves whether the instruction of the Church truly applies to their specific situation, and if so how. They will need to clarify, to apply, and to nuance that teaching for their own use.

In the third place, the Church's role in moral matters is limited by the possibility of inadequacy. Conscience/1 demands that human persons seek to do the really, objectively, good thing in life. But persons are tempora beings subject over time to evolution and change. It is distinctly possible that what once was good, truly helpful to persons, truly serving their humanization and spiritualization, may someday become the opposite. Thus, while a Church teaching may well have been both adequate and accurate at one time, it does not follow that it will always be so. On the contrary, there may well be need for revision and rearticulation.[10] What was once adequate teaching has become inadequate. And we ought not to be surprised.

The Church therefore has an important and responsible role in the process of moral education. But it is a limited role. It is limited by the possibility of error, the possibility of incompleteness, and the possibility of inadequacy. The prudent person acknowledges this, and yet seeks from the Church whatever wisdom it is able to give him or her.

We can put all this one last way. The Catholic Church claims the right to teach in matters of faith and morals. And we affirm that right. But in so doing we also acknowledge that faith and morals are quite different realities. The truths asserted in the realm of faith are perduring truths, touchstones of unchanging belief. To the extent that they capture the reality of our unchanging God, they constitute unchanging and perennially true statements. The truths asserted in the realm of morals are quite different. They do not describe an unchanging reality such as God is, but rather the consummately changing reality of the human world. They are tools for the illumination of contingent realities. Thus they hold within themselves the potential for that mutability which is the destiny of all contingent things. To say that the Church was correct in asserting that Jesus is both divine and human is to say that Jesus always was and will be both divine and human. But to say that the Church was correct in asserting the immorality of charging interest on a loan is simply to say that this practice was once in a particular context immoral.[11]

In a fundamental way, then, the Church finds itself in the same situation as the individual moral person. Just as the individual's conscience/2 must search for the truth of its situation and, once found, must kneel before that truth, so must the "conscience" of the Church. We look to that ecclesial conscience with a certain confidence and trust, but we do not ask of it what it cannot give. Throughout the whole exercise of conscience/2, as we maturely and prudently listen for whatever wisdom we can receive, we never forget that we are looking, not for "the approved," not for "the permitted," but for "the good." We and the Church together search for the true values of our situation, and once we find those values we accept them as challenges for our own lives. It is that truth, that goodness, that is supreme; and to that both Church and moral agent must bow.

In the final analysis, then, the wisdom and the judgment of the Church are important, but they are not ultimately important. Therefore, the genuinely important role of Church teaching must never be allowed to deteriorate into a "loyalty test" for Catholics. Is a Catholic who finds himself or herself able to agree with the judgment of the Church a better Catholic than one who cannot? We must never say so. For just as to use Church teaching properly is to celebrate it, to ask it to be more than it is is to destroy it. And to make of that valuable and cherished source of moral wisdom a tool for ecclesiastical discipline or a measure of religious fidelity is to betray it. Indeed, to see the moral teaching of the Church as a test of Catholic loyalty is ultimately to violate the nature of the Church, the nature of humanity, and surely the nature of conscience.[12]

9

RELATED DOGMATIC THEMES

At the beginning of this book we mentioned that one of our sources would be the dogmatic traditions of the Church. This is because the "gift" and "challenge" dimensions of Christian experience always remain intimately related.

However, as we have pursued our reflections upon the meaning of the human person, we have largely neglected this dogmatic aspect. Instead, we have maintained a focus that was almost exclusively that of moral theology. Given our objectives, this was inevitable. Still, the profound understanding of virtue and sin that has been developed here makes it clear that we are ultimately talking not about mere ethical rectitude but about human redemption. And that is a clear dogmatic concept. Indeed, it is not simply a single concept; it is a component of an integral dogmatic vision.

So, before we bring the first half of this book to a close, it is important to take notice of that dogmatic vision, to become conscious of the ways in which our understanding of human persons and their acts must be nuanced and completed by insights from dogmatic theology. In fact, it is important to do this both in order to be complete and in order to be accurate. For as we shall see, to ignore these dogmatic components is to render what has been said thus far inaccurate and possibly misleading.

We shall consider two aspects of Christian dogma: original sin and grace. And in each case we shall seek to move from traditional data to contemporary articulation.[1]

Original Sin: The Data

> If the universe is so bad or even half so bad, how on earth did human beings ever come to attribute it to the activity of a wise and good creator? . . . The spectacle of the universe as revealed by experience can never have been the ground of religion.[2]

These words of C. S. Lewis speak to something very real in human experience: the brokenness of life. That the world is somehow out of sorts, that evil has a way of perduring despite the best of intentions, that even within our highest idealism lurks a dark side of fear and cruelty: all this can hardly be denied. In our earlier terminology, experience presents us not only with our acts of sin and freely chosen state of sin, but also with the unavoidable "fact of sin." And this reality is what Christian theology means by original sin.

From the earliest moments of human reflection this reality has demanded attention. In the third chapter of Genesis there is presented a creation myth that seeks to explain the "mystery of iniquity." In contrast to the myth that is presented in the first two chapters of Genesis, with its humanistic optimism, this story is extremely conscious of evil. There is a serpent, source of evil. There is the fruit of the tree, with its potential for causing evil. There is the man and the woman, accepting evil and occasioning it in each other. There is their nakedness, creation rendered somehow evil in the process. In sum, there is here a powerful image by which to address the facts of life which we would prefer to ignore.

In the New Testament, Paul returns to this story and interprets it. His primary concern is to celebrate the saving reality of Jesus. But salvation only makes sense where there is bondage. What is more, the unique power of Jesus can be highlighted by comparing him with that other man, Adam. So Paul proclaims that

> through one man sin entered the world and with sin death, death thus coming to all men inasmuch as all sinned. . . . If by the offense of one man all died, much more did the grace of God and the gracious gift of the one man, Jesus Christ, abound for all. . . . If death began its reign through one man because of his offense, much more shall those who receive the overflowing grace and gift of justice live and reign through the one man, Jesus Christ. To sum up, then: just as a single offense brought condemnation to all men, a single righteous act brought all men acquittal and life. Just as through one man's disobedience all became sinners, so through one man's obedience all shall become just. (Rom 5:12, 15, 17ff)

Now, this text includes more than the usual number of exegetical problems, most notably in the final phrase of the first sentence. Is the reality of original sin primarily the result of Adam's act, or is it caused by every one of us in our personal sin? But for our purposes it is sufficient to note Paul's interest in the *ongoing* reality of sin, a reality addressed and conquered by Jesus.

Throughout the history of the Church the notion of original sin has been subjected to theological analysis and magisterial pronouncement. As early as the year 418 it was affirmed in response to the Pelagian heresies. And in 529, at the Second Council of Orange, the Church rejected the views of anyone who asserted that

> it was not the whole man, that is, both body and soul, that was "changed for the worse" through the offense of Adam's sin, but believes that the freedom of the soul remained untouched, . . . (DS371)

or that

> Adam's sin was injurious only to Adam and not to his descendents. (DS372)

But it was especially in the Council of Trent (1546) that the magisterium took a strong stand on this theological concept. In addition to restating the commitments mentioned above, Trent also took a position opposing the idea that

> this sin of Adam, which is one by origin, and which is communicated to all men by propagation not by imitation, and which is in all men and proper to each, is taken away either through the powers of human nature or through any remedy other than the merit of the one mediator, our Lord Jesus Christ. (DS1513)

Trent likewise rejected the opposite extreme: that "through the grace of our Lord Jesus Christ conferred in baptism the guilt of original sin is not remitted." And in a significant sentence the Council went on to say that "it is the mind of this council that it professes that concupiscence or the tendency to sin remains in the baptized" (DS1515).

Finally, the issues of original sin itself and of the understandings of the beginnings of the human race that are connected to this concept were addressed by Pope Pius XII in 1950. His document was strongly worded, intended to respond to numerous "errors." On this subject he declares that he is *not* opposed to research

> with regard to the doctrine of evolution in as far as it inquires into the origin of the human body as coming from pre-existent and living matter. . . .
>
> When, however, there is a question of another conjectural opinion, namely polygenism, the children of the Church by no means enjoy such liberty. For the faithful cannot embrace that opinion which maintains either that after Adam there existed on this earth true men who did not take their origin through natural generation from him as from the first parent of all, or that Adam represents a certain number of first parents. Now it is in no way apparent how such an opinion can be reconciled with that which the sources of revealed truth and the

documents of the Teaching Authority of the Church propose with regard to original sin, which proceeds from sin actually committed by an individual Adam and which through generation is passed on to all and is in everyone as his own.[3]

The Pope then footnotes the texts of Trent cited above.

These citations have been repeated here at some length because they serve as the underpinnings for all of the theological reflection which has been given to the topic of original sin through the centuries and which continues in our own time. Indeed, in contemporary theology this idea has been reconsidered in a particularly extensive way. To take just one example, the words of Pius XII led theologian Karl Rahner to assert at one point that the Church was irrevocably committed to the idea of monogenism, that the whole human community is descended from a single person because, among other reasons, fidelity to the doctrine of original sin required it.[4] Yet later in his theological career, Rahner reversed himself.

We are of the opinion that on a more exact interpretation of the Church's dogmatic teaching on original sin we do not have to hold that the theory of monogenism is contained in it either as a necessary premise or as a direct doctrine.[5]

Similar reversals or developments have occurred in all the theological issues related to original sin, as these have been considered by a number of theologians.

Original Sin: Synthesis

It is beyond our scope to report on all these developments, and it would not serve our purposes. So perhaps our desire to note the dogmatic input to a Christian anthropology can best be achieved by simply offering a summary list of the present understandings on original sin.

On the one hand, it seems to be the clear teaching of the Church, supported by current theological reflection, that:

(1) there was a primeval fault at the earliest stages of human development;
(2) this fault had the twin effects of removing something in the human person that was "more than human" and of reducing that person to a situation somehow "less than human";
(3) this state of affairs is now experienced by all mankind;
(4) the capacity to overcome this state of affairs comes to mankind only as a gift;
(5) this state of affairs has two distinguishable aspects: the "fault" itself (sin, alienation) and its "effects"; and
(6) removal of the "fault" does not necessarily mean also removal of the "effects."

On the other hand, this theological core leaves open for further debate a number of related questions. Among these could be mentioned the issues of:

(1) what the fault was;
(2) whether the fault was the work of a single person, a group, or perhaps even a single person on behalf of a group;
(3) whether the line of succession by which this fault became the possession of all mankind is one of strict biological generation; and
(4) whether the fault, as it resides in human persons, is better conceived as a simple "state of alienation from God" or rather as a "situation of alienation" in which all people somehow freely participate and to which they contribute; that is, whether original sin can appropriately, and perhaps better, be understood as the "sin of the world."

So there is much that is debated, much that is unclear. It is often difficult to discern the point at which a genuine, perennial human insight ends and metaphorical terminology to express the insight begins. But it is at least clear, as a doctrine of Catholic faith as well as a painful fact of human experience, that evil is not solely a matter of one's own free choice. There is also a "fact of sin" which confronts the person even prior to individual election. There is an alienated state of being in which we find ourselves, alienated from one another and from ourselves and (perhaps *because* of these) also from God. So, the seeking for responsible living which should characterize the Christian person is a truly demanding task. Even though Christians find themselves in a world that is fundamentally good, still they find themselves in a world "out of sorts." It is as if they were confronted with a magnificent machine, whose gears were filled with sand. Struggle will therefore always be a religious, moral, and spiritual theme in Christian theology.[6]

Grace: The Data

But "despite the increase of sin, grace has far surpassed it" (Rom 5:20). These words of St. Paul spotlight the importance of grace and, indeed, the intimate connection between grace and the reality of sin we have been discussing. So it is clearly important that we develop some understanding of this mysterious theological concept in order to complete our Christian anthropology.

But to sketch out an authentically Catholic understanding of grace is no small thing. For, in the first place, the central idea is profoundly paradoxical. It asserts that the achievement of human hopes and dreams, of the deepest yearnings of the human soul, is something we are radically unable to create. It is something we can only receive and accept as gift. But at the same time, this achievement is also something we must participate in. It demands our active and free cooperation. Or to put this another way, the doctrine of grace asserts that the arrival of humankind at its ultimate goal is completely the result of a divine, unmerited initiative. But at the same time it is also the result of a genuinely free human response.

What is this ultimate human goal? It goes by many names: fullness of life, the overcoming of isolation and alienation and the achievement of union with God and reality, personal and complete fulfillment, happiness, heaven, immortality. But no matter what the term used, the central assertion is the same: it comes to us only as gift (*charis*, which is the Greek word translated as grace), and still this giftedness does not compromise the reality of human freedom.

And this twin assertion is surely paradoxical, which is our first difficulty with articulating the Catholic theology of grace. A second difficulty arises from the fact that the Catholic doctrine was largely developed in response to various heresies. The positions of Pelagius (b. 354) and his followers were viewed as overly biased toward human freedom. So in a series of documents in the fifth century, a "strong" view of grace was proclaimed by the Church. On the other hand, the positions of Luther (1483–1546), Baius (c. 1513–1589), Jansen (1585–1638), and Quesnel (1634–1719) were seen as involving an excessive protection of divine initiative and a pessimistic vision of humanity. Thus, the Church responded by emphasizing human goodness and the reality of freedom at the Council of Trent and in subsequent documents. But the systematic integration of these two emphases, the achievement of some synthesis without loss of the necessary tension, was left to theologians through the centuries.

A third reason for our difficulty lies in the related questions which present themselves. Does not God's goodness require that he desire the salvation of all? That is, is there not a "universal salvific will"? And if this is so, and if God's power is preeminent, then are we not confronted with "positive predestination"? If some human beings are actually not saved, does this not lead us to also assert "negative predestination"? And if so, how can this be squared with divine goodness? With human freedom? Finally, can this whole line of thinking be synthesized with the doctrinal assertion that salvation comes also as a result of "human merit"? How can merit be conceived so as to avoid Pelagianism?

All of these difficulties complicate our efforts to articulate the basic but paradoxical reality of grace. But the attempt must nevertheless be made. For apart from grace everything we have said throughout these pages is no more than partially true. So, while we cannot deal here with all the many questions that have been raised, some general comments must be offered.

Grace: Synthesis

Catholic theology has traditionally used several distinctions in discussing grace. And we should take note of these. First, they distinguished actual and habitual grace. Actual grace is that divine gift which empowers the human person for specific acts. Habitual (or sanctifying) grace is the person's ongoing state of "giftedness." Secondly, habitual grace was itself distinguished into uncreated grace, which is the Trinity itself as present to us, and created grace, which is the resulting (or prerequisite) modification within the human person.

Articulated this way, however, these traditional distinctions seem arid. How can they be understood? If it is true, as St. John said, that God is love, then perhaps the human reality of love can give us a way to understand them. For love, too, is always a gift.[7]

The notion of required or coerced love is a contradiction in terms. I can make you *treat* me well, but I cannot make you really love me. On the other hand, even if I can only accept your love as gift, still I must at least accept it. That is, I retain some freedom, for I can always reject your gift. I can actively close myself to your gift, turning away from its message of union and favoring the proud foolishness of isolation.

Still, I clearly should accept your gift, for my own sake as well as yours. And if I do, then several things immediately begin to take place. First, you become present to me in an entirely new and far richer way. You become part of my world of meaning; you become important to and for me. You move from the status of an object occupying the physical space of the world to the status of a fellow subject now inhabiting also my own personal world of existence. Secondly, this presence makes a difference. It changes me, transforms me, calls forth from me powers of love and concern and generosity I didn't know I had (and indeed did not have before your love). You make me able to respond in love, both to you and to the others who also touch my life. You act, for me, as a "life-giver." My oneness with you makes me somehow also one with all creation. And the "intercourse" of our love gift generates the pulse of life far beyond our exclusive relationship.

The implications of this informal phenomenology of love for the theology of grace should be obvious. God offers the gift of his love and of himself. Nothing we do can require that gift. The most we can do is accept it. And accept it we must, for our freedom always permits us to reject it. If we accept this God-gift, then he becomes present to us (uncreated grace) and transforms our very being (created grace). We are new, with a new being and new powers of life. We become sanctified, made holy, and that holiness moves through us into all our world.

Our resultant state of being, then, is one of union: union with God, with our world, and somehow even with ourselves. It is one of affirmation, of acceptance, of embrace. As such it is life-giving. But to say all this is obviously to speak much as we did when we analyzed the notion of fundamental stance. And that is no accident. For the relevance of the theology of grace to our project in this book occurs especially at that point.[8] The positive fundamental stance, and the positive fundamental option by which that stance comes into being, are only possible through grace, through gift. It is only the free self-offer of God that can render us capable of affirmatively responding to all of life as it confronts us. It is only God's self-gift that can transform us into the positive beings, the fulfilled and ultimately happy beings, we yearn to be. And it is only this free divine initiative that can lead us to accept the presence of God in our own personal world not as some categorical "object," but rather as the transcendental Thou who is truly a partner in love.

Since this is so, it is of profound importance that we nuance everything that has been said in the previous chapters by this consideration of grace. The fundamental stance, if it be positive, is only possible through grace. The fundamental stance, if it be negative, can truly be called sin because it involves (indeed is constituted by) a rejection of grace. Consequently, among those human persons who are truly "adult," who have in fact made their first fundamental option, there are none who are "merely human." All adult human persons are either more or less than human. Either they are more than human because they have accepted that self-gift of God which is utterly "supernatural" in the sense that no human could demand or expect it, or they are less than human because they have rejected that love relationship which alone can lead to the fulfillment of their deepest human dreams. In "frustrating" the love-initiative of God they have ultimately chosen to frustrate even themselves.

This, then, is the vision of grace which must be integrated into our understanding of the human and Christian person. But before we conclude, one final question must be asked: How can all this be applied to those who have never heard the Gospel message? How can we conceive of grace operating in their lives? And here we recall the vision of Christ that was developed in Chapter Four.

For God does not approach us directly, in some reflexive or even merely categorical manner. Rather God approaches us through his sacraments, through his world. Inasmuch as everything in the world speaks his Word, everything likewise is a potential opportunity for response to God's gift of love. And thus, without in any way compromising our dogmatic commitment to the gratuity of grace, we can still repeat what was said earlier: whoever says "yes" from the depths of his being to anything, says "yes" to everything. Whoever accepts reality as a sacrament of love, accepts the Being of love who is himself signed and sacramented in reality. Whoever is gifted by the invitation to loving response, as all people surely are, and also accepts that gift as they experience it within the categorical realities of their life, such persons live no longer just their own life, but also the life of Christ in them, the life of God himself. They are truly gifted (graced) persons. In the deepest sense of the word, they have been saved.

Conclusion

> God's love and sin may readily be viewed as fields of force, as opposing polarities influencing man and drawing him in one direction or the other. From the time of the rise of his consciousness he is brought into contact with the effects of these two fields. His free will is poised between submission to the one or to the other. But whereas sin, like gravity, because of the ubiquity of its effects is the more intrusive of these fields and more easily captures the flitting consciousness, the field of God's love is the more dynamic and better fitted to the modality of man's being itself. For the business of a human being is to exist.[9]

These words admirably summarize the insights and the tensions of this chapter. They succinctly express the dogmatic truths which must be part of our Christian anthropology. They advert both to the "bad news" and the Good News of the Christian faith. On the one hand there is original sin, the fact of sin in our world. We cannot avoid it, or its effects. It colors our lives, increases our struggles, challenges our faith. It weighs us down and fills our world with a burdensome ambiguity. And on the other hand there is grace, God's loving and life-giving gift. It transforms us, heals us, strengthens us in love. It unites us with God and with ourselves. It allows us to penetrate the ambiguity of life, to see God's world as still profoundly good. It empowers us to commit ourselves to that world and to our fellow travellers within it. It gives us the courage to face death for love, to give ourselves up in our own self-gift to one another. And it shows us, too, the way to all the things for which we dream.

Who is the human person? He or she is the person of the world; the person, therefore, who is confronted by, and affected by, sin as well as grace. The faith and joy of Christians comes not from the immediate presence of the totally fulfilled kingdom. No, it is more subtle. Our joy, and our faithful hope, come from that deep and strengthening truth: "despite the increase of sin, grace has far surpassed it" (Rom 5:20).

10

THE CHRISTIAN VOCATION

A s we saw early in this book, the notion of covenant is one of the primary images for understanding the way people should live in the Judaeo-Christian tradition. For this idea highlights the dialogical character of that living; it focuses on the dynamic dialectic of call and response. But to say that as Christian people we have been called, that we have a calling, is literally to say that we all have a vocation (*vocare*—to call). So we will conclude this analysis of the Christian person by several reflections on the Christian vocation.

The use of the term "vocation" may at first seem strange. For some time it has had only a limited meaning, being identified with the entrance of individuals into the clerical state or religious communities. But the fact is that every Christian does have a calling, an invitation to enter into relationship with God, to respond by authentic living, and to adopt a life-style of fidelity and sincere generosity. Thus it is worthwhile to rehabilitate the idea of vocation, to free it from the tragedy of past limitations and to return it to its place of ethical and religious centrality.

So we reflect on the meaning of the Christian vocation, and in so doing we discover four themes which complement and complete the Christian anthropology we have developed so far. We find that the Christian life is temporal, cumulative, communal, and unique. Let us attend to each of these in turn.

Temporal
In Chapter Six we called for a vision of the Christian person which is three-dimensional. That is, we sought to become conscious of the depth dimension of human life. We cannot know ourselves as we truly are if we advert only to our actions. We must advert also to that which lies beneath those actions, gives them meaning, and shapes them according to its pur-

poses. So beneath the human act, we noticed and sought to understand the human person.

That insight surely led us to a more accurate picture of ourselves. But not altogether accurate. For if the picture was relatively rich, still it was also static. It did not change. It did not include the reality of time. It did not acknowledge that the Christian life truly is a vocation: a call-ing, a do-ing, a be-ing and a becom-ing—a verb far more than a noun. It did not advert to the fact that we all stand within a process of living, a process which is ongoing and not yet at all complete. If it noticed that the Christian life is not lived in a single act, still it did not sufficiently notice that this life is also not lived in a single moment.

So to the three dimensions of length, width, and breadth we must now add the so-called fourth dimension: time. In a sense, the picture we have developed to this point has been a sort of snapshot of the human being (or perhaps a hologram, to keep the three-dimensional idea). But including the reality of time makes us realize that we have actually been viewing a single frame of a motion picture. We have been "stopping the action" in order to understand the actors. But to really understand them we must also watch them move. Human life is temporal life, changing life. And the pursuit of the Christian vocation is an essentially temporal enterprise. There is a past and a future to Christian living, and they are at least as important as the present.

Heightening our consciousness of the temporal dimension of the human person can have immense pastoral significance, too. In the past, there has been an almost exclusive concern with helping people to discern accurately the moral significance of their past actions. Within the Sacrament of Penance, for example, there was the expectation that people would be quite specific about those actions and in naming them would also express sorrow for them. True, both sacramental practice and general pastoral ministry expected people to develop a "firm purpose of amendment," a commitment to avoiding these actions in the future. But even here a certain static, or at least cyclic, vision of the Christian life was evidenced. The implied question was: When you pass that way again, will you act differently? Time was not taken seriously.

And it must be taken seriously. We do not "pass that way again." We move forward (or backward). Change takes place, and it is change that must be pastorally encouraged. Past actions may sometimes deserve repentance; they should always occasion learning. The real tragedy would be if a person's Christian life really were static. For then it would not be life at all, but rather death. And it would surely not be a vocation. So, from a pastoral point of view, the temporality of the Christian life makes us realize that the important question is not "What did you do?" but rather "Where are you going?"[1]

Cumulative

This notion of time implies another idea: that of growth. For the change we have been noticing is not merely change on the same level. Rather it is cumulative. The Christian life is not only a process, it is also progress. As we live our individual lives we inevitably grow. We develop. We evolve in our consciousness of the issues of life and in our responsibility in dealing with them. We become progressively more free; but at the same time we also become progressively more accountable. Our lives are cumulative, with each new moment standing on the shoulders of all that has preceded.

This is not, of course, to say that we necessarily become better persons as we grow older. We always remain able to choose the evil as well as the good. But it is to say that the depth with which we choose increases with time and age. As our lives proceed and as we grow, we take hold of ourselves more and more. For better or for worse, the various components of our lives increasingly cohere. We know more, we feel more, we perceive and experience more. Consequently, the profundity with which we choose at the present moment surpasses whatever we may have done before. So, paradoxically, we become increasingly capable of both good and evil as the years go by.

At the transcendental level, this growth means that our fundamental stance is progressively deepened as we take hold of our lives and increasingly affirm them. Indeed, even the reversals of mortal sin and conversion (which we discussed before) are not mere shifts of direction. Rather they are increasingly deep appropriations of one's life, in either the positive or negative direction. Where a positive fundamental stance, for example, is reaffirmed in a new option, this deepening is obvious. But it is equally true that a person who once lived the life of grace, then turned away in freely chosen sin, and now has been converted, has "grown" through the experience. The positive stance of the present is not the same as that of the past. It is deeper, more mature, more emphatic.

At the categorical level, the law of growth means that we develop styles of life and skills of living which increasingly manifest themselves as time goes on. For the process of life involves a reciprocal causality, where the agent shapes his or her acts and the acts shape the agent. In a certain sense, life is like playing tennis, performing a job, or loving a spouse; it is a matter not just of decision, but also of facility. There is skill involved, an increasing fluidity and spontaneity that actually leaves one more free while also more automatic. Thus, in the process of life we develop "habits," in the richest Thomistic sense of that word. We develop a progressively integrated identity, a constellation of virtues or vices that represent our chosen selves. We develop character: "the qualification of man's self-agency through his beliefs, intentions, and actions, by which a man acquires a moral history befitting his nature as a self-determining being."[2]

This being the case, assisting people in the development of a truly Christian character is a more important task. It is no doubt of some importance that people be instructed in the specific moral value of individual actions. It may even be useful to articulate the sort of Christian anthropology that has been developed in these pages. But most important is the facilitation within the person of a freely affirmed and actively developing Christian character. It is the development of this character that is the real objective of moral education and that ought therefore to dictate moral pedagogy.

Such a character must, by definition, be the free choice of the individual. So we are clearly not speaking here of any sort of indoctrination. But we are suggesting the specific focus and the particular question by which a person should be challenged to that choice. The cumulative character of the Christian life suggests that our focus ought to be preeminently the *shape* that people's lives are taking over time. And the question that we ask ought to be not only "Where are you going?" but also "Who are you becoming?"

Communal

No man is an island, entire of itself;
Every man is a piece of the continent,
    a part of the main.

These words of John Donne poetically articulate a truism of human experience. We are all shaped by our experiences within the human community, we are radically social beings. And that sociality, if it does not entirely constitute our particular human lives, nonetheless profoundly and extensively affects them. Thus, to accurately assess the meaning of the Christian vocation we must look not only to the individual, in his or her progressive Christian life, but also to the group, with all its myriad influences.

A precise delineation of these social dynamics is far beyond what can be attempted here. But it is interesting to at least note the greatly increased attention they are receiving in theology today. Catholic scholarship, from the Marxist liberation theologies of Latin America to the sociotheology of Canadian Gregory Baum, is giving more and more attention to the social factors in Christian life.[3] Protestant theology, in a reversal of the historical tendency toward individualism, is attempting to develop a positive theology of ecclesial community.[4] And on the other hand, the social sciences themselves are spending considerable attention on religious phenomena.[5] Even psychology, a science traditionally oriented toward the individual, is becoming increasingly sensitive to these social realities.[6]

And this is as it should be. Even our line of argument in the previous chapters of this book, despite its general neglect of the social theme, would suggest as much. For the Christian life, as we saw, is dialogical. And the dialogue between God and the human person is primarily transcendental, taking place through the mediation of creation's sacramentality. Thus it is no surprise that the pursuit of the ethical life involves a pivotally important corporate dialogue as well. Whether the dialogue is between two individuals, between the individual and the group, or between various groups, the result is a process of growth or decline which is tremendously significant.

Indeed, this author would wonder whether "morality" is even a meaningful term apart from the social situation. If there is no "other" in my life, no person who is important to me and to whom I am important, does it really make any difference how I behave? Would there, if we can put it this way, be any such thing as morality if I were the only human being on a desert island? Or would my action truly have no value? Is there, in other words, any such thing as "responsibility"? Or is it rather always a matter of "responsibility to/for another"?

It is true, of course, that God can function as an "other" in my life. Indeed, he is the ultimate "other." But as we have seen, God enters my life most profoundly and effectively not as a single categorical object next to other objects, but rather as the transcendental "within" of all the objects that I confront. Indeed, God enters my life in the deepest way as the within of the various other *subjects* in my life, of the human persons whom I encounter in a really human, interpersonal way. Thus it is at least dubious whether there would be any such thing as morality apart from this interpersonal, thoroughly social context.

This essential communality of the Christian vocation has, of course, immense implications for pastoral practice. It suggests that the promotion of a genuine Christian community in the parochial setting is a necessity. The protection and nurturing of healthy family life, in a modified form if the times truly demand it, must become a priority. Concern for individual morality must be matched by attention to the overall moral flavor of the society. It may be difficult to assess the overall moral fiber of the society, and the effort may be open to all sorts of hypocritical abuses. But the task can be avoided only at the price of moral, and therefore existential, injury to the individuals who dwell there. And, in general, the Church must incarnate in its pastoral practice this central insight: that for people to realize their own potential, they must be rooted in a community where support and challenge make clear the significance of their behavior and the importance of their growth. For apart from this community moral behavior becomes at least difficult, and perhaps truly meaningless.

We, too, must remain conscious of this insight. And in the awareness of it we must again modify what has already been said. Our vision of the

Christian life is inadequate if it is seen as a "snapshot"; it is also inadequate if it is seen to include only a single person. Rather our vision, inasmuch as it truly perceives the reality of the Christian vocation, is a "motion picture" involving many people. In some sense, together they live only a single Christian life. In large measure the individuals who comprise this community grow or decline together, they find the strength to affirm the goodness of life and the loving presence of God or they capitulate to suspicion and distrust and fear. While no doubt the individual always retains ultimate control of the fundamental stance that shapes his or her life, still the corporate life exerts tremendous, and perhaps immeasurable, influence. So we must ask not only "Where are you going?" and "Who are you becoming?" but also "Who are you with?"

Unique

Finally, in seeking to understand the Christian life as vocation, we must acknowledge the high degree to which each one of us is unique. This assertion of uniqueness may seem to contradict what has just been said. But actually it complements our reflections on communality. For even as we participate in community, we each do so in a personal and very unique way.

This fact is extremely important to our reflections. For it suggests a whole other dimension to the pursuit of the Christian moral life, a dimension too often overlooked. So often discussions of morality develop an almost exclusive focus on the common elements, on actions which all persons should do, postures which all should adopt. Even the understanding of fundamental option and fundamental stance which was developed here had a certain common focus. And, of course, that is not entirely avoidable. On the one hand, there is indeed much that is common in all human beings; there is such a thing as human nature, and it does generate a certain number of universal moral obligations. On the other hand, if we are going to go to the effort of sharing ideas with one another, there is a tendency to emphasize those ideas which will be applicable to all. So a certain emphasis upon commonality is probably inevitable. But that does not mean it is exhaustive. Quite the contrary.

Early on in these pages, we contrasted the human act with the human person, and we saw personhood as a principle of continuity in the individual life, as an ongoing font of self-consciousness which directs behavior and assumes responsibility. To that extent we implied that each human person is to some extent unique. But it must be granted that we did not emphasize this uniqueness. Rather we suggested a basic similarity among all human persons. By noting a number of transcendental characteristics of human personhood, we suggested that persons are fundamentally similar. In saying this we came close to implying that persons are nothing more than individual instances of human nature, that they are mathematically disparate but essentially identical. And this implication we must now reject.

As persons we are not mere instances. We are also at least partly unique. The dynamics by which we guide and shape our lives through self-consciousness, the Christian character which we develop over time, all this conjoins to differentiate us from one another and to highlight our utter particularity. We are not totally interchangeable with one another, totalitarian ideologies notwithstanding. We are from the beginning special and different, and over time we become increasingly unique.

But if this is true, and if it is also true that the call of God is addressed to the human person, that it is an interpersonal call to interpersonal relationship, then it follows that at least some moral demands may also be quite unique. After all, in the process of making a fundamental option a person does not merely say yes to life in general. He or she says yes to the concrete, specific, and therefore partly unique reality of *this* life. Thus, inasmuch as one's relationship to God is dependent on the grace-empowered response of the fundamental option, it is quite possible that one's salvation may be mysteriously worked out in terms of some action which would have no moral import at all to someone else.

Take, for example, the selection of a profession, a life-style, or a spouse. It has often been asserted that such selections are not the stuff of moral obligation, that they are free choices, that (to use an often cited instance) one is never obligated to become a priest or minister. Now, this sort of position makes considerable sense from the perspective of human nature, of what is common to all human persons. For about a matter so personal it would be highly inappropriate to formulate moral norms of one kind or another. It would be completely out of line to attempt to say, in some general formulation, what people should or should not do.

But not so from the perspective of the unique human person. Is it not possible that I, being who I am, could not reject a felt impulse to ministry without at the same time rejecting the God-present-in-life that I encounter? Is it not possible that the uniqueness of myself, with talents and liabilities, with inclinations and attractions, might not also present itself to me as obligation? Is it not possible that in experiencing myself in this way, I am quite correct, quite in touch with the reality that I am, not a victim of some neurotic scrupulosity but rather a healthy respondent to the prophetic dimension that must always remain part of the Christian life? Therefore, is it not possible that in articulating the challenge to "be what you are" we are actually summarizing the most profound and most far-reaching dictate of Christian morality?

From the perspective of Christian vocation it is indeed possible. For we are at least partly unique; our vocation is at least partly specific to our personhood. And even if such obligations will never be able to be formulated in any helpful way, that does not mean they are any less real.[7]

Conclusion

We bring these reflections on Christian anthropology to a close, then, in this challenging and inspirational context. The Christian person is a person called by God to relationship through and in this world we inhabit. He or she is called to live the Christian life. But this life is really a vocation. That means it is also temporal, cumulative, communal, and unique. It is dynamic and profound. And it is ultimately mysterious.

At the conclusion of this Christian anthropology this author is struck by that mysteriousness. In the course of these pages we have seen that human beings are rational animals; free animals; conscious and self-directing animals; personal animals; conscientious animals; temporal, social, growing animals; unique animals. But despite all that has been said here, despite the assertions made and nuances added, we have not succeeded in utterly plumbing the depths of who we are.

It is probably true that no matter how many details we were to add, we would always fail. For we are the creatures of the divine, and therefore mysteries in every sense of the term. And the completely exhaustive, thoroughly adequate words we seek are probably in fact the Word which is the only total expression of anything.

Still, we must try to understand ourselves, and to articulate that understanding as best we can. For human beings are also questioning, searching, wondering animals. And to the extent that we succeed, the understanding and articulation can serve us well in shaping the way we should live. But we will never completely succeed.

No, in the end we are reduced to silence. We are reduced to a silence which is humble but not abject. We are reduced to a silence that is pregnant, that is alive, that pulses with the richness of all that went before. We are reduced to a silence that speaks the final, ultimate thesis of a Christian anthropology: human beings are the animals that adore.

PART III

THE MORAL WORLD

11

AN INTRODUCTION TO OBJECTIVE MORALITY

The German philosopher Martin Heidegger captured a profound insight in his famous definition of the human person as *Dasein*. The human person is not simply being (understood either as a noun or as a verb), but located being, limited, circumscribed, contextualized being. The human person is Da-sein (being-there), being-in-the-world.[1] And if it was important to spend the first half of this book looking inward, as it were, in order to understand the operative dynamics within the human person, it is equally necessary to look outward, to analyze the context within which the person exists and by which the person is somehow constituted.

Indeed, we acknowledged as much in Chapter Eight when we noted that the inner sense of responsibility that is conscience/1 inevitably drives the moral agent out into the world of values in the search that is conscience/2. For the most part, however, the first half of this book was concerned with conscience/1 and with the person as characterized by that sensibility. Now, however, we must try to grasp what it is that persons seek when they pursue the search for moral values.

For there is a real world out there. There is a world that is somehow radically independent of human intention. There is a world that quite literally exists whether we like it or not. We did not create it and we cannot make it not be. Just as denying the reality of gravity will not make us fly, so also ignoring the world of objective morality will not make it disappear.

Objectivity
But what do we mean by objective morality? Philosopher Dietrich von Hildebrand offers a helpful response to that question. In his *Ethics* von

Hildebrand pursues a phenomenology of human living, a nonjudgmental attempt to merely describe how we experience the various aspects of our lives.[2] In so doing, he begins from the notion of "importance."

To be human is, in fact, to find some things important and some things not. What is more, not all things are considered important for the same reason. Some of the things we cherish are important to us simply because they are subjectively satisfying. They feel good, and therefore we like them. Other aspects of life, however, are considered important because of their utility. They are objectively good for the person. Visits to the dentist, the pursuit of an education, or regular exercise may or may not be fun. But most people consider them somehow important nonetheless.

However, these two categories of importance do not, in von Hildebrand's judgment, exhaust our experience. On the contrary, he finds that some things are considered important by members of the human community simply because they are good in themselves. They have a kind of life of their own, independent both of our wishes and our needs, and human persons cherish them for what they are. Truth, for example, may be mightily inconvenient. It may even oppose my best interests, at least in the short term. But try as I may, I cannot bring myself to consider it unimportant. And the same can be said for beauty. I may personally be bored by a Beethoven symphony, I may not be in the mood to contemplate a golden sunset, I may rarely take time to read a novel. But I would consider it tragic if the world were purged of these realities. They are important, apart from me, and they should in all events survive.

So also with ethical goodness. Honesty is important. So are fairness, compassion, chastity, justice, and all those realities we have traditionally named "virtues." I may not always succeed in embodying them; I may not even particularly want to. But that does not mean I really consider them unimportant. No, they are important and, in fact, important in themselves.

To these realities which fall into this category of independent importance von Hildebrand gives the name "values." Whether they be intellectual, aesthetic, or moral, values have this common characteristic of independent importance. Values are there, present in our experience, whether we like it or not. But that does not mean that all values are the same. Von Hildebrand notes that if certain people lack the ability to discern the truth, we merely call them poor scholars. If they fail to appreciate a particular work of art, we consider them uncultured, perhaps even boors. But if they have no sensitivity to the importance of justice or fidelity, we consider them poor human beings. They are failures not only in a certain respect, but also in the central meaning of their humanity. So of all values, moral values are by far the most important, not because we say so, or even because we wish it so, but simply because we phenomenologically find it so.

So it is not sufficient to say that the human person is *Dasein*, located being. It is not sufficient to note that we exist "within a world." We must also note, with von Hildebrand, that our world has a certain objectivity, a certain intransigence. It has a certain quality of self-existence which we cannot dominate. Instead, it demands our acceptance and affirmation and, indeed, appreciation.[3]

To speak of these moral values as having importance in themselves is not necessarily to say that they would exist apart from the existence of human persons. To question whether this would be so is like questioning whether a falling tree in an unpeopled forest makes a noise. It all depends on how the question is exegeted. And there is no doubt that the moral values we have listed indicate modes of *human* living. Dogs and cats, after all, cannot really be "honest." But the point is that despite the fact that these values are part of the human world, they are not human constructs. Such values are not created by us, they are found by us. And having been found they must be respected if we are to be our best selves.

At the same time, everything that has been said thus far also does not answer the many questions about the nature of these values, their specific characteristics, and how they are to be concretely lived out. Indeed, these sorts of questions will be our concern in the coming chapters. But the vision of scholars such as Heidegger and von Hildebrand does at least establish the context for our investigation. Our interest is the world in which human beings live. In particular we wish to see it as a moral world, as a world of responsibility and accountability, a world of obligation and duty, a world of challenge and opportunity, a world of values. And we wish to discover precisely what all this means.

For if the insights of these philosophers tell us anything, they tell us that the world is there. Whether we like it or not it is there. And it will not go away.

Scholastic Vision

It has been our practice in this book to link our contemporary reflections to the traditions of Catholic moral theology. And that practice should be maintained in this present context. For Catholic moral theology has given tremendous attention to the reality of objective morality. Indeed, some might maintain that it has focused on objectivity to the neglect of subjective factors. Inasmuch as we began with the subjective, we cannot be accused of this neglect. Now we must not neglect the objective. For what we discovered in the first half of this book is that a proper appreciation for the subjective itself functions as a challenge to move outward. In the very moment that we discovered the preeminent importance of being sincere, we also discovered that sincerity demands a concern for finding the good. And this search for the good is what now claims our attention.

So once again, we begin with a brief summary of the Scholastic tradition. We do this not because this tradition will answer all our questions. Rather we do it because it will provide us with a very helpful perspective, and because it includes a number of insights that will greatly enrich our own reflections as we proceed.[4]

The starting point in the well-ordered universe of the Scholastics was God himself. And since God is the source of all reality, it follows that he is also the source of our moral obligations, of the moral "ought" or "law" that exists in our experience. What is more, the various names that we give God in theology (e.g. creator, omniscient, omnipotent, Esse, etc.) never really capture the mystery of his being. Rather they simply describe aspects of himself as they pertain to us. Since this is the case, there is no reason why we cannot create also a name for God-as-source-of-moral-law. And this the Scholastics did. Their starting point in objective morality, then, was the eternal law. But as we have intimated, this law is not law at all. It is God himself as the source of moral law and obligation in our world.

Natural Law

God is the creator of the world, the source of all its being. And so, as God brings about the human world and human nature, so the eternal law brings about "natural law." Or to put this another way, as the eternal law is God under the aspect of law-giver, natural law is human nature under the aspect of its inherent obligations. Natural law is that reality of our situation whereby things are, in fact, good or bad, right or wrong. In von Hildebrand's terms, natural law is the reality of moral values as these impinge upon our consciousness. Natural law is not arbitrary; or at least it is no more arbitrary than creation itself. Natural law, in fact, is not anything added on to creation. Rather it is creation itself as obligating and obligatory. It is coexistent and coextensive with creation.

But this general definition of natural law raised several questions which were typically addressed in the manuals.[5] For one thing, it prompted the question of whether the natural law is really law at all. Their answer was: "Yes and no!" Inasmuch as the natural law is a source of true obligation, inasmuch as it somehow stands outside of persons and pronounces judgment upon them, it can rightly be described as law. The natural law does involve demand; consequently, it can be experienced as a coercive force. And again, in this regard it is truly law. But inasmuch as the natural law is not a written law, does not exist in books or in official pronouncements, but rather is "written in their hearts" (Rom 2:15), it is not aptly termed law. The natural law can, of course, be formulated, though the degree to which it can be summarized with real accuracy is a question to which we will have to return. But it does not primarily exist in such formulations. Rather the natural law is the demand of creation, experienced in the lives of human persons and promulgated through the light of human reason. So while it is a law, it is a law of a special sort.

A second question was this: the natural law is rooted in the eternal law, that is, in God himself. But if we were to try to specify this grounding further, would we be more correct in locating the source of the natural law in the divine intellect or the divine will? Now, to a certain extent this is a strange and useless question. But it is significant for us in that the answer given tended to symbolize the overall philosophical bias of the respondent. These biases will demand a good deal of our attention later on. Some authors, working from the analogy of human legislation and noticing the fact that in medieval life the existence of particular laws depended upon the *will* of the monarch, concluded that the natural law, too, is an exercise of will. They judged that we should obey the natural law, as found in creation through the use of right reason, because that law reveals to us the *will* of God. Other authors, however, noted that the whole content of the natural law is oriented toward the fulfillment of creation as it exists. That is, that God's creation ought to achieve the fullness of being toward which it is pointed. Thus the existence of the natural law is nothing else than one aspect of that exercise of divine wisdom that is the shape of creation itself. It is thus an exercise of divine intellect with which we are expected to cooperate.[6]

A third question investigated whether the natural law ever changes. Or is it rather universally applicable to all mankind and permanently unchanging throughout history? Obviously the first answer to this question is that the natural law is just as static as creation, no more and no less. Well, then, is creation static? Here the manualists answered with a qualified affirmative. But let us note their qualifications.

First of all, the Scholastics acknowledged that human nature has been substantially changed in some ways by the theological situation of the human race. That is, human nature in the present fallen-redeemed situation is different than human nature before the fall (prelapsarian man), than human nature fallen and still unredeemed, and then fully blessed human nature in the next life. The result of these differences is that moral obligations change. Thus, for example, many Scholastics asserted that the natural right to private property exists only because of our fallenness. Otherwise it would be unnecessary if not undesirable. Then again, perhaps the right under the natural law of governments to coerce their citizens into socially acceptable behavior likewise is premised on the reality of sin. So for the Scholastics there was at least this slight element of change in the situation of human nature and, consequently, of natural law.

In the second place, the authors of the manuals willingly acknowledged that the more concrete and technical questions of ethics require considerable skill to judge. They distinguished three levels of natural law norms: universal principles, immediate conclusions, and concrete applications. Universal principles, such as "Do good and avoid evil," are known and appreciated by all human beings. Indeed, principles such as this are self-evident in the practical realm in the same way that the principle of contradiction is self-evident in the speculative realm. Immediate conclusions, such as the norms articulated in the Ten Commandments, were also considered easy to apprehend. Only a perverse stubbornness can prevent an individual from appreciating the correctness of these moral laws.

But in the case of concrete obligations, the Scholastics were willing to grant that the correct action is often difficult to discern. Some particular course of behavior is objectively correct, of course, and others are wrong. But the clear perception of this right behavior is not easy. Given the intricacy and ambiguity of human life, to say nothing of the "darkness of intellect" which follows from original sin, moral agents often err in their judgments. And where experts have, through subtle reasoning and high intelligence, come to see what should be done, their conclusions will often be difficult to communicate in a convincing and self-evident manner. So the natural law, as it is known by us, will doubtless change.[7]

In the third place, the manualists also affirmed "change" in the natural law in the sense that different objective situations may ground different moral obligations. The Christian is always obligated to do what is right. But that rightness is rooted not only in the general nature of human persons but also in the objective but concrete details of the specific situation. To put this another way, obligation can arise not only from human nature as such, but also from one's "state in life." Thus, correct sexual behavior will be quite different for married and unmarried persons. The right handling of money will be different for the banker and the laborer, for the wealthy bachelor and the poor father of several children. So, at the level of concrete applications, different moral obligations may sometimes apply.

In this limited sense, then, even the moral theology of the manuals can be aptly termed a "situation ethic." But notwithstanding these details, there is no doubt that the manualist tradition generally emphasized the universal and unchanging character of natural law. They might briefly grant a certain amount of existential diversity and a considerable amount of epistemological difficulty, but the weight of their argument always returned to the permanent and the absolute.

Positive Law

It is clear, however, that the natural law by itself is insufficient for the ordering of human life. Given the obvious fact that we are social beings, beings who must coordinate with and relate to our fellows, it is obvious that there is also a need for a variety of regulations by which to organize common life. So, in accord with the data of experience, the manualists spoke of a third general category of law: positive law.

This term is ambiguous in contemporary English, but it was coined for the simple reason that such laws are "posited." They are the creations of human ingenuity, not given self-evidently by the fabric of creation as is the natural law. Positive laws can be expressed in both affirmative and negative propositions (and hence are not necessarily "positive" in that sense of the word). But in either case they constitute the tools of the human enterprise of societal living.

Scholastics envisioned several subdivisions of positive law. First, they distinguished divine and human law, on the basis of the particular law's creator. Divine positive law is a category difficult to justify today; it largely resulted from naïve scriptural exegesis. But from the manualists' point of view it was clear that the Old Testament contained numerous ritual requirements which, while not at all derived from natural law, nonetheless appeared to be God's will. So they had no alternative but to view these as "rules made by God." What is more, the manualists sought to explain the demand of Christ that Christians make use of the sacraments by a similar construction. After all, there seems to be nothing in the nature of things that would make baptism truly necessary for salvation. We will leave to sacramental theologians to decide whether this way of expressing things is most appropriate; we simply report the historical fact that Scholastics had this understanding.

Human positive law is much easier to comprehend. In fact, its existence is both self-evident and self-justifying. But that did not prevent many of the manuals from pursuing an analysis that was tremendously lengthy and detailed. In part because of the intimate relationship between traditional moral theology and canon law, the introduction of the category of human positive law became the occasion for a lengthy excursion into the variety of laws, the nature and characteristics of different jurisdictions, the obligations of good citizenship, and so on. They not only distinguished human positive law into civil and ecclesiastical. They also proceeded to subdivide each of these categories several more times. As a result, despite the clearly more central importance of natural law to the task of moral theology, many of the manuals spent exponentially more pages on their consideration of positive legislations.

Methodology

We will attempt to avoid this distortion in our discussions here. On the contrary, we will try to make the issues of natural law our primary focus. We will consider the idea of natural law in the Scriptures in Chapter Twelve. We will recapitulate the history of the idea of natural law in Chapter Thirteen. Then on the basis of this data we shall attempt, in Chapters Fourteen and Fifteen, to develop a systematic understanding of natural law which will be appropriate to our contemporary situation. This understanding will force us to reconsider several common maxims of morality in Chapter Sixteen. Finally, in Chapter Seventeen, we shall add a number of important related ideas having to do with the limits of our human ability to know the natural law.

Only after this entire investigation is completed will we return to the question of positive law. We will, of course, return to it, for positive law inevitably plays a significant part in the conduct of our daily lives. But our consideration will attempt to make clear that no matter how immediately relevant, the question of positive law is a subsidiary and tangential question at best. Even when we do pursue that consideration, our focus will still be that of moral theology. We shall not try to speak as lawyers. Instead, we shall try to develop some specifically theological insights into the nature, purposes, and limits of human positive law in a Christian and Catholic context.

12

MORAL LAW IN SCRIPTURE

Before we begin to develop a contemporary theory of natural law, or even to see if such is possible, we ought to be sure we are in contact with the insights of our tradition. Both the pages of Sacred Scripture and the theological developments of the historical Church offer a richness of context which we dare not overlook. In the next two chapters, therefore, we will attend to this context and try to penetrate those themes and developments which can serve us in our task.

In investigating the biblical source, however, we cannot limit ourselves to the precise term "natural law." In order to appreciate what the text has to offer, we must adopt a broader stance and think in terms of law in general. And this both because the more general term is logically prior and because those references to natural law which do exist, as we shall see, themselves relate it to law in general. Thus we will begin by asking about the notion of law in the Old Testament. This will lead to a detailed consideration of the Ten Commandments. Moving into the New Testament we shall examine the two great commandments of Jesus. Paul's many discussions of law will follow, and then we will conclude with his comments precisely on natural law.

Old Testament Law

At various times in the history of Israel, and in various strata of Old Testament writing, the term law (*torah*, *nomos*) had somewhat different meanings. It could refer to individual moral precepts, to the Book of Deuteronomy, to all the sayings of Moses, or to the whole collectivity of obligations imposed by Yahweh. Ultimately, indeed, the entire scriptural library came to be summarized as "the Law and the Prophets." There were various types of law: moral demands, dictates of religious ritual, and legal stipulations for the conduct of social life.[1] And although references to law abounded throughout the Old Testament, there were several preeminent collections of laws: the Book of the Covenant (Exod 21–23), the entire Book of Deuteronomy, the Holiness Code (Lev 17–26), and what is known as the Priestly Code (Lev 1–7, 11–15; Num 28–29).

But no matter what the diversities of content, style, or context, the notion of law always had certain characteristics for Israel. Several of these should be isolated. First of all, law was not a separate reality, but rather was a consequence of *covenant*. It was only because of the relationship between Israel and God that the various laws were important, only because of Yahweh's commitment to the people that the laws were given, and only because of their commitment to him that they were observed. The laws were not symbols of some abstract moral order, nor were they the arbitrary demands of a cruel and distant deity. No, the laws (and the general reality of "law") were seen as symbols of the intimacy between God and his people. And obedient adherence to them was seen as an expression of that intimacy.

Following from this, the second common characteristic of Old Testament law was that it was a manifestation of Israel's *election* by God. Inasmuch as the law followed upon the divine initiative of the Covenant, it was a point of pride for Israel. The giving of the law and their right and duty to accept it were privileges which they cherished and celebrated. The unusually long text of Psalm 119 is a classic example of the "joy in the law" that was part of the Israelite heritage.

The emphasis upon *obedience* was a third salient characteristic. In some ways, the entire religious life of Israel was conceived as an exercise in obedience. Not blind obedience, to be sure, but a free and humble response to the love of God. This is why, as we have seen, the Old Testament always viewed sin as an offense against the Lord, not primarily as an offense against the injured party. The people were bonded to their God, and all the aspects of their lives were to express their singleminded obedience to his demands.

But to focus upon obedience is not to imply that the laws were seen as empty rules. On the contrary, the law was seen as a divine *gift*, as a series of demands whose observance was in Israel's own best interests. As one author beautifully puts it:

> God's election had, indeed, meant "political" freedom for the seminomadic tribes that came out of Egypt, and this liberation was deeply, ineradicably impressed upon Israel's historical memory. God had rescued them from servitude to men, and from the disaggregation and chaos of their life in Egypt; the law, by ordering their life, gave them justice and security, and by pre-empting their service for God, put a seal upon their freedom. The Decalogue was their "bill of rights."[2]

Saying this, of course, is much like saying that the law was a summary of some sort of natural law. And one might well argue, *post factum*, that this was the case. But we must be clear that this was not Israel's way of thinking. They simply acknowledged two central truths: that happiness and fulfillment were impossible apart from the Lord their God, and that God had enjoined these commandments upon them. Thus for the pious Israelite, even if immediate prosperity and success were not forthcoming, the law remained the divine gift whose observance was, in some ultimate sense, in his own best interests. And this was precisely because it came from the hand of a near and loving Lord.

All of this leads to a last characteristic of Old Testament law: that it generated a strangely beautiful and compelling sort of *legalism*. This term, reserved as it usually is for empty and fear-motivated ritualism, is generally conceived negatively. And in our own systematic reflections here we will often use it in that way. But we nonetheless ought to acknowledge that there is a different sort of legalism. There is a posture which primarily evaluates actions, not in terms of their objective and immediate significance but rather in terms of their potential as symbols of love, which sees behavior less as a tool for the accomplishment of tasks and more as a word speaking the language of love. For one who adopts this posture, even the most apparently empty of actions is full of devotional potential. Such a person is a legalist, but a legalist of a tremendously rich, poetic, and saintly sort. For the best of the Old Testament tradition this is precisely the significance which the law always had.[3]

Ten Commandments

But of all the laws in the pages of Scripture, perhaps those most celebrated are the laws of the Decalogue. To our own day the Ten Commandments remain an element near the center of the lived and celebrated faith. So we should give them some particular notice in this summary.

The first thing to be noted about the Decalogue is that it is not a single, tidy biblical statement. It appears in a quite complete form in two different passages in the Old Testament (Exod 20:1–17; Deut 5:6–21), and various portions can also be found elsewhere (e.g. Exod 12:15–17; Exod 21; Deut 27: 15–26; Lev 19: 11–18). What is more, there are several different ways of dividing the text, with the result that even today three different enumerations are customary with various religious groups. Nonetheless, the basic structure and content of the Commandments is sufficiently clear and well known to permit some further analysis. And this we do through a series of questions.

How old is the Decalogue? There was a time when scholars judged these commandments to be the product of late Israel. The argument was that they seemed to presume a settled agrarian society and to possess a subtlety that could only come after considerable development. Now, however, the weight of scholarly opinion seems to have gone the other way. It appears that at least significant parts of the Decalogue not only are not the product of a period *after* its alleged source at Sinai, they are actually the product of a period *before* Sinai. On this basis, then, the Decalogue continued to evolve through the periods of Israel's history.[4]

Was the Decalogue unique to Israel? No. At least the concrete requirements of Commandments IV–X can also be found in the Egyptian "Book of the Dead" and in Babylonian literature. It is true that there are no other lists exactly like the Ten Commandments. Most of the others are much longer. But they do include among the prohibited behaviors the same familiar items. Indeed, some are even more stringent. The Code of Hammurabi, for example, gives wives a number of rights which were not recognized in Israel. So the notion that the moral dictates of the Decalogue are either unique or particularly enlightened simply cannot be supported. (This suggests that it may be appropriate to view these moral demands as being, in fact, some sort of natural law.)

But does this mean there is *nothing* unique about the Ten Commandments? No. On the contrary, these statements are quite special in two ways: their context and their function. As regards context, it is very noteworthy that the Decalogue is not really a moral document; it is a religious document. The various moral strictures are placed, quite powerfully, in the context of covenant. They are justified by and related to the First Commandment: "I am the Lord your God." As some have put it, there is really only one commandment. And that commandment is followed by nine consequences.[5]

Secondly, the Decalogue is quite special because of its function. Scholars tell us that this text is far more liturgical than ethical. It was proclaimed at the Feast of Tabernacles as a way of expressing and celebrating the mystery of covenant. And this proclamation was part of a liturgy of rededication, by which the people recommitted themselves to the faithful Lord. The pivotal First Commandment was announced, the obvious consequent prohibition of idolatry was asserted ("no other gods before me"), and then some of the more obviously seductive "other gods" were specified.

These specifications were no surprise to the people; common sense would lead one to much the same conclusions. And the Israelites were under no illusion that these prohibitions might express the totality of their moral responsibilities. Clearly the good person must do far more than is mentioned in this list. But the proclamation had a powerful effect nonetheless. No matter how much diversity there was among the people, no matter how widely dispersed across the countryside they might be, they were still one people. For they shared the one God to whom they were committed, and they shared a willingness to respond to that God through right living, some of the more obvious examples of which could quickly be outlined.

To describe the Decalogue in this way, as a cultic text with some minimal ethical components, leads one to wonder about the specific prohibitions. Are they really so minimal? What, after all, was really prohibited? That is our next question.

Scholars tell us that the more concrete commandments were, indeed, minimalistic and that the texts had meanings quite different from those we naïvely presume. For example, the Fourth Commandment only forbade cursing one's parents (for to do so would, by implication, be to curse the source of one's own life, therefore oneself, and therefore the Lord who is Lord of life). The Fifth prohibited killing (whether intentional or accidental) within the community. Nothing was said about respecting the lives of foreigners. The Sixth Commandment really supported the "property rights" of a husband by forbidding sexual involvement with a married woman. Liaisons with single women and recourse to prostitutes were unmentioned. The Seventh prohibited the kidnaping of Israelite freemen while the Ninth and Tenth gave the same protection to the man's dependents (wives, children, slaves) and property. And the Eighth Commandment opposed only perjury in a court of law.

From all of this, then, it is clear that the Decalogue did not present a particularly sensitive ethic, that the revelation of God's election of Israel neither included a revelation of moral specifics nor guaranteed that the people would quickly perceive the ideal of human behavior. But, as we have indicated, this was not a cause for any special concern. For the Decalogue was never expected to express the ultimate in morality. Indeed, a careful reading of the text makes clear that the Decalogue was not particularly concerned about *individual* morality in any form. Rather its consistent focus was the needs of the *community*, and it prohibited those actions which might injure the community. It was the survival and flourishing of God's people as a group that was important. And this precisely because they were God's people. So the Decalogue was a tremendously important document, indeed a primary statement of Israel's life. But its importance was not precisely ethical.[6]

Two Commandments

We now move to the New Testament. We have already seen, in Chapter Three, the aspect of "demand" that was integral to Jesus' message, so there is no need to return to that more general theme. But there are several ideas which immediately pertain to our search for natural law and which should now be pursued. We begin with Jesus' teaching of the two New Commandments (Mt 22:34–40; Mk 12:28–34; Lk 10:25–28) because these are so often contrasted with the Ten Commandments of the Old Law.

This opposition is, of course, a great exaggeration. For one thing, that posture of love which was summarized in the New Commandments was also a clearly central reality for the life of Israel. To understand the Decalogue in a way that makes love irrelevant is a travesty which only later generations of Christians would dare to think. For the people of Israel, the love-intimacy of covenant was the only thing that gave meaning to their moral and religious lives. So, for this reason it is an exaggeration to oppose the new and old commandments.

It is also an exaggeration for another reason. And that, simply, is the fact that the new law is *part* of the old: "You shall love the Lord, your God, with all your heart, and with all your soul, and with all your strength" (Deut 6:5). And "You shall love your neighbor as yourself" (Lev 19:18). What is more, the existence of these two commands, and their preeminence as a summary of the "whole law and the prophets," was well known in the time of Jesus. We can only presume that Jesus himself was well aware of them.

Consider, for example, the text in Mark (12: 28–34). A scribe questions Jesus about the heart of the law. Jesus answers with the two commandments. And the scribe responds: "Excellent, Teacher! You are right." Now, if Jesus were really introducing some radically new concept (as people sometimes seem to suggest), the scribe's response would be either absurd or outrageous. But it is neither. In this episode he has been testing Jesus on his knowledge of legal scholarship. And Jesus has passed the test.

So the proclamation of the New Commandments does not represent the introduction of any radically new ideas. But to say this is not to say that Jesus made no contribution whatever in this teaching. Rudolph Schnackenburg, in a classic statement, makes clear that this is not the case. He says that Jesus'

> action was threefold: he revealed the indissoluble interior bond between these two commandments; he showed clearly that the whole law could be reduced to this and only this chief and double commandment; and he reinterpreted "neighborly love" as "love of the nearest person," that is he interpreted it in an absolutely universal sense.[7]

So perhaps the most balanced conclusion would be that Jesus did not introduce an altogether new concept in his preaching of the dual commandment of love. But he did move the Jewish tradition ahead by a sort of quantum leap. He took the materials of his own heritage, he shaped them according to his own vision, and in so doing he produced a special focus and thrust for his own moral teaching. He produced a moral ideal that St. Augustine could summarize quite accurately in his famous dictum: "Love and do what you will."[8]

Paul on Law

One last series of reflections upon the reality of law is required. And these revolve around Paul's thought. We will begin by noting the overall thrust of Paul's understanding of law, and then we will look at his specific references to natural law.

That Paul was in continuity with the Gospel tradition which we have just considered is clear. In his letter to the Romans he declared that

> the commandments . . . are all summed up in this, "You shall love your neighbor as yourself." Love never wrongs the neighbor, hence love is the fulfillment of the law. (13:9f)

But he did not merely mimic the teaching we find in the Synoptics and in John. Rather Paul developed ideas particularly his own. And surely one of the most powerful of these is his conception of the opposition between the law and the Spirit. As is well known, Paul insisted on rejecting any myth of self-righteousness held by his readers. We do not save ourselves; neither ritual purity nor moral correctness can purchase the gift of divine grace and love. Therefore, to the extent that the law is a symbol of that presumptous independence, the law must be rejected as well. We are saved not by the law but by the Spirit of God. "Now we have been released from the law—for we have died to what bound us—and we serve in the new spirit, not the antiquated letter" (Rom 7: 6; cf. also Gal 3: 13f).

This new life of the Spirit can, of course, be called a law. It does not represent a life-style of license; rather it demands its own style of generous love. But it is a law in a very different sense.

> The law of the spirit, the spirit of life in Christ Jesus, has freed you from the law of sin and death. (Rom 8:2)

> My point is that you should live in accord with the spirit and you will not yield to the cravings of the flesh. . . . If you are guided by the spirit, you are not under the law. (Gal 5:16, 18)

The law of the Spirit, the law of the Christian's new being, is an inner law. It is not a law imposed by God on unwilling humankind. Rather it is, if we may put it this way, the result of intimate communication between the heart of a loving God and the heart of the believing human person. Indeed, viewed most profoundly this law is a kind of revelation, a gift of God, that far surpasses the revelation and gift of the Old Law. For this law of the Spirit is the Lord himself. Thus, in this law is found a very real and very profound sort of human freedom. "The Lord is the Spirit, and where the Spirit of the Lord is, there is freedom" (2 Cor. 3:17).

In a certain sense, then, Paul stands as a culmination and synthesis of that process we noted in Chapter Three, the move to the interior. Any taint of superficiality, of legalism or ritualism, must be rejected. The arena of God—his kingdom, his call to conversion, his discipleship, and his law—is to be found in our hearts. The covenant between God and his people is a relationship, indeed. And like any genuine relationship it is primarily a matter of the heart, of the inner personal intention. Of course this intention needs to be expressed in behavior. But this does not mean that behavior, by itself, can ever suffice. Behavior is at most the consequence. The core reality lies much deeper. It lies at the level of the Spirit.

Paul on Natural Law

This emphasis on interiority is evident in a special way in the first and second chapters of Paul's Letter to the Romans. For there he speaks of something very like our idea of natural law itself, the law which is not announced from the outside but which rather is heard and experienced in the depths of one's own heart. Let us begin by quoting the two salient texts in their entirety.

> The wrath of God is being revealed from heaven against the irreligious and perverse spirit of men who, in this perversity of theirs, hinder the truth. In fact, whatever can be known about God is clear to them; he himself made it so. Since the creation of the world, invisible realities, God's eternal power and divinity, have become visible, recognized through the things he has made. Therefore these men are inexcusable. (Rom 1:18ff)

> Sinners who do not have the law will perish without reference to it. . . . When Gentiles who do not have the law keep it as by instinct, these men although without the law serve as a law for themselves. They show that the demands of the law are written in their hearts. (Rom 2:12, 14f)

So here we find Paul making a number of related, and very significant, assertions. He claims that God makes himself known not only through direct revelation but also through "the things he has made." From this we can presume that we are capable of knowing God in this natural way, too. Moreover, Paul believes that even those pagans who are not gifted with the Old Law know what they ought to do. For these moral demands are proclaimed not only by revelation but also by instinct. Similarly, the requirements of morality are heard not only by the ears but also by the heart/conscience.

Now, we must be clear that Paul is not "doing" philosophical ethics in these passages. He is neither proposing the concept of natural law nor supporting the somewhat optimistic view of the human person that goes with that concept. Indeed, his actual intent is quite the opposite. Paul's emphasis in this part of the Letter to the Romans is on the mystery of our salvation in Christ. And in the process of developing that theme he wishes to strongly assert the *insufficiency* of any other humanly accessible reality. Paul proves this by the fact that "all have sinned." Those who possess the law are not thereby saved; for by highlighting their evilness the law has simply become an "occasion of sin." Indeed, "no one will be justified in God's sight through observance of the law; the law does nothing but point out what is sinful" (Rom 3:20). But this line of argument would seem to suggest that those under the law are worse off than others; knowing what is right only gives them more chances for failure. But Paul rejects this conclusion. No, he says, all people are equally burdened by sin. For what the Jew knows through the law, we all know in our consciences.

Thus Paul's proclamation of general moral knowledge is actually part of his proclamation of general need for salvation. His reference to natural law is a symbol not of our right to be proud but of our need to be humble. But perhaps this Pauline emphasis only serves to make his texts more interesting. For we certainly would not claim that we are able to consistently do the good by our own power. Indeed, reflecting, in Chapter Nine, on the realities of original sin and grace, we said just the opposite. So we have no quarrel with Paul on this account. But if, while maintaining this God-focus, Paul nonetheless suggests that we can truly know the good and that this good is a human, this-worldly good, then he has said something very important. He has articulated a vision of reality into which a concept of natural law most surely fits. And he has given no small basis on which to build on our own reflections.[9]

Conclusion

We have seen that the notion of law meant many different things at different points in the development of Scripture. On rare occasions it seemed to mean something very like our idea of natural law. Much more commonly it meant the Mosaic Law. But even these latter demands are, upon examination, seen to be quite human insights into the good that one must do. Indeed, they are found to be insights not unlike those of Israel's pagan neighbors. Thus they, too, can somehow be understood as part of the natural law.

But to assert this is obviously to maintain a very colloquial understanding of the term "natural law." And for the overall purposes of this book that will not suffice. The history of secular thought and the history of the Church's reflections upon its own identity reveal considerable sophistication in the handling of that term. So the next step in our investigation will be to recapitulate some major intersections along the road of that extensive history.[10]

13

THE HISTORY
OF NATURAL LAW

We have seen the ways in which the notion of natural law, if not the term, was exploited in the pages of Sacred Scripture. And these reflections inevitably involved references to the history of secular thought. But now, before we synthesize an understanding for our own time, we ought to give explicit consideration to that wider history. The purpose of this chapter, then, is to provide a general outline of the evolution of the idea of natural law. It will be impossible to be complete, of course, but perhaps we can isolate certain highlights which will not betray the more subtle flows of history and will nonetheless suffice for our purposes.

Greeks
Probably one of the more amazing things about the notion of natural law is the fact of its early emergence in the history of humankind. Indeed, one could plausibly argue that *some* sense of moral accountability is absolutely coextensive with human existence as we know it. Be that as it may, the specific idea and term of natural law first emerged in the midst of Greek civilization. While the earlier Greek tragedies, for example, had turned on the capricious will of the gods, the later plays seem to have grasped in a compelling way the unyielding reality of objective obligation. As has often been noted, it is precisely the disproportion between ill will and ill effects that provides the tragic experience in these plays. Morality, they seem to be saying, is not merely a matter of intention. It is also a matter of responding to life as it is. And failure to do so, even unintentional failure, wreaks havoc for those involved.

The notion of natural law was also considered by Greek philosophers, but to varying degrees and in varying ways. In a certain sense Aristotle's *Nichomachean Ethics* depends upon some idea of natural law for its whole validity. Aristotle does use the term or some equivalent in a number of cases. But curiously enough, he does not develop a theory of natural law as such. On the contrary, it was left to the later Stoic philosophers to explicate these ideas. And for them natural law was precisely the objective demand placed on humankind to conform to the givenness of reality. We find ourselves in a cosmos that is fundamentally static, rigid, and unyielding. If we wish to survive, let alone to develop as we ought, we must accept these facts of life. We must learn to live with life, not resisting, not pretending to control it, not attempting to mold it to our will, but rather accepting its domination and demands.

Given the general Greek commitment to a cyclic view of history, of course, this understanding of natural law is not surprising. Even less is it surprising if we realize how much this vision resonated with their experience. In a world without easy access to heat and light, in a world where preservation of food was difficult at best, conformity to the demands of reality and cooperation with the rhythms of life was indeed the key to survival. Thus the extrapolation of this experience into a theory of natural law was an eminently reasonable project. In any case this extrapolation is what occurred in Greek civilization.[1]

Romans

The Roman world, as is well known, was quite different in style from the Greek. If we may put it this way, the Romans were the activists of the ancient world. They were the conquerors, the pragmatic rulers, the politicians of a sort. Because of these "expansionist" commitments, they were also the lawyers. To this day scholars revere Roman civilization for its gift to the western world of an appreciation of law and of its development. Thus it is to be expected that the Romans would build on the Greeks, modify the earlier views, and greatly expand the understanding of natural law. In fact perhaps the Romans are the fathers of natural law, if one puts the emphasis on the second term. For while the Greeks primarily reflected on the realities that confront us—human nature and the world—the Romans spotlighted the *law* of the natural order and of human nature and, in fact, compared and contrasted that law with the other laws of their experience.

One can hear this Roman activism, this optimism toward life, in the way Cicero (d. 43 B.C.) emphasizes things when he speaks of "true law which is right reason in agreement with nature."[2] There is, indeed, something natural, to which we should conform ourselves. But what is natural is right reason, human intelligence, prudent and thoughtful action directed to humane ends. Here no abject capitulation to the facts of life. Instead we find a willingness to take on life, to use common sense and intelligence to solve its riddles and control its caprices. The legal philosopher Gaius (c. 160) betrayed a similar vision. He distinguished *jus civile* (civil law) from *jus gentium* (law of the peoples). He saw the former as including all those regulations and customs that are particular to a specific group or society. *Jus gentium*, on the contrary, referred to laws that are, as experience shows, the common possession of all. They are rules of behavior that are pandemic, and that therefore provide the basis for the interaction of various cultures. But while Gaius noticed and acknowledged this sort of universal law, he did not emphasize its necessity. We do not hear him speaking in the passive, almost fatalistic terms of the Greeks. Rather he simply acknowledged the empirical fact of these universal laws, these natural laws, and sought to appreciate their utility.

As Roman history proceeded, however, a certain amount of the Greek influence began to emerge. (It would be fascinating to speculate on the relationship between this shift and the deterioration of Roman culture.) And it is well exemplified in the categories of Ulpian (d. 228). For while Ulpian accepted Gaius' terminology, he so modified its meaning and so added to it as to fundamentally shift the perspective. For Ulpian there were three sorts of law. *Jus civile* was for him, as for Gaius, the collectivity of particular and specific laws devised by various communities for their own reasons and purposes. Ulpian also spoke of *jus gentium*. But for him this term referred to those somewhat arbitrary laws which nonetheless transcend the boundaries of particular societies. Ulpian's *jus gentium* was not unlike our contemporary notion of international law, clearly a human construct, going beyond self-evident moral demands, and yet reasonable enough to justify general acceptance and appreciation.

But the real contribution of Ulpian was a third term which he added: *jus naturale* (natural law). He described this term as a "rule of action common to man and all the animals." Apparently Ulpian considered man far more like other animals than unlike them. He seemed to feel that what was fundamental was the brute facticity of our being-in-the-world. The givenness of reality impressed him. Thus he saw the natural law as the demand placed upon human beings (as upon all beings) to be what they are, to conform themselves to the facts of life, to accept themselves and their fate, to be docile fellow-animals in the world.

Gone is Cicero's celebration of human reason. Gone is Gaius' vision of intelligent beings shaping the openness of the world to their own envisioned ends. For Ulpian, reason's only task is to discern the facts and laws which are then obeyed. It is true that we are different than other animals. But the difference lies, we might say, at the level of means and not ends, of method and not meaning. Whereas other animals know and pursue their natural functions by instinct, we must discover these by intelligence. But having discovered them, the proper response is the same: obedience. That is the implication of Ulpian's understanding.

With the close of the Roman period we have the terms of a perennial debate well established. And before continuing we should try to articulate it in a strong, concise form. Are we fundamentally identified with the animal kingdom as the Greeks and Ulpian said? Are we basically the beings who use our intellect in order to conform to the facticity of nature? Or are we primarily different, as Romans such as Cicero and Gaius said? Is our task to shape and control our world, to guide it to our own ends? Or again, looked at from the perspective of the world, do we live in a situation that is basically closed, predetermined, univocal in its meaning and possibilities? Or do we live in an open creation, filled with multiple possibilities, a creation possessed of ambiguous and malleable meanings?

Granted that these alternatives are matters of emphasis. After all, in Heideggerian terms human persons are *both* "being" and "world-context." We are both creativity and facticity. Still the emphasis which one elects is significant. And probably such an election cannot be avoided even in a definition that attempts to incorporate both the Greek and Roman visions. Shall we understand natural law as "the obligation (perceived by reason) to conform to nature"? Or shall we see it as "the obligation (built into nature) to use reason in moral judgment"?[3]

These are the questions we inherit from the Greeks and Romans. They are the questions to which succeeding cultures have repeatedly returned.[4]

Medievals

For example, Isadore of Seville (d. 636) reflected on these questions, and on the very terminology developed by Gaius and Ulpian, and sought to bridge them. Ostensibly he accepted Ulpian's tripartite conceptualization of law: *jus civile, jus gentium* and *jus naturale*. But he significantly modified the definition of the last term. Isadore viewed the natural law as being the sum of laws shared by all cultures and societies everywhere. He easily granted Ulpian's idea that *jus naturale* is not a mere formulation of human conventions, a somewhat arbitrary solving of pragmatic problems. Thus it is indeed quite different than *jus gentium*. But he rejected (or at least pointedly avoided) the description of natural law as "common to man and all the animals." Isadore seemed to view the *jus naturale* as a peculiarly human reality, a specifically human exercise of specifically human reason. Natural law is what distinguishes human beings from the animals.

Thus Isadore aligned himself to some extent with Cicero and Gaius. True, his adoption of the tripartite division of law gave him a superficial connection with Ulpian. And indeed it is possible that his emphasis on the difference between *jus gentium* and *jus naturale* may indicate some allegiance to a conception of a closed universe. But his celebration of human reason nonetheless established him as being also in continuity with the Roman approach.

Later history makes clear the importance of this commitment of Isadore's. For the early Scholastics, Alexander of Hales (d. 1245) and Albert the Great (d. 1280), present similar understandings. In fact, they acknowledge a debt to Isadore and forthrightly accept his theory as their own. Bonaventure (d. 1274), however, did not. The great Franciscan, whose Platonic perspective, behavioristic focus, and somewhat pessimistic flavor we have seen before, opted for Ulpian's point of view. But even he, in so doing, felt obliged to take account of Isadore and respond to him in the course of developing another understanding.

Thomas Aquinas

Among medievals, however, Thomas Aquinas (d. 1274) demands special attention, and not only because of his eminence in Catholic theology. On the question of natural law, Thomas is important primarily because of the enigmatic character of his loyalties. Study of the *Summa Theologiae* reveals a genuine ambivalence on Thomas's part. Sometimes he appears to support the open-ended vision of the Romans and Isadore. At other times, however, his loyalty to Ulpian and the Greeks manifests itself quite clearly.

For example, Thomas's general understanding of the human person as a rational animal, his commitment to human law as a "determination of reason" (to which we will return in Chapter Eighteen), even the appeal to reason implicit in the very style of his writings, would all support a Roman approach to natural law. Indeed, in his general discussion of natural law Aquinas asserts that "to the natural law belongs those things to which a man is inclined naturally: and among these it is proper to man to be inclined to act according to reason" (I-II, 94, 4). And he goes on to say that "as to the proper conclusions of the practical reason [i.e. concrete moral judgments], neither is the truth or rectitude the same for all, nor, where it is the same, is it equally known by all" (ibid.). Thus, whereas Thomas admittedly holds a certain skepticism about the accuracy of human knowledge (his last point), which is Greek in flavor, he also assets that the *rectitude* of particular actions may well vary in different situations. And this reflects a much more open, Roman perspective on life.

Still, it also remains true that in many places Aquinas appears to support Ulpian by referring to natural law as "common to all animals" (I-II, 95, 4), by including the demand to conform to animal facticity under the rubric of natural law (I-II, 94, 2), and by the way in which he deals with many concrete ethical questions. Thus it must be granted that

> the Thomistic natural law concept vacillates at times between the order of nature and the order of reason. The general Thomistic thrust

is toward the predominance of reason in natural law theory. However, there is in Thomas a definite tendency to identify the demands of natural law with physical and biological processes.[5]

Later Scholastic Synthesis

Our general survey of the history of moral theology (Chapter Two) dwelt at length on the nominalist movement of the fourteenth and fifteenth centuries. We also noted the behavioristic shape taken by moral theology when it emerged as a separate discipline after the Council of Trent. So rather than belaboring the obvious, let us simply summarize this period by saying that the perspective of the Greeks and of Ulpian almost completely dominated the scene. Indeed, it is saying the best one can of this period to assert that it adopted the more restrictive elements of the Thomistic vision of natural law. In many cases, it even forsook that degree of rationality in favor of a voluntaristic and legalistic conception. Human law often became the paradigm, and natural law was seen simply as "rules made by God." But as we will have occasion to see again, this kind of formulation does not deserve to be called natural law at all.

In any case, the final outcome of the debates of these centuries was the Scholastic synthesis in the manuals of the late nineteenth and early twentieth centuries. And the kind of understanding that was theirs we have seen in Chapter Eleven. Indeed, in sketching out in that chapter the manualist vision of natural law we were viewing the final stage in the history of the theory that has been our concern here. There is no need, therefore, to repeat all of those details.

But just because we have completed our overview of the understandings of natural law to be found in Catholic theology up until recently, it does not follow that everything important has been said. On the contrary, at least one other line of thought demands our attention: the developments outside of theology which have influenced recent reconsiderations of natural law. For particularly in the last two centuries, a number of insights from various other disciplines have been highly influential. So, before concluding this chapter we will pause to notice these related developments.

Attacks on Natural Law

In the last century or so, western civilization has experienced a number of intellectual events which summarily constituted a substantial attack upon the notion of natural law. Not just an attack upon some particular theory of natural law; rather a much more thoroughgoing attack upon the idea of the human person and of human nature that underlies all such theories. Perhaps these attacks were a necessary reaction to the excesses of the Enlightenment, with its naïve optimism about the human race. Perhaps they were the inevitable concomitant of the scientific advances of this era. But whatever the explanation, the simple fact is that natural law was rather completely discredited. And this occurred as a result of attacks upon our freedom or our intelligence or both.

Three attacks in particular should be noted. And they are associated with three major figures in modern thought: Sigmund Freud (1856–1939), Karl Marx (1818–1883), and Charles Darwin (1807–1882). Each of these men was, of course, brilliant in his own way; and we do not wish to denigrate their importance. But whether appropriately or not, their contributions did function as sources for a popular rejection of natural law and human nature. This should not be overlooked.

So we begin with the Freudian attack. Freud's typology of the human person as composed of id, ego, and superego is well known. For our purposes the really significant point is the emphasis upon the id. This cauldron of libidinal energy, this source of life force, was viewed as the central reality of our existence. The id may be controlled by the superego; its energies may be channelled by the ego. But it cannot be denied. Our image of ourselves as free of these drives, or as master of them, is illusion. In fact, true freedom resides precisely in coming to know these forces which cannot be controlled. We are the victims of our own being, and it is naïve to pretend otherwise. Our unconscious is what rules our life.

In the Marxist vision the human person is similarly unfree. But here the source of the unfreedom is not the depths of the inner person but the forces of surrounding society. Because of ideology (which we will discuss again in Chapter Seventeen), we see life not as it is but as we wish it to be. We are betrayed by our situation, deceived by its shared and supported untruths. Thus, even though we may pretend to rule our life by intelligence and reason (because it suits our purposes to so pretend), in reality we are victims to the core.

Charles Darwin's discoveries likewise contributed to a disinterest in natural law. But in this case the reason for the disinterest was the simple realization that we are not only *like* the animals (as Ulpian might assert), we *are* animals. The continuity of human evolution with animal evolution is so thoroughgoing that the correct categories with which to understand and deal with the human person are the categories of zoology and related sciences. The Darwinian thesis, of course, offers a felicitous basis for the psychological theories of B. F. Skinner and other behaviorists. A common theme of their writings is that our illusion of freedom and dignity must be recognized and accepted. We are beings who can be trained but not truly educated; we are beings who can be manipulated but not respected. We use each other, not because of nastiness but simply because there is no alternative. The admirable human creature envisioned by even the most conservative of natural law theorists does not exist. And there is no use pretending it does.

Thus the doubtlessly correct scientific discoveries of these men and their followers led, by immediate implication, to the undermining of one or another of the premises of natural law. They either denied our ability to know and understand ourselves or they rejected the reality of that freedom which alone can justify the call to ethical responsibility.

More recent developments, particularly in psychology, cultural anthropology, and the social sciences, have continued to reinforce these ideas. Many schools of philosophy have, too. One thinks of the British philosophers, with their commitment to empiricism. The assertion that only what is measurable is real clearly makes any discussion of ethics and value difficult, if not impossible. The even more pessimistic premises of linguistic analysis, that we never really achieve contact with "underlying reality," that the proper task of philosophy is not the myth of metaphysics but only the phenomenological consideration of how we express ourselves, all this adversely affected natural law theory with immediacy. Even the American pragmatism of John Dewey and others had that effect. It discouraged the kind of long-range reflection that is characteristic of moral theology. It asked about what "works," it celebrated the "technological criterion," and it attempted to avoid tarrying over the abstractions of evaluation. Or at least, that was its effect in the popular mind.

Indeed, in all of these cases we are focusing more upon the actual results of the theories than upon the subtleties of their originators. For subtleties have a way of not surviving the process of idea dissemination. And there is little doubt that the result of these various innovations was a modern cultural climate in which natural law theory, no matter what its stripe, was not well received. Indeed, until quite recently, it exercised almost no influence whatsoever.

Rebirth of Natural Law

We say "until quite recently." For the last ten to fifteen years have been characterized by an astonishing rebirth of interest in natural law, a renewed respect for the objective reality of human nature, a reawakened appreciation for the limits of our malleability on the one hand and for the possibilities of our power for self-direction on the other.[6] Let us note just a few examples of this phenomenon.

Given the widespread influence of the psychological theories of the Freudians and the behaviorists, it is of more than passing interest that a number of developmental psychologists have claimed to isolate patterns of personal growth that transcend geographical and social boundaries. One thinks of Jean Piaget, Erik Erikson, Lawrence Kohlberg, and Eric Berne. There is tremendous variety in the approaches and conclusions of these men, but there is also something they share in common: the fact that they assert the existence of *patterns*. Not culturally derived patterns, not patterns by which we are victimized. Rather patterns which seem intrinsic to

the human constitution and which are both a challenge to human intelli
gence and freedom and an opportunity for those faculties to realize thei
potential. No doubt these psychologists would hesitate to view themselve
as proponents of some sort of natural law theory. But it is not altogethe
inappropriate to describe them in just this way.[7]

Other sciences also provide examples of this shift in approach. In cul
tural anthropology—a field long dominated by relativistic schemas and b\
the conviction that one must study each culture only on its own terms an(
without any attempt to make comparisons between cultures—there is
new interest in the "universal" in human behavior. Indeed, structura
anthropologist Claude Lévi-Strauss has spent most of his career studyin(
precisely this sort of general dynamic. And in the related discipline o
linguistics, the radical innovations of Noam Chomsky have been highl\
influential. Chomsky's thesis—that there are underlying ways of humar
thinking and speaking which are neither relative to culture nor malleabl(
by human intervention but which are or appear to be rather intrinsic to th(
constitution of the human person—is as strong an assertion of humar
nature as one could fairly expect. And this thesis is not without its owr
potential for interesting extension. Musician Leonard Bernstein has use(
Chomsky as a starting point for his own investigation of the nature o:
music.[8]

So, in a number of areas developments have taken place which have
significantly altered the state of the question regarding the existence and
relevance of natural law. The posture for the last century or so was one of
relativism and pessimism. Relativism, in that many sciences held the view
that human beings were infinitely malleable, without any inner constitution to set limits on their potential or to preestablish the direction in which
their most rewarding growth would occur. And paradoxically, pessimism.
in that scientific views often held that people were not truly in control of
their own fate. Intelligence and/or freedom are myths, it was said. The
human person is perhaps a machine, perhaps a mere animal, and most
certainly not the rational and free being that classic philosophy envisioned.

But both of those perspectives have changed. In the work of people like
Piaget, Lévi-Strauss, and Chomsky relativism has itself been relativized.
The realization has emerged that the human is some particular sort of
being. We possess a nature which is both characteristic of us, wherever and
whenever we may live, and distinguishably ours, setting us apart from
other creatures of this planet. This commitment to a substance lying beneath all the relativities of culture has generated a certain sort of pessimism
of its own. Or at least it has led to a new realism. We cannot (or should not)
become just anything. There are laws of nature, whether we like it or not,
in terms of which the future must be shaped. But this new understanding
has also rejected that other sort of pessimism. If our possibilities are now

seen to be limited, they are nonetheless real. We are in charge of this fact-being which is ours. If we cannot do everything, we can do something. We are free; our intelligence is real. And that, after all, is no small thing.[9]

Conclusion

So, at the end of this thumbnail history of the concepts of human nature and natural law, we are left with a certain irony. For in the flow of theological and Christian-philosophical thought we saw a movement toward quite a rigid conception of natural law. It was a conception that felt very much at home in the rationalistic context of the Enlightenment. Perhaps too much so. For at the end of that era secular culture strongly rebelled against what was seen as a prevailing naïveté. And as the various fields of science and art moved away from natural law and toward the pessimistic and relativistic conceptions that we have discussed, the manuals remained locked into their traditional formulations.

But then came the new period. On the side of theology, we have the strong conciliar call to renewal that was highlighted in Chapter Two. And on the side of the secular sciences we have a new interest in these traditional themes. There is no doubt that the old formulations will not satisfy the cravings of today's thinkers. But it just may be a special moment in which to rethink the ethical notion of natural law. Perhaps we can tap into the openness of our culture and attempt to offer a theological vision of the human person, a concept of human nature and of its ethical aspect, natural law, that will speak to thinking people today. Perhaps there is a way of extrapolating from the best of our tradition those ideas which appear to have perennial validity and of complementing them with ideas derived from the long road traveled by the history of thought.

Perhaps this is just the right moment to once again, in a new context, ask the old question: What is the nature of natural law? At least one can try to formulate a contemporary answer to that question. The next chapter is dedicated to that task.

14

THE NATURE
OF NATURAL LAW

The last two chapters have had as their function to give us a genera
sense of natural law theory, to provide us with a scriptural and historical context for our own reflections. The time has now come to begin those
reflections. This chapter and the one to follow will attempt to develop ar
overall systematic understanding of natural law, an understanding tha
resonates with our experience, satisfies our intellectual need for coherence
and logic, and funds our personal moral decisions in the life-situation
Toward that end, this chapter will sketch the outlines of a contemporary
natural law theory. The next chapter will develop some of the implications
of that theory, particularly as it expresses itself in moral norms.

So we begin by articulating an understanding of natural law, of the
reality of objective moral obligation, for our time. And this we do by
isolating five characteristics of natural law. Or, to put it another way, we
assert that natural law is the term used to express the conviction that moral
values are: real, experiential, consequential, historical, and proportional.[1]

Real

If anything is clear from the perspectives developed in the previous chapters, it is that natural law theory has functioned through the centuries as a
summary statement for the vision of Christian realism. By Christian
realism we mean the fundamental conviction that what makes things right
or wrong is precisely and solely the fact that they truly help or hurt the
human persons that inhabit this world. Christian realism says that the
moral task of the human person genuinely makes a difference, that it is not
an exercise in futility. Nor is it a game that we play only because God
wants us to. Whether I do the right thing or not truly affects the quality of
life that I live in the midst of the human community.

To put all this more theoretically, the tradition of Christian realism stands in opposition to both subjectivism and legalism. For instance, it opposes the notion that particular actions are moral or immoral simply because I judge them to be so, that what gives actions their moral value is merely my perception of them. Christian realism denies that actions are valueless apart from human intentionality, that in the end it makes no difference what one does, that the only issue is why one does it. Consequently, Christian realism supports the statement of the Catholic magisterium which rejected that situation ethics whose authors hold "the decisive and ultimate norm of action to be not the right objective order . . . but a sort of intimate judgment and illumination of the mind and of the unique individual" (DS3918). Christian realism does not deny the central importance of personal decision, an importance that has been emphasized repeatedly in these pages. It does deny, however, that this decision is the ultimate and absolute source of moral value.

But Christian realism equally opposes legalism, and this is a fact often overlooked or insufficiently considered. If it is not my own interior judgment that makes something right or wrong, it is also not the proclamation of the law that makes it such. For Christian realism, the natural law (as law) is justified only by the fact that it expresses what *is*, by the fact that it articulates with some degree of accuracy the reality of moral value. This reality, as it is the basis of natural law, also preexists that law. Thus natural law norms proclaim that something is right *because* it is good, that something is wrong *because* it is bad, in and of itself.[2] Any legalistic theory that attempts to begin with the statements of the law, or argue to moral value from a preexisting statement of moral law, is totally opposed to the vision of Christian realism. And this is true whether the law is divine or human. The Christian life is not, ultimately, a matter of following the law; it is not an exercise in obedience. Instead the Christian life is a matter of doing the good, an exercise in love. And the moral law achieves its dignity simply and precisely because it expresses for the moral person the preexistent reality of objective moral value.

More will have to be said about both subjectivism and legalism as we proceed. In particular we will have to ask about the exact role played by personal decision and about the actual potential of moral norms to express that objective value. But for now it suffices to assert the basic commitment of Christian morality. Christian realism is our starting point; and that realism opposes both subjectivism and legalism in all their forms.

Experiential

The assertion of Christian realism leads us, then, to a second assertion: namely, that natural law theory is an expression of ethical "experientialism." What does this mean? It means that since deeds are judged to be right because they are, in fact, good for human persons, the process of moral evaluation is, in principle, a public, measurable, quasi-experimental process. The process may not be empirical in the technical philosophical sense. Indeed, some empiricists might reject the attempt to justify moral evaluations precisely because value judgments are not utterly quantitative and thus not, in that sense, empirical. But the process is empirical in a more general sense of the term. That is, moral evaluative judgments are conclusions derived from concrete perceptions of human reality, of what truly helps or hurts human persons.[3]

Why do we assert this experiential basis for moral judgments? We do so simply because the alternative is untenable. For this alternative is a subtle but nonetheless real form of legalism. For example, one sometimes hears it said that what makes certain actions wrong is that they violate the natural law. Or, to put this another way, that it is wrong to go against the nature of man, to deny or attack the reality of human nature. This seems reasonable enough. But then other questions occur: What is human nature? How do we know that a particular action contradicts that nature? Here only two answers seem possible. Either we know the nature of the human person as a result of some divine illumination or revelation, or we know it as a result of ordinary human observation, as a result of reflection upon the collective experience of human selfhood.

It may well be that revelation offers us some particular insight into human nature. Indeed, even though scriptural and ecclesial research make clear that no one consistent vision of human nature is systematically detailed here, it is possible to discern general human qualities in these sources. But even if that is true, such legalistic sources cannot be the only (or ultimate) foundation for our perceptions of the human. For if it is in any sense true that human beings are rational animals, that they are the physical beings who know, then it must surely be true that they know, or can know, what they themselves are. At least in general outlines, we must be able to sketch our own reality and to discover the challenge of our own facticity.

Consequently, the discovery of human nature must itself be at least in principle and in part an experiential process. To ultimately root the challenge of moral decision and of prerequisite knowledge of the facts of life on anything other than experience is, in the last analysis, to reduce the moral enterprise to a series of hoops through which the Christian person is commanded to jump. It is to reduce the dignity of moral living to an empty and dehumanizing game. And that is the insidious implication of a legalistic moral theory.[4]

Consequential
To hold the real and experiential approach to the discovery of moral values is also to assert that ethical value is consequential. So, in the third place, we

must now speak of "consequentialism." This term, much discussed in contemporary theological literature, suggests that specific actions are to be evaluated from a moral point of view by considering their actual effects, or consequences, in the arena of human life. If it is wrong for me to take a sum of money left unguarded on my neighbor's table, it is wrong precisely because it does injury to my neighbor (and perhaps also to myself), because the consequences of this action are generally injurious to human persons and the development of human community.

In many questions of Christian morality, this commitment to consequentialism is well accepted and quite traditional. For example, in the case mentioned above, if I were starving and had no other recourse, traditional Catholic morality would be quite prepared to approve of my "theft." That morality would argue that property rights are relative, and that in certain cases my neighbor's right to his money must be balanced against my right to continue living. This analysis can be expressed in our terms by saying that in the particular case at hand the good consequences of the theft outweigh the bad, and thus the action is morally right. Indeed, the analysis makes clear that in this case we simply do not have theft, in any meaningful sense of the term. My neighbor does not reasonably oppose my taking of his money. In fact, in all probability, he has a moral obligation to see to my desperate need. Consideration of the consequences is what brings us to this ethical conclusion.

Other examples could be offered, and will be as we proceed. But at this point we simply want to present the general notion of consequentialism and to respond to two serious objections.

In the first place, it is occasionally argued that at least some human actions reveal themselves as immoral, not because of their consequences but because of the very significance of the action in and of itself. The area most often alluded to is human sexuality. That is, authors assert that sexual activity apart from the situation of a permanent and genuine commitment violates the very significance of the sexual capacity in man, and thus no matter what the specific consequences of the act, it is immoral. This argument is telling, particularly since it resonates with the common judgment of many men and women. And so it must be considered.

But a question arises for us: Is the perception of this intrinsic significance truly nonconsequential? That is: How does one know the purpose of the sexual capacity if not by observation of the results of its being "used" in various ways? And is not this, at least in a general sense, an investigation into consequences? But, one might say, it is in no way a consideration of consequences. Rather, it is a mere observation of the anatomical and biological facts of human sexuality which reveals that capacity's significance. Once again, however, a response suggests itself. First of all, it should be noted that even this analysis grants the experiential nature of the judgment. So Christian ethics is at least experiential. But beyond this, one cannot resist asking why it is so wrong to make various alternative uses of these biological facts. Why must we acquiese to these facts and conform our behavior to them? There are only two answers to this question. One to argue from authority, to say that God (or nature) has given us these facts and expects us to conform ourselves to them. But this line of argument is reductively, legalism once again. The other response is to argue that experience proves that when we go against these facts, when we attempt to mold them to our own desires, the result is the dehumanization of the human community. This, evidently, is an argument from consequences.

The second objection holds that a consequentialist approach to moral theology leads to absurd conclusions. Or at least that it leads to concrete moral judgments which are at variance with the spontaneous evaluations of good people. Examples to demonstrate this include a number of colorful cases. In one, it is asserted that a consequentialist, having contracted with young boy to mow the lawn, might well have to give the promised payment to someone else instead, if it appeared the money would "do more good" that way. In another, the idea of a sheriff handing over an innocent black man to a lynch mob in order to avoid general riot is alleged to be something a consequentialist might have to support. And in a third, it is questioned whether a consequentialist would have any objection to an individual failing to vote in an election when he supports the candidate who will clearly win anyway. After all, his vote is useless, and therefore more good will come of his using his time otherwise. On the basis of examples such as these, and the related arguments, some assert that consequences do not constitute an adequate grounding for moral value and that moral rules are a much more dependable guide for action.[6]

In response to this objection three points can be made. First, consequentialism leads to these absurdities only if it is viewed in an extremely narrow fashion. That is, if the basis for moral value is a sort of "microconsequentialism." Where I decide what to do solely on the grounds of what is best for you and me here and now, then the conclusions I draw may well be abhorrent to virtuous people. But that is not the consequentialism we are describing. On the contrary, it is nothing more than a naïve and solipsistic sort of hedonism. What we propose might better be described as "macroconsequentialism," where one attempts to take into account the results of particular acts in *both* the near and long term.[7] On that basis, the actions described in the three cases would all have to be condemned. For while appearing to be immediately useful, all three actually attack the very fiber of society and encourage the dissolution of the bond of trust and fairness on which the human community depends. Of course, in our cases the sheriff attacks this bond far more forcefully than does the absent voter. Thus, on consequential grounds, the former's behavior would be far more objectionable. But then, it would probably be far more criticized on any grounds.

Some actions are, after all, worse than others, no matter how one explains things.

Secondly, this objection should be countered by clearly asserting that this presentation of consequentialism is a discussion of the nature of values, not their communication. What this means is that our question is "What makes things right or wrong?" and not "How do we find out that something is right or wrong?" There is no doubt that moral values are commonly and effectively transmitted by means of moral rules. Thus I may find out that something is morally wrong by listening to such rules. Indeed, given the personal limitations that all men and women possess in the guidance of their moral lives—limitations of time, of expertise, of objectivity—prudence may often dictate that one simply accept the judgment of such rules and abide by them, especially if one trusts the agent of such rules: the Church, the wider culture, one's friends. But to say all this is to describe the process of ethical value-transmission. And our point is otherwise. Our question is "What is it that these rules transmit?" And the answer, the reality of moral values, is: the cumulative human perception of good and evil consequences.[8]

Thirdly, the objection seems to imply that consequentialism looks only to the pragmatically useful, to the pleasure-giving, the need-fulfilling, the self-satisfying. But that is naïve. To assert the propriety of a consequentialist basis for moral norms is not to deny the need for some wider criterion. Even less is it to accept a cheap and selfish criterion. After all, if we are going to judge particular actions on the basis of whether their results are good or bad, we have to answer the question: Good or bad for whom and in what way? To formulate this question is to seek a criterion. At least in the context of this book, which is about principles of *Catholic* morality, that criterion is shaped by a commitment to the dignity and destiny of human persons. As Christians we do have a prevailing understanding of what the world is and where it is going.[9] In terms of this understanding, then, we evaluate particular actions. And this sort of Christian consequentialism aptly grounds our moral value judgments.[10]

Historical

We must now proceed to a fourth point. It is one thing to discover what is right and wrong, to isolate what truly helps and hurts other human persons and the self. It is quite another to ask about the general perduring validity of the conclusions reached. What we have in mind here is the very important and controversial question of the universality and immutability of the natural law. Granted that we can, as human persons participating in an ethical community, discover what we ought or ought not to do, to what extent can our conclusions be generalized to other situations? Can we presume that our conclusions will be equally valid in other places, other parts of the world? And can we presume that our conclusions will continue to be true in the future?

The answer to these questions lies not precisely in our reflections upon natural law. It is rather the underlying idea of human nature that demands our attention. For we have seen that natural law, as real, is nothing but the formulation of the *ought* contained in the reality of *is*. If we all share the same human nature, then our obligations will be the same. If the human nature which we discern (through an experiential and consequential investigation) is a fully formed and relatively unchanging human nature, perhaps even a static human nature, then we can presume that our conclusions will continue to be valid in the future. And clearly, if either of these statements is not true, if these are not the facts, then our confidence will be greatly lessened. We will be required to reinvestigate and reformulate our conclusions in these new geographical or temporal situations.

So we must ask: What is the human person? That question, of course, admits of many answers. But there is no doubt that at least a component of any answer would be that the human person is the intelligent and free animal. These two qualities are central to our self-understanding. As human persons we are the beings in this world who think, who are self-aware, who have the capacity to imagine options and opportunities and possibilities. And having conceived these alternative futures, we are the beings who can make them happen. We are the beings who not only "live in the world," we are the ones who participate in the "creation of the world." We are the beings whose presence "makes a difference." For in the very act of responding to the world as it is, to the realities with which we find ourselves confronted, we change that world. We reshape it, we guide its evolution, and in so doing we cocreate it.[11]

How do we know all this to be true? Arguments for this vision of the human can be gleaned from several sources. First of all, there is the simple fact of our experience. What is the meaning of work? What is the goal of the political process? What drives us to pursue science and technology? In all cases the answer is the same: to understand and control the environment of this world, to "humanize" the world for the sake of its various inhabitants. No doubt the word "control" needs to be nuanced. Naïve beliefs about our human ability to have it our way, to manipulate our environment to suit our whims, have been discredited. It is now acknowledged much more widely than in recent years that part of the ability to control is the willingness to cooperate, to accept the world as it is. The formula for successful living involves not only dominion but also respect. Idealism must be tempered by realism.[12]

But this is not to say that the drive to control has been forsaken. Quite the contrary, it is simply being pursued in a more sophisticated way.

There exists now a willingness to acknowledge that there are some things we do not at present control. Perhaps we never will. But the move toward knowledge and control remains active. For that move is inevitable with beings of intellect and freedom, as our experience teaches.

Secondly, the reality of man as cocreator is verified by the data of the historical sciences. Paleontology, cultural anthropology, political science, and history itself, all testify to the difference human beings have made. We have not simply been present in the world; we have not merely interacted with our environment. Our presence has been a creative presence, our interaction an evolutionary force. Our culture has changed, and we have changed ourselves. Thus the significance of intellect and freedom, as forces for change in the world, is certified.

In the third place, theology itself supports this vision of the human. In particular, the Hebraic, biblical vision of the world argues for a linear conception of history. There is a difference between past and future, there is an historical dynamic which suggests an essential openness to the being of the world. Granted that this linear vision is not the only perspective to be found in the pages of Scripture, but it is still there, and it gives additional credence to our understanding of the human person, not conformist but creator.

The point of these reflections upon ourselves as intellect and freedom is to highlight the essential historicity of the human person. It is to take note of the central openness of ourselves and our world, of our fundamental capacity (and challenge) to change. But if the world situation of the moral person can change, if we ourselves can change, if, therefore, human nature is not so much a finished fact as it is a project and an experiment, then it follows that the natural law is likewise open to change.[13]

If a particular action has been found to be good for human persons and for the development of human community in the past, if the experiential and consequential investigation has (correctly) concluded that this action has value, then there is surely some likelihood that it will continue to be good in the future. But there is no certainty of that. It is at least possible that the human situation and the structure of human living will so change in the future that this action will no longer be truly helpful. And should that come to be the case, then clearly the moral judgment will have to be revised.

This line of argument often leads theologians to speak of the "mutability" of the natural law. But we will avoid that term. For it sometimes seems to imply that one is convinced that particular norms of the natural law will change. And this is not the case. The essential openness of human persons and their world makes it just as impossible to prove change as to prove permanence. We simply do not know in advance whether a particular action will continue to function in the future in the same way as it does now, whether it will function in another situation as it does in this situation. Thus, instead of speaking of the mutability of the natural law, we speak of its "historicity." And by this term we indicate, not that the natural law *will* change but that it is in principle and of necessity *capable of change*; that change is a possibility, not that it will be a fact.[14]

Proportional

We have therefore found that the natural law, as it is understood in our time, is real, experiential, consequential, and historical. One final characteristic must now be isolated. And that characteristic may be highlighted through the consideration of a series of questions. How does one find the right thing to do? Once one has begun to perceive these real, empirical, consequential, and historical goods, what does one do with that information? How is this data converted into behavior?

It is clear from what has already been said that we are called as human and Christian persons to do good to our neighbor. That is, we are challenged to do that which is genuinely good, truly helpful to others. In theory, this seems completely reasonable. But the briefest reflection on our experience will reveal how actually unreasonable it is. If we are truly expected to do all good things to others, and no bad things, then all of us are doomed to failure. The traditional moral maxim, do good and avoid evil, may have some colloquial significance. But as a precise description of the living of our lives it is simply and inevitably impossible.

This is so for three reasons. First of all, as human beings we are finite. We are limited in our capacity for action and energy. There is only so much time; to read this book is not to read another. We have only so many resources; to contribute to one charity is not to contribute to another. We are the physical captives of geography; to be in one place is not to be in another. In so many ways we are limited. And the result of this is that our best hope is to do as much good as possible, and as little evil as necessary.

Second of all, we are social beings. There are many of us, and our presence together places an inevitable limit on the freedom of the individual. We have already seen the example of the starving person who comes upon some surplus money. Our Christian intuition, as well as our tradition, clearly tells us that the right to life of the starving person outweighs the right to property of the person of wealth. We realize in this example that human rights are relative, that, in the words of the old cliché, my right to swing my arm ends where your nose begins. So it is not simply a matter of *the* good. There are many goods, sometimes complementing each other but often competing and conflicting. And in this situation our best hope is to do as much good as possible, and as little evil as necessary.

Third of all, we are temporal. Perhaps this term is not altogether accurate. What we mean is that all of our actions have multiple effects, that those consequences of which we have spoken do not present themselves in a tidy and logical way. There are many consequences of our actions. And in no situation are all of them good. We may speak of our actions as right or wrong. (And there is a sense in which these terms are quite properly used, as we shall see.) But such terms seem to imply a black-and-white approach to morality, whereas in reality our human experiences of action are almost entirely gray. I stay up late to finish a mystery novel. I get great pleasure from the experience, but I am also quite tired the next day. Or on the other hand, I submit to the pain and indignity of the dentist's drill, and I am rewarded with teeth that are better able to fulfill their natural function. We do good and evil comes of it. We do evil that good may come of it. This is the common experience of men and women throughout the world. And that experience makes us realize that our best hope is to do as much good as possible, and as little evil as necessary.

These reflections upon experience, then, lead us to the answer to our questions. What ought we to do? We ought to do that action which maximizes the good and minimizes the evil. How do we discover the right thing to do? We discover it by balancing the various "goods" and "bads" that are part of the situation and by trying to achieve the greatest proportion of goods to bads. What constitutes right action? It is that action which contains the proportionally greatest maximization of good and minimization of evil. Finally: What is the fifth characteristic of the natural law as it is understood in our time? It is its proportionality. Not only is the natural law real, empirical, consequential, and historical. It is also proportional.[15]

One final note. This notion of proportionality, and of our moral obligation to pursue it, is by no means new in Catholic tradition. "Proportionate reason" is a notion dear to that tradition. It is introduced in the discussion of the Principle of Double Effect; in the consideration of situations in which one is permitted to cooperate in the evil of others; in specifying the individual's rights to forego, or his obligations to accept, certain medical procedures; in justifying the withholding of information in certain circumstances; and in the discussion of property rights.

Moreover, Aquinas makes a point in his *Summa Theologiae* of the centrality of the Christian virtue of prudence (I-II, 61, 2). Many people (including this author at one time) are offended by this statement of Thomas. Is not *love* the central Christian virtue? No, says Aquinas. Love is the "form of all the virtues," it is what gives all virtues their "energy." But even love is of no good if persons do not have common sense, if they are not able to deal intelligently and wisely with the ambiguous situations of their lives. Christians must be able to judge well, to be prudent, in pursuing their moral life. And in the light of our analysis, we can see how right Thomas was.

Moral judgments are exercises in proportionality. They are not mere syllogistic applications of general principles. They are difficult concrete decisions. Persons who judge rightly will be persons who judge prudently. They will be those who are able to perceive their situation truly and know how to maximize the good and minimize the evil. They will be those able to achieve the best possible proportionality of good to evil.

This then is the contemporary understanding of natural law. It is real, experiential, consequential, historical, and proportional. The outline that has been presented in this chapter is still highly abstract, of course. It is really little more than a skeleton. The task now is to flesh out this understanding with additional terminology, with other perspectives, and with many examples. The next chapter will be dedicated to that project of incarnation.[16]

15

MORALITY:
VALUES AND NORMS

In the last chapter we approached the natural law in a rather schematic way. Instead of looking for the content of that law, we tried to describe its shape. Just as one could discuss pyramids, not in terms of their function as burial places but in terms of their three-dimensional triangular shape, so we have approached the natural law in an abstract and formalistic way. This has had the advantage of giving us some criteria by which to evaluate various statements about the natural law which people might make, various expectations of the natural law which people might have.

But if an abstract analysis of natural law is valuable, it is not sufficient. Probably no one would ever have built pyramids if there were not an interest in suitable burial for kings. Similarly, the reality of natural law would have no interest for us if we were not concerned about the actual conduct of our lives. So now we must try to render the general description of natural law into a strategy for living; we must translate the language of characteristics into a language more suited to the guidance of our lives, into the language of values and norms.

Premoral Values

"There is a real world out there." That is the basic presupposition of the natural law vision of life. It is a world that exists on its own terms, a world that operates according to its own laws. What is more, it is a world of values, of "goods" and "bads" that simply are. It is a world of life and death, prosperity and poverty; a world of truth and error, knowledge and ignorance, understanding and confusion; a world of harmony and friction, union and alienation, companionship and loneliness; a world of health and sickness, comfort and discomfort, fertility and sterility; a world of possession and loss; a world of beauty and ugliness. In these ways, and in many more besides, it is a world of values and disvalues.

And it is a world where these values and disvalues compete. Just listing so many of these goods and bads should make it clear that no one can attain them all. In fact, in the process of concretely "doing" our lives, the decision to reach for one value can often mean forsaking another. It may even mean attacking another. So, for example, telling the truth may turn two friends apart. Bearing children may lead to relative poverty. Finishing an important job may make the worker sick. And as the cliché points out: "That's life!" Indeed, this insight, a real and often painful fact of life, is what led us to see the natural law as proportional, as involving the challenge to maximize the good and minimize the evil.

So while these concrete values, these "doing-values" are real and important, they are not moral values. That is, achieving them is not absolutely essential to the project of being a moral human being.[1] In fact, achieving them may in some cases be proof that a person is quite immoral. Thus, if a woman stays awake through the night to care for her ailing child, we would hardly brand her a bad mother or a bad person. The most we would say is that her fatigue is "too bad" in the sense that it is unfortunate, regrettable. It is hardly a good thing in and of itself, but in this case it is far better than the alternative of getting her rest and neglecting her child. So, in a way that might be paradoxical if it were not so commonplace, *doing* the bad thing is often necessary in order to *be* a good person.

Thus, we might speak of the values descibed here as nonmoral. Except that this is not altogether accurate either. For one cannot completely ignore these values; they are not morally irrelevant. If the mother were staying up most of the night on a regular basis, and only because she loved the late movie, and if this practice were making her sick or unable to fulfill her other responsibilities, then surely we would claim that there was a moral issue. So while all those "doing-values" we listed are not moral in the sense of being absolutely essential to the living of a virtuous life, still they are morally relevant. Or, in the terminology preferred today, they are "premoral values."[2]

The exact reason for this terminology will become evident as we proceed. For now it is not particularly important; what is important is the underlying insight. We live in a value-laden world. We cannot realize all the values in our experience simultaneously. But we must at least attend to those values, take them into consideration. The virtuous person is the person who realizes those values as much as possible, while neglecting or attacking them as little as necessary. That is, morality is a matter of maximizing the premoral goods that we encounter and of minimizing the premoral evils. And premoral values, simply defined, are the concrete good things that ought, to the extent possible, to be done. They are the real values of our world, values to which we must always attend even though they cannot always be realized.

This underlying insight, moreover, is something most people intuitively realize. Married people will talk about the difficulty of deciding how much time to spend with their families, how much on community affairs, and how much on outside personal interests. Business people point out the tension between their responsibilities to stockholders, to employees, and to consumers. Doctors often experience some conflict between the value of getting their patients home as soon as possible and the value of doing tests which may lead to discoveries that will help others. All of these people intuitively know that living as one ought, being moral, entails the proper balancing of these premoral goods and evils. All we are doing is raising this intuition to consciousness, giving it some clarity, and pointing out that it truly summarizes the strategy of moral living.

Material Norms

It is now obvious that in order to implement this strategy we have to properly assess the importance of the various values we encounter. Often enough that is no simple thing. Of course, if the two competing values are fatigue and the health of one's child, then the priority is clear. But the cases of the married people, the business people, and the doctors exemplify that priorities often are not clear. Hence, the assessment of particular concrete premoral values has always been a major concern. It is a concern of people in general, and it is a concern of moral theology as a science.[3]

As that assessment process is completed, the results are quite commonly summarized in pithy form. They are articulated in a way that is easily communicable, readily accessible to others. And these summaries are norms of morality.

"Do not kill." "Get enough rest." "Do not take what belongs to another." "Tell the truth." "Repay your loans." All of these are norms. They are formulated in different ways, but they have the common characteristic of articulating values in terms of how we should behave. They tell us what, if possible, we ought to *do*. They point at a specific, concrete human situation, and they tell us where the values reside in that situation—or at least where one of the values resides, for there could be others. If I am starving, I do not repay my loans. If I am asked an intruding question about a client of mine, I do not tell the truth. If I am accosted by a deranged knife-wielder, I may kill. But still the norms do point to values. And they remind us not to take them lightly.

Norms like these, norms that point at the premoral values to be found in our world, are commonly called "material norms." That is, they seek to be quite specific, to describe concretely the material from which human situations are made, and they try to name and assess the premoral values that reside there. They try to inform us about those values so that we can correctly and more insightfully proceed to the proportional judgment we must make. Indeed, they attempt (whether successfully or not) to make that judgment for us. We know we must maximize the premoral good and minimize the premoral evil. Material norms call our attention to the various values we must take into account in doing precisely that. And conscious of those values, material norms attempt to write a very specific *script* for the living of our human lives. They bluntly announce precisely what ought to be *done*.

Such norms are not absolute, of course. As we have seen, there may be times when I encroach on another's property rights, when I should withhold the truth, when I may have to kill. There are, in other words, times when every script may have to be revised. But such norms are nonetheless very useful. For they give us some concrete input. In fact, it is their very concreteness that prevents them from being absolute. One cannot have it both ways. Either a norm remains very general, describing the sort of people we should *be*, and in its generality is absolute; or it becomes quite specific, describing the actions we should *do*, and in its specificity stands open to exception. Either I say "Do what's right!" and speak in absolutes, or I say "Do your homework!" and acknowledge that there will be exceptions. And material norms, forced to choose between specificity and absoluteness, serve us by pursuing the first.

Moral Values

The objective of all our moral judgments is to do the good. Or, more precisely, to do what is right. And, as we said before, that rightness is constituted by doing as much good as possible and as little evil as necessary. It is not a matter of doing what one feels like. It is not even a matter of being sincere. Good and sincere people regularly do things that injure themselves and those around them. And while we may appreciate their sincerity of intention, we still offer judgment on the behavior they perform. So, without denying the dignity of human persons, the rights of personal conscience, or the importance of inner sincerity, it is still appropriate to speak of moral success and failure. In any particular situation there is, in fact, some action that is the right action, some action that really does maximize the premoral good and minimize the premoral evil. Other actions, no matter how well intentioned, are objective failures of the moral enterprise. Indeed, perhaps the fact that people argue so forcefully about ethical issues proves they know how true this is.

So it is not surprising that, in addition to everything we have discussed so far, there also exists a whole language of moral success and failure, a language of human ideals. We speak of honesty, of justice, of chastity, of reverence for life. And on the other side, we speak of cruelty, of lust, of disrespect, of injustice. We speak of those qualities which characterize the person who is both sincere and objectively correct, or who is not. We speak of the virtues, and the vices they oppose.

The qualities we have listed here are, of course, good or bad things. They are important in themselves, valuable in their own right, so it is certainly appropriate to call them values. But they are also clearly values of a different sort.

On the one hand, they are values which we consider truly essential to proper human living. If a person fails to get a good night's sleep, that may be good or bad. But is a person fails to be honest, that is always bad. These values, then, do not just describe things we should attend to in our daily living. They describe things we should, indeed must, possess. They are really alternative ways of describing moral living itself. And so they are called "moral values."

On the other hand, these values differ from those we saw earlier in that they do not so much point "out there" as "in here." They do not name aspects of a particular situation which should be noted and taken into account. Rather they describe qualities of moral persons themselves as they confront and correctly deal with their situations. They describe the kind of persons they should *be*. If we name these values by using adjectives (fair, honest, just, chaste, etc.), then the adjectives are most appropriately modifiers of moral agents themselves. They describe their way of *being*, they report their success and failure in maximizing the premoral good and minimizing the premoral evil in a particular area of life. For this reason, again, they are called "moral values."[4]

Thus, we find in our experience two different sorts of values: not only premoral "doing-values," but also moral "being-values." And as we compare these two, we find that, paradoxically, moral values are both more and less than premoral values. They are more in that they point at qualities that are absolutely essential for proper human living. They are less in that they are so obvious and so lacking in specific content, really little more than synonyms for goodness itself. This fact, that they are both more and less, is precisely what explains their existence. We know that the goal of human living is to be both sincere *and* correct in our moral judgments. So it is the most natural thing in the world that we should create a vocabulary to describe this goal. Inasmuch as this goal must be sought in a variety of different dimensions of our lives, it is utterly natural that we should create terms to describe the goal in each. In the area of interpersonal communications we call it honesty. In the area of mutual rights and duties we call it justice. In the area of sexual behavior we call it chastity. And while these terms do not wrestle with the total complexity of the various situations, they do articulate the ideal that should always be sought.

Formal Norms

Moral values, too, are often proclaimed in normative language: Be honest. Respect life. Give to each his due. Honor your father and mother. But they are obviously norms of a different sort, not at all in the nature of a script. They are so vague, so totally lacking in content, that they hardly seem to deserve being called norms at all. If we are going to consider them norms, then they will have to have a special name. Theologians today refer to them as "formal norms," for they describe the form, the style, the shape that one's life should have in a particular area of ethical concern. While material norms try to grapple with the concreteness of the situation, with its material, in order to assess the various values, formal norms try to point out the character, the form, that will be possessed by the successful moral agent. Or to put this in other ways, while material norms seek to write a useful, albeit tentative, script for life, formal norms proclaim the *goal* to which every script ought to conform, the *dream* which every script ought to incarnate. Or again, while material norms tell us what we should *do*, formal norms tell us who we should *be*.

The reader may have noticed that the examples of formal norms used above were all affirmative in character. Are there no formal norms which are prohibitions? There are, but we avoided them at first because they are a bit problematic. Do not murder. Do not lie. Promiscuity is wrong. Stealing is wrong. Are these norms formal or material? That is, do they describe the form or shape that one's life should take in a particular area of ethical concern, or do they describe a specific item of premoral material and point out its value or disvalue? In answering these questions, one might well be tempted to view these prohibitions as material norms. They are, after all, more specific than the affirmative commands with which we began this section. They are more like a script, and less like a goal, than the others. There seems to be a world of difference between "Respect life" and "Do not murder." But is there really?

Take the case mentioned earlier, where I am accosted by a deranged man on a rampage with a knife. In self-defense I kill the man. Have I murdered him? Most people would say no. They would say that I had committed a justified homicide. In fact, even the civil courts would say that. Well then, what is murder? Perhaps it can be defined as unjustified killing. But if that is the case, then the norm we are considering really declares: "Do not kill without justification." It points out quite literally that wrong killing is wrong.

In other words, this norm really does not give us any information, it is not oriented toward the material of a particular situation. Rather it, too, in its own way spotlights the form or style that moral living should have. It, too, proclaims the sort of person we should *be*. Despite the apparent differences between "Respect life" and "Do not murder," they are really exactly the same sort of norm. They are both formal norms.

This sort of analysis could be pursued with the other prohibitions. Lying is precisely those violations of the truth which are unjustified. Promiscuity is irresponsible sexual behavior. Stealing occurs when one takes the possession of another without a proportionate reason.[5] In all these cases, the norm does not actually give any information about the real premoral values of a particular situation. It does not really attempt to write a script for our lives, to tell us what to *do*. Rather it denominates the posture of the moral agent who successfully deals with those values as they confront him in his life. It tells us who to *be*. It proclaims the nonnegotiable goal that applies to every situation.

Implications

So there is such a thing as formal norms. But having said this, and having defined what formal norms are, two further questions arise. One simply asks why formal norms exist at all. The other asks why it is so important to distinguish them from material norms. We ask both these questions because our objective is a strategy for living the Christian life. We are not interested in idle distinctions, and so we legitimately ask: What difference does it make?

So, to the first question. It may well have occurred to the reader by this time that formal norms are really tautologies. That is, they repeat themselves and somehow involve circular logic. We found that "Do not murder" really means "Wrong killings are wrong." Since this is so, one wonders why we should have such norms. There is no doubt that we do. This entire discussion of values and norms has merely been describing what people do and how they talk. We have created nothing, we have merely noticed what is. But still, it may be worth inquiring why people think and talk this way. Why do people make such contentless statements?

The answer, and it is a very significant answer, involves returning to an insight discussed much earlier in this book. In Chapter Five we discussed the difference between speculative and evaluative knowledge. We discovered how important evaluative knowledge is, but also how neglected it can be in our technological culture. The distinction comes to mind once again in this context. For if one's goal is solely and precisely to get *information* about what one ought to do, then clearly formal norms are of little use. But is information the only need of the human moral agent? Is it really true that my only moral problem is to discern what I ought to do, that once I have that information I always obey it? By no means.

At least as important as information for the moral enterprise is *motivation*. I do not need only the data, I also need encouragement. I need formulations of my own values, formulations which in their conciseness and directness help me to remain faithful to those values. And here is the specific (and very important) function of formal norms. They take the meaning of humanity, with its challenge of intellect and freedom. They apply that meaning to a particular area of human life (for example, property rights). And they declare, in pithy form, what I already know but tend to forget or neglect: Do not steal. By presenting me with that challenge, almost in aphoristic style, formal norms serve me in those moments of human weakness and temptation which are so much a part of our sin-affected situation.[6]

Formal norms are the homiletics of the Christian moral life. Indeed, it is no accident that much preaching is in the language of formal norms, challenging the people to responsibility, urging them to fidelity, calling them to generosity. And it could hardly be otherwise. The preacher cannot get into the minutiae of the unique situations that confront his people. He cannot make their decisions for them. He cannot conclude the proportional evaluation of the various premoral values for them (though in many cases he can assist in that process). So he speaks the only language that is applicable to all, the only language that is general enough to apply in all situations. He speaks the language of formal norms.[7]

So formal norms exist because ethical discourse has not one function but two. That is the simple answer to our first question. The second question asks why it is so important for us to distinguish formal and material norms in our analysis. Again the answer is simple. Indeed, it has already been implied, but it should be said clearly. The distinction is important for us because only formal norms are absolute and exceptionless.

Inasmuch as formal norms specify styles of living that are characteristic of the moral person, they speak without fear of contradiction. It is always right to be honest; it is never right to be promiscuous. But inasmuch as material norms point at concrete values that reside in the moral situation, and inasmuch as those values coexist with others which may sometimes have to take precedence, such norms must always be open to exceptions. Generally, one should not kill, but sometimes it may be necessary. Generally, one should speak the truth, but sometimes deception must occur.

This does not mean that there *will* be exceptions to all material norms. The statement "Do not drop a bomb that will kill a million people" would probably never admit of exception. At least we pray that it would not. But the reason for its exceptionless character is not anything intrinsic to this specific norm. Rather the reason is that we cannot conceive of any other value so pressing as to take precedence over that of a million human lives. But since we cannot see into the future or imagine the infinite number of conflict situations that might occur, we cannot *prove* that no exception could occur. So while some material norms may highlight values which, in the general run of situations, must always take precedence and which, for all practical purposes, must therefore always be preferred, and while such norms may therefore be viewed as "practical absolutes," still material norms are never truly and demonstrably absolute.

Thus the importance of drawing the distinction between formal norms which describe qualities of the moral person and material norms which specify values in the moral situation is that only in this way can we keep clear what is absolute and what is not. And that, obviously, is important to the development of a strategy for Christian living.[8]

Conclusion

We can now bring together what has been said in this chapter and thereby summarize the strategy we have been seeking.

As human persons, and all the more as Christians who understand the dignity and destiny of our world, we are called to goodness and responsibility. We experience ourselves as accountable, as challenged by ourselves and our world, as worthy of praise or blame depending on how we respond. Whether this phenomenon is viewed as conscience/1, as Heldeggerian located being, or as von Hildebrand's experience of importance, it is a central aspect of existence.

This call to be moral, moreover, makes itself heard across the length and breadth of our lives. No matter what the situation, no matter what the concrete issue, we experience ourselves as called and challenged by the real. We must do what is right. We must find and pursue the good. We must cultivate and nurture existence, we must be agents of creation and not of destruction. This is what it means to be moral. And these images describe the most fundamental of all moral values.

But we can be a bit more concrete. We can speak of the sort of people we should *be* in particular areas. We can talk about honesty and justice, about chastity and temperance, about love and respect, about generosity and concern. These, too, are moral values, for they are good things and, indeed, good things without which one is really a failure as a human being. They are virtues, and the virtuous person is the *goal* of human living.

So we can speak of these values. And having found them for ourselves, we can proclaim them to one another. We can cast them in the language of norms. Such norms are formal, of course. They are general and abstract. They do not tell us precisely what to do. They do not really give us any new information about our specific situation. In fact, they give us no information at all; they tell us nothing we did not already know. But they are important nonetheless, for they focus the goal of our endeavors, they challenge and motivate us, they urge us to carry on. And, in describing the kind of people we should *be*, they are utterly absolute.

Still the question returns: "What should I *do?*" And the answer is very clear: "There is a real world out there. Deal with it." And as we do, we find that it is a world of values, of "goods" and "bads." We find that these values are real; but we also find that they are in competition with one another. We find that we cannot realize all of them, that sometimes we must even *do* something harmful that good may result. But for all that, we cannot ignore them.

We find, in other words, that it is a world of premoral values and disvalues. And we sense that the term "premoral" introduces both a negative and a positive tone. There is a negative tone, for the term reminds us that these values are less than moral. Their achievement is not utterly essential to being a good person. And in some cases it may be expressive of a bad moral person. But there is also a positive tone. For the term "premoral" reminds us that these values are the input for our moral lives, they are the content with which we deal, the reality to which we respond. They lead to the moral judgment.

These values, too, are something we talk to each other about. They are something we seek to communicate, especially since such values can often be overlooked. In a society where elective abortion is increasingly common, someone must speak out regarding the value of fetal life. In a time of sexual confusion, the meaning and value of physical intimacy must be rearticulated. In a situation where technological skill can outrun human control, specific values and disvalues in medicine, in scientific research, in cybernetics must be isolated and proclaimed. In all these areas, precisely because they are so important, we must at least attempt to write a script. We must at least attempt to say concretely what we ought to *do*. When we formulate this script, we have material norms. Concrete, informational, instructive; but also debatable, often tentative, open to exceptions. Such norms do not settle personal issues. Rather they point to values. They shed light on the situation. And in so doing, they specify for moral agents at least some of the factors they must take into account in reaching their final judgment.

For that is what agents must do. They must deal with that world, with its values and disvalues. To be moral persons they must maximize the goods and minimize the evils. For only in that way can they fulfill themselves and their world. If they are sincere, then their life as a religious enterprise is safeguarded. But for moral persons, precisely because they are sincere, sincerity is not enough. They yearn also to be correct. And this not in order to be self-righteous but that good may truly flourish, that the neighbor may be treated as he or she deserves, that values may be protected and disvalues avoided, that the situations they encounter may be better as a result of their presence.

That is the strategy for the moral life. For there *is* a real world out there. And it is the world that God has made.[9]

16

TRADITIONAL
MORAL MAXIMS

The last chapter completed our systematic presentation of a contemporary vision of natural law. But it did not answer all the questions. In particular, for those versed in the formulations of the Catholic manuals of moral theology, several issues remain. For the vision of natural law we have developed, while it is in continuity with much of Catholic tradition, does seem to deny a number of positions held in our recent past.

For two different reasons we should not avoid this conflict. On the one hand, the traditional ideas did incarnate significant wisdom; and if we are going to disagree with them to any appreciable degree, we should take particular care not to lose what wisdom they incorporated. And on the other hand, it will become clear as we proceed that the conflict between the vision of natural law developed here and these traditional formulations is not just apparent, it is real. The fact that we, at least partly, reject the formulations is not accidental, it is quite intentional. Since this is the case, we owe an accounting of the grounds on which we are making this change and a clear delineation of its scope.

Therefore, in this chapter we shall deal with three traditional concepts of Catholic moral theology: the idea of *intrinsice malum*, the "three-font principle," and the "principle of the double effect."

Intrinsice Malum

One of the notions most identified in the popular mind with the moral theology of the manuals is that of "intrinsically evil acts." The question is whether there are any specific acts which a Christian person ought never, under any circumstance, to do. Are there any acts which, if freely done in any situation, always constitute moral wrong? The answer, at least in many books, was that there are. What are those acts? The first thing that is interesting about the answer to this question is that very few acts were eventually mentioned. For most of the areas of our moral lives, it turned out, the kind of division between moral and premoral values which we have seen, and the use of proportionality, was affirmed. That is, particular concrete acts were seen as good or bad, and therefore to *generally* be done or avoided. But it was recognized that there were exceptions, that the case might arise where the act would have to yield to another, more important, value.

However, in certain areas this was not the case. In certain areas specific, concrete, material acts were viewed as intrinsically evil and therefore never to be done. So again we ask: What were those acts? There were three. The first was violating the marriage contract. In the view of recent Catholic theology, the prohibition of divorce and remarriage was absolute and exceptionless. At least in the case of sacramental and consummated marriages, remarriage was absolutely prohibited. Or to put this another way, the prohibition of divorce and remarriage in these cases, despite the fact that it was a material norm, was nonetheless viewed as an absolute and exceptionless norm.

The second area was the direct taking of innocent life. It was recognized that one sometimes had to indirectly take such life. For example, the cancerous uterus of a pregnant woman might have to be surgically removed even though the fetus would consequently die. Or a wartime pilot might have to drop bombs knowing that some noncombatants might also be killed. But to directly take such lives was forbidden. To once again put this in our terminology, the prohibition of the taking of innocent life was seen to be a material norm, describing a quality of the situation, which was nonetheless exceptionless.

The third area involved sexual morality. The free exercise of the sexual faculty, apart from normal sexual intercourse within a marriage relationship, was prohibited, no matter what the intention or the situation. So, again, we have a material, but exceptionless, norm; we have a description of a material act which is nonetheless viewed as *intrinsice malum*, intrinsically evil.

Now, the obvious question revolves around the grounds for these assertions. For only if we understand the reason these positions were taken can we determine if they are valid. This understanding is difficult to achieve, for different explanations were given by different authors. What is more, the reasons for the absolute prohibition were different in each of the three cases. But we can offer at least a brief summary of the common presentation.

In the case of divorce and remarriage, two justifications are possible; and both were offered at one time or another. Indeed, as E. Schillebeeckx has shown, the history of this prohibition is extremely complicated.[1] On the one hand, it can be argued that divorce and remarriage is prohibited because it violates the natural law, because it is intrinsically opposed to the meaning of human life properly lived. But if this is true, then it is hard to understand the Catholic practice of granting divorces "in favor of the faith." (This is the so-called Pauline Privilege, based on 1 Cor 7:12–15.) But on the other hand, if one argues that the natural law should be understood here as in the other situations we have seen in these pages, namely as expressing real but relative values, then the practice of the Church (and the words of Paul) makes sense. The perdurance of a marriage truly is a value. But it is not an ultimate value, and it is not the only value. It must sometimes yield to other values, for not all values can be simultaneously served in a finite human world.

If one follows this line of thought, then the next question is why such a practice is not also permitted in the case of sacramental and consummated marriages. In answering this, the second ground for the absolute prohibition emerges. What is that ground? It is the meaning of the Sacrament of Matrimony, the real and ontological bond which exists between the partners in such a marriage, which not even the Church can countermand.

Is such an assertion valid? Here this present writer must exercise some humility and say that he simply does not know. It must be left to sacramental theologians to determine whether this is an appropriate way to understand the Sacrament of Matrimony, and to biblical theologians to determine whether this is appropriately concluded from the often quoted words of Jesus prohibiting divorce (Mt 5:31f; Mk 10:1–12; Lk 16:18). All we can say here, as we have already said, is that there is no apparent reason why the objective, material fact of divorce and remarriage should be understood any differently from the perspective of the natural law, that is, in the context of objective morality. Whether the reality of *Christian* life as prophetic, whether *Christian* marriage—not only as a natural fact but as a religious symbol, as a sign of the relationship of Christ and the Church (Eph 5:22–33)—demands this utter and exceptionless fidelity, we cannot say. But that it is not forbidden in such an absolute way by the *natural* law, that it is not a material disvalue so evil that no other good could ever justify it, we can and must affirm.[2]

In the case of the direct taking of innocent life a somewhat different line of argument was followed in the manuals. Here, it was argued, we are confronted with absolute rights of human persons, rights which it is never permissible to attack. But why is this so? The fact that human persons have such absolute rights is, at the very least, not immediately evident. After all, both Church and state have long recognized the legitimacy of capital punishment. And here an individual's right to life is definitely violated.

But, it could be responded, this analogy is fallacious. For capital punishment occurs in the case where an individual has, by his behavior, given up the right to life. There are two answers to this objection. One is that in the real world we are rarely *certain* that the criminal is guilty; no doubt we have often executed the innocent. More importantly, even if the defendent is guilty as charged, he may not have *known* that his act constituted a sacrifice of the right to life. Can one give that right away accidentally? No, the justification for capital punishment, if there is one, is not that the criminal has "given us permission" to execute him. Rather it is that the common good of society demands that his right to life be violated. That is, the justification for capital punishment is precisely that another value, the value of societal peace and order, must take precedence over the value of this individual life. It is, in other words, a thoroughly proportional justification.[3]

The absolute prohibition of the taking of innocent human life is therefore by no means self-evident. It may still be correct. But if it is, it is correct on consequential and proportional grounds. That is, such killing may have such terrible consequences upon the victim (in the case of both direct and indirect killing) and upon the killer (in the case of direct killing) that no other value could possibly outweigh it. But this is in principle an experiential judgment. We can discuss whether it is true in all cases; we can try to imagine alternative scenarios, and then we can hold this conclusion if it seems justified (as it surely is in many cases, if not all).

In any case, the issue of directly killing the innocent is fundamentally no different than any other ethical issue. It involves premoral values expressed in material norms. It involves relative values, not absolutes. And it does not, in any meaningful sense, involve an *intrinsice malum*.

Finally, we look at the case of sexual behavior. But in doing so we merely reiterate what was already said in Chapter Fourteen. Sexuality is a very important area of human life, and a very challenging one as well. That norms should exist to guide our behavior in this area is eminently reasonable; that the various premoral values and disvalues should be highlighted is a great gift. But that this area of human life should be viewed as involving absolute and exceptionless standards different from those of the rest of life does not make sense. Such standards could be justified only by appeal to the natural law, understood in some juridical sense, or to commandments of some kind. In either case, we have a legalism which does injustice to both the Creator and his creation.

No, sexuality is like all the other areas of human life. It involves premoral values and disvalues which are real, experiential, consequential, historical, and proportional. Perhaps the disvalue of sexual behavior, apart from normal sexual intercourse within a marriage setting, is so great that exceptions should be very rare. Perhaps it is so great that they should be nonexistent, that no other value could, or will, ever outweigh them. But it certainly does not involve an *intrinsice malum*.

Therefore, our conclusion is that the concept of intrinsically evil acts, of material and concrete acts which nonetheless constitute moral evils, must be rejected.[4] And this for two reasons. First of all, we have found that there are no examples of such acts. Second of all, as the example of sexual behavior particularly showed, appeal to such a concept involves a subtle but real "legalization" of Christian morality. We are called to do the good as best we can, to avoid evil to the extent we can. Morality is not a legal enterprise. It is a human dealing with the values of our human world. And nothing less will do.[5]

Three-font Principle

The second principle that we must consider speaks of the "three fonts of morality." We discussed this principle briefly in Chapter Seven. And the remarks that must be made here are really just an extension and completion of what was said there. But first we must summarize the prinicple again. It pointed out that human action involves three components: the deed itself, the relevant circumstances, and the motive of the agent. It asserted that to morally evaluate a human action one must evaluate each of these components. One must judge whether the deed itself is morally good, bad, or indifferent. One must consider whether any of the circumstances alter the moral quality of the act. Then one must judge whether the agent's motive is moral. And this maxim declared that an action is truly moral only if all three of the components are moral. If any one of them is not, then the action is immoral. (The trenchant Latin read: *Bonum ex integra causa, malum ex quocumque defectu.*)

Now, this traditional principle is impressive for its clarity, and often it is a helpful tool in dealing with the ambiguity of human life. But, as we saw in Chapter Seven, the dictum also contributes some ambiguity of its own. So, at this point in our reflections it must be critiqued on two counts.

First of all, by including motive (or intention, as it was also called) as just one of three fonts of morality, the maxim risked confusing a number of different things. Does one mean motive in the sense of the purpose of the action? If so, then it may be quite relevant to our consideration of objective morality. For often enough we cannot really evaluate a specific action unless we know why it is being done, what the intended goal is. But in that case, the motive is simply the backdrop against which the usual consequential judgments must be made. Is this action really an apt way to achieve that goal? Is it the best way, involving the most good and the least evil? If this is true, then the motive is really just one of the relevant circumstances that must be taken into account, and there is no reason why it must be mentioned as a separate third font of morality.

On the other hand, does one mean motive in the sense of the purpose of the agent? That is, is one focusing on the subjective reality of inner decision, on the fundamental desire to do good or evil, as one sees it? If that is the case, then the notion of motive, as we saw in Chapter Seven, is a symbol for the whole reality of subjective morality, of sin and virtue. Understood from the side of subjective morality, motive is not one of three fonts of morality, it is the only font of morality.

It is hard to avoid these confusions, for agents and actions always go together. So the notion of motive will always have these two important meanings. Indeed, trying to find a different term does not help, either. Whether one speaks of intentionality, goal, purpose, objective, or reason, the idea can still be understood from the two sides. And while both sides are important, they are quite different. So we would assert that in order to minimize this confusion, the three-font principle should itself be avoided.

Second of all, the three-font principle must be critiqued in that it spoke of various action-components as "moral." That is, it declared that a human action is moral "if all three components are moral." But we have already seen that such components are only premoral. That is, they are, in view of their consequences, either premoral values or disvalues. They become moral only when, viewed proportionally, it becomes clear that they are predominantly values rather than disvalues. For example, if the deed itself is taking money, we know well enough that this is a disvalue. But we are not yet in a position to say whether it is immoral. Only when we add the circumstance that the money is being taken from a pauper by one who has sufficient funds himself or herself are we in a position to make the moral judgment: This is wrong.

Some might object (as we have considered before) that if murder is the deed, then we know it is immoral no matter what the circumstances. But of course the point is that we describe a particular killing as murder only *after* we have taken into consideration the relevant circumstances. "Murder" is, indeed, our term for those killings which are not only premorally evil but also morally wrong, because the deed and circumstances, taken together, yield a predominance of premoral disvalue. So, to express this line of reasoning more theoretically, the one and only font of objective *morality* is the deed itself and the relevant circumstances *taken together*. These two fonts taken separately, on the contrary, are merely the loci of premoral value and disvalue.

Double Effect

The third traditional formulation which deserves our attention at this point is the well-known Principle of the Double Effect. This principle stated that, when confronted by a prospective action which will have two effects, one good and the other evil, I may do the action only if four conditions are satisfied: (1) the action itself must be good or indifferent, (2) my motive (intention) must be the good effect, (3) the good effect must not occur by means of the bad effect (for otherwise I truly *intend* the evil, however begrudgingly), and (4) there must be a proportionate reason for tolerating the evil effect. Once again, we should freely acknowledge the pragmatic usefulness of this principle. It did give the sincere moral agent a way to sort out and analyze the complexities of the human situation. But that usefulness did not remove the substantial theoretical problems inherent here.

For one thing, we have seen that *every* human action involves both good and bad effects, that this "grey" quality is an inevitable by-product of the finite, social, and temporal nature of man. Of course, some might object that the Principle of the Double Effect did not have in mind just ordinary bad effects but rather morally bad effects. However, as we have seen, effects taken by themselves are neither moral nor immoral; they are pre-morally good or bad. Effects (or consequences, as we have called them) provide the input for a moral evaluation. They do not constitute that evaluation.

Secondly (and given the first point), human experience teaches that often we allow evil to function as the means for the achievement of good. Parents lose sleep in order to care for their sick children. Doctors inflict pain in order to heal their patients. Christian ascetics do penance in order to become more focused on the transcendent mystery of God. In our ordinary experience we judge as moral an action whose prevailing direction is toward the good, an action where, viewed proportionally, the good outweighs the evil. Whether the evil arises as a coeffect or whether it is the means to the good is not of any relevance. The predominance of good is what counts.[6]

So the Principle of the Double Effect, as it was traditionally taught, must be rejected. That does not mean that all the wisdom it contained is now to be jettisoned. Quite the contrary. The second condition of the principle remains important. While motive, as we have seen, does not immediately contribute to our evaluation of the objective morality of an action, it is nonetheless central to the actual pursuit of the Christian life. So its inclusion in a practical dictate is quite understandable and commendable. Similarly, the fourth condition is to be maintained. Indeed, the notion of proportionate reason lies at the very core of the vision of natural law which these chapters have developed. Rather than being one of four conditions, we now see proportion as *the* condition for moral behavior. It is the proportional prevalence of premoral goods over premoral evils that characterizes and, in fact, constitutes the reality of moral action for the Christian person.

One last point. The Principle of the Double Effect is often articulated through a more colloquial formulation: "The end does not justify the means." This formulation, precisely because of its familiarity, deserves a bit of analysis. We would suggest that the problem here is the ambiguity of the word "end." This term can be understood to refer either to motive ("I did it to help you") or to consequence ("The action ended up helping you"). But, as we have repeatedly seen, motive and consequence are very different things. Likewise, this maxim means very different things depending on how "end" is understood. If we mean that one's motive does not justify the means, then the maxim is altogether true. "The path to hell is paved with good intentions," and there is hardly anything clearer in human experience than the fact that good people, guided by good intentions, are forever doing objective injury to one another. So a good motive in no way provides an objective justification for the means (or, for that matter, for any other element of the total action). The action is objectively justified only by the fact that it really, truly does contribute to the good of the neighbor and the self.

But if the maxim means that the consequences do not justify the means, then it must be rejected. For it is precisely the consequences, where they are predominantly positive and premorally valuable, that justify the means. Nothing else. And this for all the reasons that have been developed through the last several chapters.

Some time ago, a newspaper editorial provided an analysis of the American tragedy involved in the Watergate affair. And the author asserted, in the process of his wide-ranging critique, that Watergate was the inevitable result of a naïve and self-serving ethic willing to believe that "the end justifies the means." If the author is correct, then this is a telling objection to all that has been presented here. But is he?

Consider for the moment the deceptions perpetrated by those involved with Watergate, and compare them to the deceptions of Dietrich Bonhoeffer and his coconspirators in their attempt to assassinate Adolf Hitler. What is the difference? Is it that the latter group had noble intentions, while the former did not? Perhaps. But it is risky business trying to judge the motives of other men's souls. Our criticism of Watergate dare not base itself only on the insincerity of the participants. Rather we must (and certainly do) complain that what they did was objectively *wrong*. So again we ask: What is the difference between the two groups? Is it that the Germans did not use means that are evil (at least premorally)? This is patently not the case. Both groups indulged in deception. The difference, we would assert, is precisely a difference in the envisioned consequences, and this in light of grossly different circumstances. The difference is that in the case of Watergate *these* ends (consequences) did not justify *these* means, whereas in the other case they did.

So we find that the editorial author, while no doubt working out of a valid intuition about the moral climate of Nixonian Washington, did not isolate the real enemy. The evil of Watergate was not the result of asserting that the end justifies the means. Rather the evil was the result of a profound failure in judgment, a failure to realize that, precisely because *only* the end justifies the means, the proposed action should be unequivocally condemned.[7]

Conclusion

The core of the ongoing exercise of Christian moral living is precisely the pursuit of proportional thinking. That is what Thomas Aquinas sensed in his encomium to prudence. That is what traditional moral theology intuited in its inclusion of proportionate reason. And that is what contemporary ethical thinking is reasserting more forcefully than ever, with its focus on moral and premoral values, formal and material norms.

In developing a vision of the natural law, proportion was the fifth and final characteristic we isolated. In developing a strategy for living the Christian moral life, we saw that this proportionality was central. And now, having reflected on three traditional moral maxims, we find our earlier insight reaffirmed.

The traditional maxims were admirable creations in that they tried to specify the implications of prudence and proportionality in a practical way. But they were regrettable in that this effort led to new confusions and even some errors. Perhaps there is a lesson here: namely, that it is impossible to eliminate the process of prudential judgment by which the moral person reaches concrete conclusions. Assistance can be provided, insight can be offered, the significance of the premoral values that comprise the situation can be highlighted. But the moral judgment can never be so sanitized and packaged as to free the individual from his or her burden.

And if this is true, then the challenge of moral education is clearer than ever. In Chapter Ten we talked about the development of Christian character. It now becomes powerfully evident how central that character is and how critically important is its development. The *real* search is not for values or norms, it is not for maxims or principles. The real search is for the prudent man or woman.

17

THE KNOWABILITY OF
NATURAL LAW

In discussing the natural law, theologian Karl Rahner declares that "the mutability or immutability of this law and the possibility of knowing it are an important theme in Greek and Christian philosophy.[1] In the last several chapters we have dealt primarily with the first aspect of this theme, while somewhat ignoring the second. In technical language, we have pursued metaphysical questions while avoiding epistemological. But that imbalance must now be rectified.

For Rahner is right. If our fundamental question is "What should I do in living the Christian life, and how can I discover what I should do?" then the answer requires two investigations. On the one hand, it must be asked what there is about the nature of human persons and their world that affects that answer. And this we have done. But on the other hand, it must also be asked what there is about ourselves as knowers that affects that answer. And this we have not done.

So we devote one more chapter to the topic of natural law. In so doing, we will not be entering absolutely new areas of concern. For the knower and the known always go together. Rather we will be looking again at topics which have already concerned us. But we will be approaching these topics from a new point of view. We will be tinting the picture already developed with the color of the way we human persons know.

Specifically, we will summarize some insights from the Scholastic tradition. Then we will introduce three facts about ourselves as knowers, facts that must always be kept in mind as we seek to know the natural law. We will investigate those facts and try to appreciate their significance for our Christian lives.

Scholastics

The question is: "Can we know the natural law?" And the interesting thing about the Scholastic answer is that even this tradition, which is sometimes accused of "naïve realism," gave a guarded response. They answered: "Yes and no." Let us specify their response.

The manuals of moral theology began their discussions of the knowability of natural law by distinguishing three levels of that law. First there are the most general and universal dictates of the natural law. "Do good and avoid evil." "Give to everyone their due." Norms such as these, dictates which are little more than definitions of the natural law itself, were judged by the Scholastics to be absolutely knowable. Everyone knows that these norms express truth. And everyone feels obliged to obey them. We ought not to find this surprising since these very universal norms are little else than alternative formulations of that basic dictate of conscience, the demand of conscience/1, which we considered in Chapter Eight. To be a human person is to be aware that one is accountable. Formulations of that fundamental accountability are what we mean by the first level of natural law.

The second level of natural law is comprised of norms which are more concrete than those considered above, but that are nevertheless still somewhat general. These are the norms on which people of good will generally agree, norms which function as basic rules of behavior in most situations. Scholastics suggested that the Ten Commandments of the Old Testament provide us with a typical list of such second-level natural law norms. "Adultery is wrong." "One ought to tell the truth." "Thou shalt not steal." These are second-level norms; and they, like the norms of the first level, were in the Scholastics' view knowable by all. It is possible for people to deny these norms, particularly in the absence of good will. Nonetheless, most people know them and affirm them, even when they fail to obey them.[2]

The third level of natural law contains all the extremely concrete and detailed applications of the more universal norms. They are the conclusions drawn by individuals or by communities, conclusions that make explicit what ought to be done or ought not to be done in a particular case. The case may be an utterly unique situation never to be repeated, or it may be a common and widely shared case. But either way the norms describing the morality of the case are third-level norms. For they attempt to express rightness or wrongness in specific, detailed, and concrete terms. Such norms, said the Scholastics, are by no means universally known. Indeed, the attempt to formulate third-level norms is a task involving considerable risk and significant possibility of error. Why is this?

The reason lies in the intricacy of human reality. The fact of the matter is that life is complex, comprised of myriad significant factors, all of which must be taken into consideration in formulating the norms. It is extremely difficult to include all these factors and to evaluate them accurately. Consequently, even for the Scholastics, human attempts to formulate concrete moral norms are clumsy, risky, and difficult. Moreover, even when such norms are accurately formulated, their ability to be communicated to others, to be shared in a convincing way, is problematic. To use a contemporary example, all Catholic theologians as well as many Protestant theologians currently share the opinion that most (if not all) abortions are immoral. But it is a painful fact of our current culture that these theologians and religious leaders have been notably unable to convince much of the general public of this moral judgment. This would not surprise members of the Scholastic tradition, for they understood that all concrete norms, norms at the third level of the natural law, share this difficulty of certitude and communication.[3]

But if Scholastic writers frankly admitted this difficulty, contemporary theologians confess even greater difficulty. And the three topics which explain this difficulty now demand our attention.

Weakness of Formulation

We begin our investigation of current insights by distinguishing very strongly between understandings of the natural law and the formulation of those understandings. It is one thing to say that I know something; it is quite another to articulate and verbalize that knowledge. Indeed, there are many things in our experience which we know quite surely but which we cannot adequately express. Thus it is extremely important in the matter of the natural law as in other matters to distinguish between understandings and formulations.

The moral history of mankind is cluttered with the corpses of moral norms, formulations of the natural law, which failed to accurately express the reality beneath. Consider an example we have used before, the usual text of the Fifth Commandment: "Thou shall not kill." What is the meaning of this formulation? How adequate is it? Experience and common wisdom immediately respond that the norm is by no means adequate. There is the sad but recurring necessity of war which generated the Catholic just-war theory. There is the commonly accepted right of government to employ capital punishment when and if it is in the best interests of the society. There is the right of persons to defend themselves against unjust aggressors, criminals or irresponsible people who would do them harm. And all of these cases must be taken into account. It is clear that human beings possess some sort of moral obligation to respect the sanctity of life. But it is equally clear that the norm as expressed in the Fifth Commandment does not precisely isolate that moral obligation.

Thus, through the centuries people of wisdom and common sense have felt themselves obliged to nuance and clarify that general statement. In so doing they have exemplified what we now see as a basic fact of life; namely, that formulations never succeed in capturing all the intricacies and complexities of our moral obligation.[4]

There is a very clear reason why this is so. If we think about it, we realize that formulations, and indeed all human words, are clumsy and indelicate tools for the expressing of reality. Reality is subtle and fluid; words are static and rigid. Reality is individual and at least partly unique; words are abstract and universal. Reality, existing in time, always retains the possibility of change; words exist in a timeless and static death.[5] We cannot avoid the use of words, of course. They are the main way at our disposal for the expression of our insights into moral obligation. But that does not mean that words are ever genuinely adequate to the task. They are the clumsy but unavoidable instruments of moral communication. As long as people exist, then, they will express their moral convictions in formulations, but they will also continue to add subordinate clauses to those formulations in the vain but understandable attempt to achieve utter accuracy.

Therefore, we must be careful to distinguish our understanding of natural law from the formulation of that natural law.[6] Indeed, we must be careful to do so not only because the difference between these two is factual, but also because failure to be conscious of it can lead to unfortunate confusions.

For example, one will occasionally hear the argument that natural law must not exist since, if it did, people would surely agree on its formulations. We would not have all the moral disagreements and debates that we do. But in light of what has been said here, we can see how fallacious this reasoning is. Just because men and women of good will cannot agree on the formulation of the natural law, it does not follow that they lack genuine insight into its character. Even more, it certainly does not follow that this law is nonexistent. As we saw in our earlier discussion of evaluative knowledge, there are many things in life that are real which cannot be put into accurate words.

Thus, this insight reminds us to be humble about our own formulations, to anticipate the fact that they will not communicate our thoughts with perfect accuracy. It reminds us to be thoughtful and questioning with regard to the formulations of others; not to presume too quickly that real communication has taken place. And it reminds us always to protect our understandings by recognizing that they are different from the language in which they are clothed. For only in this way can we grant the weakness and inadequacy of much religious and ethical language, and at the same time continue to affirm the reality of moral obligation.

Partiality of Understanding

But what of understandings themselves? If our question "Can we know the natural law?" is taken to mean "Can we understand the natural law?", how shall we answer? In order to respond to this query, it will be necessary for us to make use of several insights derived from fields other than theology. The first of these insights comes from sociology. Sociology, of course, is the science of groups. It studies groups: their causes, their activities, and their effects. As its major premise, sociology presumes the "social construction of reality." That is, sociology presumes that groups have an effect upon individuals, that to a greater or lesser extent groups influence and determine the individuals within.

Beginning about 1850, and continuing until recent years, sociologists have spent considerable time discussing ideology as a factor in group process. What is ideology? In its simplest terms, ideology is the distortion of reality for the sake of one's own interests. It is the denial of the facts of the case; it is the substitution of one's own desires. The witty cliché, "My mind's made up, don't confuse me with the facts," is a classic statement of ideology.

Karl Marx made much of ideology in his analysis of nineteenth-century Europe. The bourgeoisie, he asserted, did not recognize the true facts of their situation, their exploitation of the proletariat and their subjugation of the powerless, precisely because it was not in their best interests to do so. The bourgeoisie were affected by ideology, and that ideology prevented them from seeing the truth. Religion, for Marx, was an example of ideology, as was also the idealistic philosophy of his time. Marx judged all these groups to be guilty of "tunnel vision," a distortion and denial of reality out of self-interest. He accused them of ideology.[7]

For many years, then, it was common to distinguish ideology from objectivity. There are those who deny reality and those who accept it, those who distort and those who see the truth. And these two groups comprise all of humankind. In recent decades, however, sociologists have denied this clear dualism. In so doing they have developed a new subscience within the field of sociology: the sociology of knowledge. This new science of sociology of knowledge offers a contribution of major importance for theology and ethics. According to these sociologists, there is a third possibility in addition to the two previously suggested: that is, accurate but partial knowledge. Just because we see what is there, avoiding ideology and affirming reality, it does not follow that we see everything that lies before us. Indeed, it is impossible for us to see everything.[8]

For example, an artist and a botanist may contemplate the same tree. They are not guilty of ideology, of distorting its reality. Rather they are attempting to be open to that reality. But this does not mean that they "see" the same tree. They do not. For the artist the tree is shape, a color, a combination of light and shadow. In a word, it is a thing of beauty. For the botanist the tree is a specimen of a particular species, having certain characteristics, capable of growing to a certain height and at a certain rate. The artist and the botanist could each provide us with descriptions of what they see, but those descriptions would be quite different. Each of them has seen the tree, the truth. But their "in-sights" are by no means the same. What they see is determined, at least in part, by the perspective from which they look. It is determined by their identity as they approach the tree; it is determined by their position in the group. Their knowledge has, to some extent at least, a sociological explanation. Intellectually speaking, they "stand in different places" and thus they see the tree in quite different ways.

But what if two viewers share common vision? What if their approach is similar? Will they necessarily see the same thing? It depends. Where are they standing? If two artists view the same tree, but from opposite sides, they will not see the same thing. They will both see the tree; what they say about the tree will be true. But it will not be all truth, truth from all perspectives. It will be partial truth, in this case determined, not by their intellectual position but by their geographical position. But the same point obtains. They see in a partial, a limited, a finite way. Though they speak the truth, they speak the truth from a point of view.

The sociology of knowledge, then, asserts that all human knowledge is influenced by one's placement. Such placement can be intellectual, social, economic, geographical, or otherwise. But it is real, and it affects all human knowledge. When we escape ideology, we touch the truth. But we never conquer the truth; we never capture it totally. Reality is bigger than our understanding. True, the knower can move from one placement to another. We can educate ourselves to other ways of understanding; we can move from one location to another. The one thing we cannot do, however, is see reality from all points of view at once. We always stand somewhere, and the place where we stand determines what we see. Human knowledge, then, is never totally objective. It is always partial, always limited. "Men were usually right in what they affirmed and wrong in what they denied."[9] That was true in the past and remains true. Just because we know the truth, it does not follow that we know all truth. Reality is bigger than our understanding, and it will always be so.

The implications of these insights of the sociology of knowledge for our study of natural law are evident. In the past, perhaps, we have been entirely too sanguine about our ability to touch, comprehend, grasp, and conquer the reality of our world. We have presumed that we could know the nature of the human beings, that we could know it thoroughly, and that we could know it exhaustively. And that was very foolish.

There is no doubt that we do have some sense of reality, some understanding of our world and ourselves. So we are by no means prepared to say we know nothing. Indeed, thinkers of the past also wanted to avoid that admission at all costs. We can appreciate how, confronted with only the two choices of being labeled ideologists or else asserting total objectivity and total comprehension, they would choose for the latter. But with the development of the field of sociology of knowledge, thinkers, and Christians generally, are provided with another option.

To avoid admitting that our understandings are nothing but ideology it is not necessary to go to the other extreme. What is more, it is not permissible to go to that extreme, not rational to do so. Do we know the natural law? Yes, no doubt we do. But do we know it comprehensively, exhaustively? No. Does our knowledge absolve us from the continuing task of searching out and pursuing the meaning of ourselves? By no means. Knowledge is much more a task than an accomplishment. It is something that is real—but it is also something partial. A little humility is going to have to be an increasingly prominent characteristic of theological reflections and discussions. And the topic of natural law is no exception.

Tentativeness of Understanding

We have been asking whether we can know the natural law. And we began our answer by coming to grips with the weakness of all human formulations. Beyond that, we also discovered that our underlying understandings are at best partial. Now we wish to make clear that our understandings are also tentative. For, as we shall see, it is always possible that a characteristic of the human person which we consider to be intrinsic, to be part of human nature as such, may actually be nothing more than an accident of historical, cultural, social, or psychological conditioning. It is always possible that while human beings "have always been thus," it is not *necessary* that they be thus. Consequently, when we set out to describe the nature of humans (and thus the natural law), our descriptions will always be characterized by a certain hesitancy, a certain tentativeness. But why is this so? The following observations may help to answer that question.

What do we mean by human nature? Do we mean people as they now actually exist? That cannot be. For one thing, historical research makes very clear the fact that we have greatly evolved over the eons. We have changed, we do change, and we presumably will continue to change. Thus the *status quo* is by no means the benchmark of nature. But surely there are certain characteristics which are common to all people throughout the centuries. Are not these characteristics the content of "human nature?" Perhaps not. For many theologians hold the opinion that God could have created the human species without the supernatural destiny which is, in fact, ours. And if we had been thus created, we would still have been humans. We would have been different from those people throughout the centuries, but not for all that any less human. What is more, the Christian belief in the resurrection of the body leads us to affirm that human existence will continue after death. Persons will still be persons. But will they be like the people of our experience? We have no way to tell.

Human nature, then, is not identical with the people who are part of our experience. In fact, in a certain sense, human nature does not exist. Persons exist. Persons possess human nature but are not identical with it. Existing persons, in the language of the Scholastics, are the composite of essence (nature) and accidents (all those qualities and attributes and characteristics of people which are but need not be). Thus human nature as such is the underlying structure to which all those accidents are connected, is that which is common to all people who have existed or could exist.

Human nature, then, is not an existential reality. Rather it is a metaphysical concept. It is not "that which exists." Rather it is "that by which we exist." It is a principle of being rather than an existing being (an *id quo* rather than an *id quod*). Human nature is a philosophical concept (*Begriff* in German), a concept grounded in reality, a thoroughly justified concept, but a concept nonetheless.

But how do we arrive at that concept? Perhaps it is not all that difficult to understand why there must *be* such a thing as human nature. But how do we decide what *comprises* human nature? In discussing above the various historical differences, as well as the theological differences, among people we have already implied the answer to that question. We discover the content of human nature through a process of subtraction. We look at human persons as they exist, as they have existed in the past, and as we imagine they might exist in the future. Under the light of faith we remind ourselves of the possible alternative modes of human existence: merely natural persons, fallen persons, redeemed persons, resurrected persons And from this selection of existential varieties we subtract out all the variables. Whatever is true of only one sort of person cannot be human nature itself. So we eliminate it from our understanding. And just as the process of subtraction in arithmetic yields a remainder, our philosophical subtraction yields a "remainder concept" (*Restbegriff* in German). That remainder concept is, presumably, identical with the content of human nature.[10]

But is it? Or more precisely, can we be sure that it is? Clearly not. For we are historical beings, we have a future. And that future is open, since we are capable of change. We cannot be certain that the person of the past and the present will be the person of the future. Perhaps something that we now consider essential will someday reveal itself as merely accidental. For example, are humans essentially sexual beings? One would think so. It is more than likely. But can we be absolutely certain? No. It is conceivable that sexuality is merely a characteristic of people as they have existed, not as they *must* exist. Thus, precisely because our understanding of human nature, our concept of human nature, is a *Restbegriff*, that understanding will always have a certain tentativeness.

This point should not be overemphasized. There are some things about ourselves that we spontaneously judge to be essential. If we were not free, or at least called to freedom, would we still be human? If we were not rational, or capable of rationality, would we be human? If we were not physical, what then? Still, if we can sketch the broad outlines of human nature with some confidence, we must also be conscious that the details are far less certain.

One further point should be made here. And it can be brought out through the following example. Until recent years, it had been the practice of architects to design buildings in such a way as to disguise the skeletal structure and to hide it under surface decoration. Most of our homes were built in this way as were many public buildings. One could look at such a building and know very well that a superstructure indeed existed. Otherwise the building would not stand. But where is that superstructure? Which walls support the roof, and which are merely dividers? One could not always be sure. In some cases one could be quite certain that a particular wall or facade or doorway was a nonessential addition (an accident). It could be removed and the building would still stand. In other cases one could be relatively certain that a post or pillar was essential. But in many cases, perhaps most, one could not be certain. Of course there was a way to find out. One could remove the wall in question, and see what happened. If the building still stood, it was nonessential. If the building collapsed, it was necessary. But in either case, absolute certitude could be achieved only at the risk of destruction.

The same is true of the nature of human beings. As we move through history we do in fact change. To an increasing extent that change is under our own control. We can plan and design that change; we can experiment. And some of those changes will no doubt indicate more precisely the perimeters of human nature. But experiments on humans, like all experiments, involve risk. And the risk in this case is the risk of self-destruction. We have the power to change ourselves, and the power to destroy ourselves. The search for human nature is a search which can result in the destruction of human nature. Thus the only road to absolute certainty regarding the nature of the human is the road of self-destruction.[11]

For all these reasons, then, our understanding of our own nature will always be tentative. The concept of human nature is a remainder concept, a *Restbegriff*. And it will always be thus.

Conclusion

Can we know human nature and the natural law? We can finally summarize our threefold answer. First, if we are talking about the formulations of our understanding, we must acknowledge that formulations are often inadequate. Secondly, if we are referring to understandings themselves, we must be conscious that such understandings are always partial; they are subject to the sociology of knowledge. And thirdly, such understandings are also tentative; they never possess apodictic certitude. We know much about ourselves, but we do not know everything. And what we do know is not always thoroughly certain.

Nonetheless, this knowledge is the basis for our moral judgments. And it must be so. For we are obligated, accountable, responsible beings. We are moral beings (seen from the subjective side as conscience/1 and from the objective side as the first principles of the natural law). And so we must take what knowledge we have and use it to shape our life. We must do the best we can. For the Christians, this is what God expects—and it is all he expects.

18

THE THEOLOGY OF HUMAN LAW

This author once had occasion to organize a program on the nature of human law. We wanted to include some discussion of the philosophy of human law, and our presumption was that we should hire a lawyer to speak to this topic. But we were quickly corrected. As a colleague said: "Lawyers are trained to be pragmatists. Their job is to know and use the law, whatever the law may be. The demands of their duties directly militate against a lawyer's temptation to step back and ask what the law *should* be. For your project you may want a political scientist, but you most certainly do *not* want a lawyer."

Perhaps the same comment could be made regarding the theology of human law. Whether one's focus is primarily civil law or the law of the Church, lawyers are not the ultimate spokesmen for the understanding and interpretations that we seek. From the point of view of the civil or canon lawyer, and perhaps also of an administrator of state or Church, the law no doubt appears to be an "ultimate." The law dictates what is or is not to be done, and that is that. But such people view law as an ultimate only because they view it from within, so to speak. They see law only in terms of itself, and there is no denying that from that perspective law presents itself as an ultimate. For viewed thus, law presents itself as an exercise in power; and power is indeed a certain sort of ultimate. The law does what the law can get away with doing.

But power and true authority are very different things, as the sad history of many nations teaches. In the words of the cliché: "Might indeed does not make right." Consider this example. If I am driving a sick friend to the hospital late at night and violate the speed limits, there is no denying that I can be ticketed and fined. I have violated the law, and the state is quite capable of punishing me. That is the prerogative of power. But for all that, it does not directly follow that I was wrong in speeding. One might well be able to make a case for the claim that I had a clear moral obligation to do exactly what I did and that I would have been wrong to obey the law in this case. The fact that authority is able to ignore this and to use its power to punish me does not change things in the slightest.

So it is important, in the context of a discussion of the principles of Catholic morality, to ask broad questions about the nature, purposes, and limits of human law. Our pursuit of these questions will have four parts. First we shall see, in sketchy form, an outline of the traditional Scholastic understanding of human law. We do this because this understanding offers us several worthwhile insights. Secondly, we shall consider in detail two alternative approaches to the question of whether, why, and how human laws impose moral obligation on us. This in turn will lead us to a series of related observations. Some conclusions will comprise the fourth part.

Traditional Understanding

Thomas Aquinas begins his entire treatise on law by developing a definition. Although this definition can in some ways be applied to any law, its most obvious relevance is to the category of human, positive law. Aquinas says that law is a "reasonable decision promulgated by competent authority for the common good" (I–II, 90, 4). This definition, which has been taken over and preserved in almost all Scholastic writings, contains four separable elements; and each is very important.

Law is a reasonable decision. It is an exercise of human intelligence, not arbitrary and capricious but prudent and purposeful. It is a decision that is promulgated. That is, it is imposed on its subjects only after sufficient notice and, therefore, with due respect for their rights and dignity. It is created by competent authority, by the person or persons who legitimately exercise this function in a particular community and over particular matters. Finally law is created for the common good. For all human law has as its general function the direction of social life among human persons. It is not primarily oriented toward the welfare of the isolated individual but rather concerns itself with the welfare of society itself.

This, then, is the generic definition of law. And in a special way it is the definition of human, positive law, those laws of Church and state. But behind the definition are a number of further points made by the Scholastics. These points are of interest to us both because of their content and because of the life-vision which they implied.

For example, by further reflection upon the notion of "common good" the Scholastics succeeded in specifying much more completely the proper functions of human law. They isolated two such functions.

First, it is common experience that many laws are actually human ratifications of precepts of the natural law. That is, a law of the Church or the state may repeat a dictate that is fundamentally moral (e.g., do not murder) and, by exercise of authority, urge its acceptance by the general populace. The justification for this function, though, must always lie in the common good. That is, it is not appropriate for human law to attempt to compel the inner reality of conscience. But inasmuch as the violation of the moral law has a real affect on the quality of human life (as we saw in analyzing the natural law), it is often necessary and appropriate for human law to attempt to coerce compliance where a particular citizen might not be personally inclined to do the good.[1]

Secondly, human law often functions as a means of particularizing and specifying the natural law. For example, it is clear that the natural law requires in justice that human persons give one another what is their due. But what is their due? In many subtle areas of economics, property rights, distribution of inherited property, etc., the answer to that question is not at all clear. In such cases people properly reach determinations which, while they do not contradict the natural law, go beyond that law in precision and clarity. And these determinations quite appropriately assume the force of human law.

Or again, the natural moral law makes clear that people driving cars must take due care to avoid threatening the lives or property of others. But in order to achieve this goal someone must stipulate which side of the street to drive on, the meaning of various signs and signals, the speed at which one ought to travel, and numberless other details. It is one of the functions of human law to make decisions about these details in order to structure the common life of citizens so that they can, to the greatest extent possible, live together in peace and harmony.[2]

These then, are the two traditional functions of human law, functions isolated by reflecting upon the reality of the common good, which was mentioned in the definition of that law. Another component of the definition which received particular attention from the manual theologians was the idea of "competent authority." Interestingly enough, their reflections upon this notion had the effect of establishing various limits to the development of human law. It was as if these theologians intuitively knew that we also need as much freedom as can reasonably be ours. Thus they were taking some pains to be sure law did not overburden the citizen in any way.

To this end, the Scholastics asserted that in order to be competent authorities must possess both jurisdiction and power. "Jurisdiction" means that they must be legislating for those *people* who truly are their responsibility. The Governor of Illinois has jurisdiction over the citizens of Illinois but not those of Indiana. And "power" means that they must be legislating on a *topic* that is legitimate for them. An academic dean ought not to attempt to control academically irrelevant aspects of his or her teachers' lives. In the judgment of the Scholastic tradition, then, human law is only justifiable when it arises from the decision of an authority possessing both jurisdiction and power.[3]

Finally, the manualists also took a closer look at the notion of "reasonable decision." Even granted that a particular law comes from a legitimate authority, it does not follow that the law is legitimate. In their opinion, for that latter situation to prevail, the law itself must have four characteristics. It must be moral, not commanding its subjects to do something immoral. It must be fair, treating all alike. And this precisely because the general purpose of law is the common good, and discriminatory law can never fulfill that purpose. Thirdly, it must be possible. To command the impossible or the unreasonably difficult is to attack the welfare of society, not to serve it. Finally, for the same reasons, it must be useful. Useless law is, indeed, worse than useless; it is harmful. Thus, for the Scholastics, it is not at all binding on those who are its subjects.[4]

What is really interesting about these four characteristics of law, as about the distinctions made before, is the sensitivity and wisdom which they imply. Even though the highly structured thinking of a Scholastic synthesis may not completely mesh with contemporary styles, it is clear that the Scholastic intention was perennially valid. It represents a concern for the commonweal, and for the maximum development of the individual, that is admirably human and thoroughly Christian in its inner dynamic.

Binding Force

Given this overall understanding of human law, however, the Scholastics were not without their differences of opinion. In particular, these revolved around the question of the precise binding force of law. This is a terribly important issue, both because of its particular details and because the two positions taken represent differing general understandings of human life. For the position one takes on this question tends to reflect a fundamental commitment on the question of whether the individual or the group is of primary importance in the conduct of human life. The resolution of this question, which we will now pursue, has immense implications for life in the Church and in civil authority in our own day.

Historically, the two approaches to the question of the binding force of human law are identified with the great theologians Francis Suarez and Thomas Aquinas.[5] Let us briefly outline the position held by each. Suarez, who died in 1617, was a theologian greatly influenced by the nominalist and voluntarist perspectives of that period. Thus, his basic understanding of law was a voluntaristic one. That is, he fundamentally conceived of law as an exercise of the *will* of the legislator by which he ruled over subjects. The validity of the law was primarily a function of the legitimacy of the legislator. For the legislator was the source and identity of authority. Or, to put this another way, for Suarez, authority referred to a person and, indeed, was identified with that person.

This did not mean, of course, that a ruler could do absolutely anything. Suarez was familiar with the four-part definition of law that came from Thomas, and he accepted it. But it did mean that the definition was understood in a particular way. Two elements, "reasonable dictate" and "common good," were interpreted very broadly. It was presumed that whatever was proposed by the legitimate authority had those two characteristics, unless the opposite was very evident indeed. By the same token, the other two elements, "competent authority" and "promulgated," were interpreted rather strictly. Since authority was viewed as identified with the person of the ruler, it was of high importance that the legitimacy of his or her rule be clearly established.

One further point will help to "enflesh" this Suarezian vision even more. Traditional Catholic theology has long spoken of *epikeia* as an important factor in handling human law. "Epikeia" is a term describing the way in which a Christian ought to deal with what appears to be a conflict between the letter of the law and the spirit of the law. Thus, to return to an earlier example, if I violate speed limits in order to get a sick friend to the hospital, it is epikeia that justifies my doing so. But how shall we understand this thing called epikeia? Suarez had an answer.

Since law is essentially an exercise of the will of the legislator and achieves its validity by that will, epikeia can only be understood as the "benign interpretation of the legislator's will." That is, in an intuitive way I judge that if the legislator were with me in my car at 3:00 A.M., he would not want me to obey the speed limits. Rather he would want me to exercise due caution for the lives of others and then move to the hospital at the maximum possible speed. Since I judge that the legislator's will no longer stands behind this law, but rather supports just the opposite (or would if he knew), I am perfectly justified in violating the law in this instance.

All of this, however, was understood quite differently by Thomas Aquinas. Indeed, as recent scholarly rediscoveries have made clear, he could hardly have disagreed with this synthesis more. So let us try to sketch out the Thomistic vision on this question.

In the first place, the Thomistic view of law was in no way voluntaristic. Quite the contrary, like all of Thomas's theology, his conception of law was determined by the notion of *finality*. Classic philosophy had asserted that one knew something if one knew its four causes: material, formal, efficient, and final. And for Aquinas, the final cause was pivotal. A thing is justified by its purpose, and by the fact that it truly achieves that purpose.

It is the actual functionality of a thing that constitutes its *raison d'être*. Thus, far from being a voluntarist, Thomas was a thoroughgoing functionalist when it came to the question of human law.

Since this is the case, Thomas also held understandings of a number of specific points that differed greatly from those of Suarez. For example, Aquinas viewed law, not primarily as an exercise of the will of the legislator but of the intellect. That is, law is the tool by which the legislator intelligently orders individual components of society so that the proper end of society can be more easily achieved. Following from this, Thomas also avoided closely identifying human law with the person of the legislator. To the extent that a law is indeed an intelligent and functional servant of the common good, the law is in a sense self-justifying. It does not derive its force from the person of the legislator, but rather from its own evident utility.

This theory of law, moreover, led Thomas to understand authority in a special way. For him this term does not refer to a person; it refers to a function. One does not say that a person *is* the authority; one says a person *has* authority. That changes things substantially, for it tends to separate the law from the lawgiver and to make consideration of the law itself more important than consideration of the way the law was made. Thus, the Thomistic understanding, while accepting the same basic definition of law, handled it very differently. Those following Aquinas dealt very carefully with the two elements focused on the law: namely, the ideas of "reasonable dictate" and "common good." The elements oriented toward the lawgiver, on the other hand, were interpreted more broadly. There was less concern about whether the source of this self-validating law really was competent authority or whether all the niceties of promulgation had been observed.[6]

Finally, and following from all this, Thomas's general vision of law led him to a much richer understanding of the reality of epikeia. He would argue in this way. Since law is essentially the intelligent ordering of means to an end, epikeia must be understood as the "correct interpretation of the intention of the law." Every human law is an attempt to concretize in the letter of the law the intention of the spirit of the law. But inasmuch as everyday life is complex and constantly shifting, it is to be expected that the letter of the law will not always succeed in serving the spirit of the law. That, we could surmise, is the case in our example of the rush to the hospital. The real intent of the law is to protect lives. However, in this particular case observing the speed limits will not protect lives. Quite the contrary, it will threaten lives. That being the case, the Christian's duty is to the spirit of the law, to the intended end which is the common good. If the letter of the law does not in fact function in service to that end, the Christian must forsake it.

Further Observations

This Thomistic understanding of human law is rich in its relevance to the Christian situation today. Several further points will help to make that clear. First of all, note that we say Christians *must* forsake the letter of the law if it does not actually serve the common good in a particular case. It is not a matter of being *permitted* to violate the law. One is morally obligated to do so because the basic moral obligation is to seek the good. If a human law does not actually serve that good, Christians must do whatever will serve that good. Thus, the notion of epikeia is not (as is often thought) a matter of replacing duty with un-Christian license. No, it is a matter of replacing one apparent duty (to the letter of the law) with another, more fundamental duty (to the spirit of the law, to its true function of serving the common good).

Secondly, since epikeia is here understood as a quality by which Christians pursue their moral obligation to the good, it is thoroughly understandable that Thomas asserts it to be a virtue (II-II,120, 1 & 2). Just as justice, fairness, and chastity are virtues, so also is epikeia. Epikeia is the virtue (power, skill, habit) by which Christian persons discern the inner meaning of any human law so as to intelligently obey it in the majority of cases and to reasonably violate it in the properly exceptional case. Epikeia is the virtue by which Christians deal humanely with the reality of human law. They respect law for what it is; but they do not ask it to be what it is not. They recognize that no humanly formulated law can be expected to cover all possible contingencies (as we saw in Chapter Seventeen), so they accept their proper responsibility and deal with those contingencies when they arise. They do not hide out in the law. They use the law, respect it, and willingly go beyond it when they must.

Thirdly, this understanding of law and of the virtue of epikeia makes clear that the opinion of the legislator is not, of itself, particularly relevant. In the Suarezian conception of epikeia as the benign interpretation of the legislator's will, it was quite possible that epikeia could be rendered useless by some announcement of the legislator. The ruler could simply proclaim: "What you view as my will is not my will. I now know your situation and nonetheless expect you to follow the letter of the law." And such a declaration would dispose of any appeal to epikeia. Not so in the Thomistic understanding. Christians could hear the legislator speak in this way and nonetheless continue to judge that in this case the letter of the law does not truly function in service of the common good. And if they so judge, Christians could (indeed, should) opt for some other behavior which they believe to more completely achieve the spirit of the law.

Of course, the legislator retains his ability to punish persons choosing to do this. Here we see again the difference between power and authority which was raised earlier. The fact that a legislator is not truly exercising functional authority in a particular case does not, in this imperfect world, guarantee that he or she will not use dominative power to coerce and to punish. But "might does not make right." So Christians may in the end have to tolerate that punishment rather than do what they honestly believe to be "not good." Deciding this will take wisdom and prudence; proportion, as we have seen, is central to the living of the Christian life. But it is a possibility which cannot be ignored.[7]

Fourthly, it should be obvious that this Thomistic vision is highly consistent with our theory of the natural law. Like that theory, it is real, experiential, consequential, historical, and proportional. In the best sense of the word, it is pragmatic. It looks not to appearances and formalistic legitimacy; it looks to the facts and to actual utility. Indeed, this is perhaps the central difference between Suarezian and Thomistic concepts of human law. And it is painfully germane in our time.

For example, should a German citizen have obeyed the laws of Hitler's government? The Suarezian would *tend* to answer in the affirmative. Until it becomes overwhelmingly evident that these laws violate the more basic dictates of the natural law, one ought to obey. For Hitler's rise to power was altogether legitimate; he had the appearance of rightful authority, and obedience was therefore both justified and expected. Thomists, on the other hand, would not be unduly concerned about these niceties. They would attempt to judge the objective value of the laws; and on the basis of that judgment they would obey or not. In either case they would seek consistently to serve the spirit of the law so that the common good might truly be achieved.

But take another case: Should a Cuban citizen obey the laws of Castro's regime? Once again the two theories would offer contradictory judgments. Suarezians would tend to say not. Inasmuch as Castro took power by violent and illegal means his authority is not legitimate. Therefore, any law he might propose, even if it is is a consummately intelligent means to the common good, does not of itself demand obedience. It is not truly binding human law. Thomists, of course, would say the opposite. Cuban citizens have the fundamental moral obligation to cooperate with any law which actually functions for the common good. It is not particularly important who formulated the law or by what means it was promulgated. The law's justification lies not in the legislator, but in itself. And thus obedience is altogether required.

Finally, a third example. One of the more celebrated political conflicts within the Catholic Church in recent years involved Cardinal Josef Mindszenty of Hungary and Pope Paul VI. Cardinal Mindszenty had been in voluntary captivity in the United States Embassy in Budapest for years. He refused to leave the country and thereby concede some victory to the Communists. Therefore, since he would not be permitted to return to his previous post and situation, he chose to remain in the embassy. However, several years ago Pope Paul VI arranged for (commanded?) Cardinal Mindszenty to leave his homeland and come to Rome. He did so, with considerable obvious displeasure.

Though it is dangerous to apply general labels to complex historical events, it seems that a good case could be made for viewing this episode as the result of a conflict between Suarezian and Thomistic theories of human law. Cardinal Mindszenty viewed the Communist Party in Hungary as his eternal enemy. They had grasped power through violent means. They were illegitimate rulers. They professed to be atheists, and so their dictates could hardly fulfill the Scholastic requirement that human law be moral. Thus he felt justified in altogether rejecting or ignoring the regime and all its works.

Pope Paul apparently interpreted the situation in a different way. We would say a Thomistic way. The undeniable fact is that this regime does rule Hungary today. How they came to power is not particularly relevant. What is relevant is the question of what will best serve the common good here and now. It appeared that the Communist regime was enacting many laws which well served the people of Hungary. What is more, it was judged likely that, with the departure of Cardinal Mindszenty, greater freedom for the Church and for religious people in Hungary could yet be achieved. In other words, a tenuous, uncertain (typically human) judgment was made that the common good would best be served by some sort of rapprochement with the ruling regime. That rapprochement, with the calling of Cardinal Mindszenty to Rome as one of its components, was therefore pursued.

If newspaper accounts can be believed, it seems that Cardinal Mindszenty never fully understood or approved of this Vatican decision. And this is no surprise. From the Suarezian perspective of his own seminary training it was indefensible. The decision could only be defended from a quite different Thomistic point of view. The theology of human law had changed in recent decades. And that shift of perspective no doubt added in its own sad way to the pain of the entire episode.

Conclusion

This brings us to a final observation, or complex of observations, which will also serve to conclude this chapter. We refer to the fact that the difference between these two understandings of human law, and of the way that law should be handled, is correlative to a differing understanding of the individual in relation to the group.

There is no denying that the Thomistic conception of human law is highly oriented toward individual Christians. It freely acknowledges their dignity, it emphasizes their right (and duty) to make independent judgments. In focusing itself in this way, of course, the Thomistic understanding runs the risk of encouraging anarchy. When legislators object to this theory on the ground that it makes their job more difficult, they are quite right. They no longer have the ability to command and to be obeyed simply because they have commanded. Within a Thomistic framework the legislator is obeyed only because the law serves, and is seen to serve, the common good. And all citizens reserve the right (and duty) to judge for themselves whether this is the case. So it is quite true that since the theory of human law which traces itself to Aquinas is undeniably oriented toward the individual, there exists the consequent threat of disorder in the group at large.

But that is a threat which must be tolerated. Why do we say this? There are two important reasons. First of all, Suarezian theories of human law are not without their own dangers. While the Thomistic perspective risks anarchy in society, Suarezian visions risk tyranny.[8] By placing such high emphasis upon the person of the legislator and upon the obligation of obeying this particular individual, these theories are in constant danger of violating both the integrity of the individual citizen and the humanity of the legislator. They are in danger, paradoxically, of giving both too little credit to the citizen and too much to the ruler. On the one hand, to deny individuals their right (and duty) to make personal judgments and decisions is to deny them a central component of their human dignity. On the other hand, to focus authority on the person of the ruler is to make him or her a member of some "privileged order" of being. It is to deny the limitations of their creatureliness and, instead, to presume that by birth, appointment, ordination, or whatever, they have inevitably acquired the skills needed to wisely guide the conduct of public life. And that is, to say the least, a dubious supposition. Indeed, both these Suarezian emphases are not particularly subtle preambles to tyranny.

So the first reason for tolerating the risks involved in a Thomistic understanding of human law is the dangers which the alternative theory itself entails. A second reason focuses on the "cosmological mood" implied by the two perspectives. What we have in mind is the fundamental optimism about the human person that is suggested by the Thomistic vision. In its willingness to tolerate the risk of anarchy, this theory is in effect asserting that anarchy is not likely to occur. It is claiming that people are not likely to take untoward advantage of their freedom, to exercise their alleged independence in a socially destructive way. At base, this theory is asserting that people are basically good, that they are inclined as human persons toward doing the good, and that good is far more likely to result from this expression of respect for them than is evil.

This optimism about people and their nature is no mean thing. It is characteristic of all of Thomas Aquinas's theology. Thomas recognized the reality of original sin, of course. But he was careful to point out that it has not altogether undermined the goodness of human nature, that nature is wounded but not destroyed. Aquinas acknowledged the reality of personal sin. But he was strong in asserting that sin is an act against the grain of human nature, that for the human person good is actually easier then evil, that one has to attack the very fiber of one's nature to choose selfishness and isolation and cruelty. As we have seen in many places in this book, an anthropological optimism is one of the foremost characteristics of the writing of Thomas Aquinas and, even more profoundly, of the incarnational vision that is Catholic Christianity.

If many people do not accept this optimism today, and if, therefore, they are far more comfortable with the pessimism of a Suarezian theory of human law, then perhaps that is one of our problems. A well-known Catholic preacher recently asserted that much of the evil that confronts us today is caused by the acceptance of the expression "I gotta be me" as a principle of life. Of course, there is no doubt that this phrase, like any aphorism, is ambiguous. It is able to be so interpreted that it represents an utterly selfish and, indeed, naïve life-program. But such aberrations should not, in this writer's opinion, be characterized as typical. The fact of the matter is that I do "gotta be me." My own personhood is what I have been given by God as the challenge and the arena for the pursuit of my Christian life. Nothing takes precedence over the moral challenges of my own unique person and my own particular life.

This can be asserted in a way that is not negatively selfish precisely because we presume that "me" is, in all our individual cases, someone good, a being of dignity and beauty, a creature loved by God and blessed with life and grace. Because we, along with Thomas Aquinas and many great saints throughout the ages, stand in awful appreciation for the dignity of the person, we can celebrate and accept this Thomistic theory of human law. We are respecters of law because we are respecters of all that is. We appreciate the need for law because we appreciate the facts of life in our human, finite, partly sinful, and honestly weak world. But we also recognize and clearly affirm the limitedness of law. It is not the ultimate norm of life; it is not an ultimate in any sense. Law is a tool that we use. It serves us, we do not serve it. When it meets our needs and the needs of others we obey it. Indeed, we obey it with joy and a cooperative spirit.

But when law fails to meet those lofty goals, we are neither distressed nor distracted. We are not distressed, for it is no surprise that law sometimes fails to express the truly good. It is, after all, only a human construct in the hands of human agents. More than that, it is static words seeking to capture a rather fluid reality. So it does not bother us that the law must at times be transcended. And we are not distracted either. That is, we do not remove our attention from its proper object: the good. If the law guides us to the good, so much the better. But if it does not, then the law must be forsaken, it must be violated, it must be ignored. The good must be sought, always and in all things.

For the good, after all, is where God is finally to be found.

PART IV

CONCLUDING ESSAYS

19

"CHRISTIAN" MORALITY

Throughout the chapters of this book we have presumably been seeking to understand Christian morality. Yet it must be admitted that relatively little attention has been given to the content of the Christian faith. In fact, the discussion has been predominantly philosophical and phenomenological.

This, of course, was no accident. In Chapter Four we presented an explicitly theological justification for this approach. But now, as we approach the end of our investigation, it may be useful to return to this topic and to reflect on it a bit more deeply. Is there, in reality, any such thing as a Christian ethic? And if so, what are its characteristics? These are the questions that concern us in this present chapter.

We will deal with the questions through a series of three reflections. First, we will consider the incorrect ways of describing our ethic as Christian. Then we shall isolate some quite appropriate formulations. Finally we shall summarize by discussing the relationship of the natural law and the law of Christ.

Not a Christian Ethic

The first step in our reflection will be to eliminate certain senses of the term "Christian ethic" which are not at all correct. And these senses are two. It is incorrect to speak of a Christian or Catholic morality if one means that we possess unique ethical obligations or a unique ethical source.

First about ethical obligations. This may be belaboring the obvious, but it should be pointed out, in light of the overall theory of natural law that has been presented in these pages, that Christians are called to do the humanly good thing and that consequently their moral obligations are generally synonymous with those of all people. One wonders if this is always clear to Catholics. This author remembers the comment of a Catholic grammar-school student that he didn't like being a Catholic because "it's wrong for me to play around with girls whereas it's all right for the public schoolers." What sort of distorted pedagogy would lead a Catholic to that notion? And yet it is common. Many Catholics, one would suspect, believe that divorce is wrong *because* one is a Catholic. Indeed, it is often forgotten that the Catholic Church holds a marriage between two baptized Protestants, once consummated, to be sacramental and just as indissoluble as any Catholic marriage.

Thus, it is worth saying clearly that whatever we hold and teach to be right or wrong, we so describe only because the action is judged to be harmful to human persons. Therefore, all moral assertions are assertions that the action in question should not be done by *any* person in a similar situation. Catholics do not have unique or specific moral obligations. Rather they participate in the moral life that is the task and challenge of the entire human community.

What is more, to hold this material identity of Christian ethics and human ethics is not to say anything new. Even though it has not been particularly emphasized in recent centuries (for all the reasons which we saw in Chapter Two), still the idea is very much part of our Catholic tradition. Indeed, it is one of the glories of the incarnational vision that is Catholic theology. For example, Thomas Aquinas, having analyzed the natural law, asks whether the law of the Old Testament added anything new from a moral point of view. His answer is that it really did not. His discussion makes clear that he sees the contribution of the Old Law as one of clarification and reinforcement. And Aquinas believes these are necessary, given the weakness of man due to original sin. But the law did not, in his view, introduce any materially new moral precepts (I-II, 99, 2).

Further on, Aquinas asks whether the law of the New Testament, the law of Christ, introduced any innovations. With one exception his answer is the same. Having asserted that the essence of the New Law is the internal grace of the Holy Spirit, Aquinas goes on to claim that

> the New Law had to make such prescriptions or prohibitions alone as are essential for the reception or right use of grace. . . . Hence Christ of Himself instituted the Sacraments whereby we attain grace. . . . But the right use of grace is by means of works of charity. These, in so far as they are essential to virtue, pertain to the moral precepts which also formed part of the Old Law. Hence, in this respect, the New Law had nothing to add as regards external action. (I-II, 108, 2)

So, except for the sacraments, insofar as these can be viewed as "commands," there is no new moral dictate in the New Law, as there was none in the Old Law. The inescapable conclusion, then, is that for Aquinas there is really no such thing as a materially specific Christian ethic. And this very traditional position of his is what is being espoused emphatically today and what has been developed here.

But if Catholics do not have special ethical obligations, do they at least have special ethical sources? Is the distinguishing characteristic of Christian ethics the fonts from which its wisdom is derived? A beginning of an answer to this question follows easily from what has been said above.

Repeatedly in these pages we have spoken of the dangerous temptation to reduce the moral obligations of the Christian to one sort of legalism or another, to suggest that certain actions are wrong *because* they are forbidden by the law. The error of this understanding is evident when one focuses on *human* law as an ethical source, and most particularly evident when one focuses on human *civil* law. What is not so evident, but just as true, is that appeal to ecclesiastical law, or even to the law of God is just as erroneous. Whether we consider the pronouncements of the ecclesial magisterium or the pages of Sacred Scripture, it is clear that they cannot be considered a special source of ethical wisdom in the sense that their judgments *make* things right or wrong.

But what if we avoid this legalism? What if we assert that these sources do not create moral value, but that they do articulate it in a special, privileged, and completely dependable way? Several responses are in order here.

First of all, we would have to assert, logically, that such ethical statements are also, in principle, available to all people through the use of human reason. That is, we would have to hold that ethical pronouncements of Scripture or magisterium are at most a species of confirmatory data. They reaffirm facts of human experience which have been, or can be, discerned and validated independently. Seen in this way, such pronouncements would be accepted as gift, as helpful illuminations of human experience, and not as a sort of burden imposed on the Christian as law. This, after all, is fundamentally the position espoused above by Aquinas.

But what sort of dependability could such pronouncements have? That is, what would one do if such pronouncements of Scripture or magisterium *appeared* to conflict with the data of experience regarding the value of certain actions? It would perhaps be naïve to presume that this experience, particularly if it is limited to personal observations, is *prima facie* to be preferred. If anything, one could well argue that, given the presence of the Spirit, one should presume that the sacred sources are more trustworthy. If those sources present a unified commitment, even more if they claim to be quite certain, then giving them the presumption of the truth would be quite reasonable. But is that the case? What, precisely, do we find in those sources? That is our next question.

With regard to Scripture, it must honestly be acknowledged that we rarely find either unanimity or independence of judgment. Rather what we find are quite diverse judgments, and judgments which often enough are rooted in various secular sources. As one Scripture scholar puts it,

> There is an eclecticism that characterizes the New Testament ethic. The sayings of the sages, the ethics of the Stoic philosophers, contemporary ethical standards, the teaching of the rabbis, the Jewish catechism, the texts of the Bible, and the good sense of the New Testament authors each contribute to the content of New Testament ethics. The result is that there is both an openness and a pluralism in New Testament ethics. Consequently, it is not easy to, nor is it legitimate to, reduce the ethical teachings of the New Testament to a single ethical view.[1]

Beyond this, it must also be admitted that some concrete moral judgments of the Bible can in no way be supported today. One thinks, for example, of Paul's dictates regarding slavery and the place of women. On the other hand, many of the more important ethical issues of our time (e.g. economic justice, medical and scientific procedures) receive no attention at all.

There is no doubt that the New Testament at least presents a relatively clear vision of the *sort* of person a Christian should be, a person of generosity and love, a person empowered by the Spirit, a person of prayer and good works. But when it comes to the crucial question of whether particular actions are consistent with that personhood or not, the simple fact is that one cannot give the biblical texts implicit and uncritical trust.

> The biblical renewal has emphasized the historical and cultural limitations of the Scriptures so that one cannot just apply the Scriptures in a somewhat timeless manner to problems existing in different historical circumstances.[2]

Similar observations can be made with regard to the magisterium of the Church. It is true that the First Vatican Council held that "the Roman Pontiff, when he speaks ex cathedra . . . possesses the infallibility with which the divine Redeemer willed his Church to be endowed in defining doctrine concerning faith or morals" (DS1839). But it is also true that, whatever the exact meaning of this declaration, it appears never to have been exercised in moral matters. Indeed, in the entire history of the Roman Catholic Church, there has never been a clearly infallible pronouncement by either pope or council on an ethical issue. All the teaching that has taken place has been of the sort known as "ordinary magisterium," teaching that does not pretend to be protected from the possibility of error.[3]

What is more, there has not even been a great deal of this sort of teaching. When concrete ethical questions have been submitted to the Vatican for discernment and judgment, quite commonly the response has been *videantur auctores probati* (consult the approved authors). In other words, the magisterium seems to have been sensitive to the complexity and ambiguity of such moral questions. It has preferred to allow the slow process of analysis and interpretation to continue rather than abort that process by premature declaration.[4]

The theory of natural law which has been developed in these pages, of course, makes us see the wisdom of this practice. Inasmuch as right action is precisely constituted by the maximization of premoral good over premoral evil, only one who is thoroughly aware of the various situational factors can dare to risk a definitive judgment. And there is no guarantee that such a judgment will continue to have validity in some new situation. So it is with good wisdom, and a very Christian sort of prudence, that the magisterium has generally chosen to avoid very specific ethical judgments.[5]

The point of all these arguments, then, is that in fact (and perhaps also in theory) the Catholic does not approach his ethical decision-making with any unique and dependable sources. Catholic moral evaluation is not some sort of gnostic exercise, where we derive concrete norms from a secret source of wisdom. Rather such evaluation is a thoroughly human process, pursued by Catholics in union with their fellows of the human community with the hope of achieving some reasonable, relative degree of certainty. Nothing more can be expected. At the level of concrete premoral values, in the formulation of concrete material norms, Christian ethics is human ethics, no less and certainly no more.

A Christian Ethic

But if everything said thus far is true, it is also true that in some sense we do have a specifically Christian ethic. And this in two ways: meaning and motivation.

First of all, as believers and as followers of Christ we are gifted with a profoundly Christian view of the meaning of the world. This world-view functions as a basis and context for all our concrete moral judgments. In particular, it contributes two things: a deeper understanding of human person's dignity and a clearer sense of his or her destiny.

We have already discussed the first of these items. The point is that, with our understanding of the mysterious reality of grace, we are in a position to grasp much more fully and more perfectly the real being and situation of human persons. Inasmuch as we know humankind to be supernatural, to be called by God in the depths of their hearts, to be, in essence, responders to revelation, we know the human mystery in ways no philosopher or social scientist can touch. We have, in Karl Rahner's phrase, a theological anthropology, a vision of the human that is shaped and guided by our theological commitments. And this vision of personal dignity contributes to our ethical judgments in that it offers us a benchmark in terms of which to judge the concrete good.

Similarly, the Christian vision of the world's meaning deeply affects our ethical thinking insofar as it speaks of the destiny of the human race. Our human hopes are not to be dashed. The human drive for interpersonal union, for life shared in love, is not to be frustrated. Indeed, these very human urges are but glimmers of the wonder which God has in store for us. Thus there is great reason for us to accept and cooperate with the call to human growth, to fidelity and generosity and honor, which we hear within ourselves. Of course, it is not a matter of doing the "unpleasant good" in order to be rewarded at the end. Rather it is a matter of knowing that the call to the good, a call which we sense as part of our human composition, is not the prelude to absurdity. It is not an invitation to develop ourselves only to be crushed into nothingness in the end. There is meaning to the best that is human. The world is ultimately benign and not perversely malignant.[6] The Christian life is not a cosmic joke but rather a joyous cosmic gift. Thus human beings have a dignity and destiny which give the Christian a very special sense of the meaning of the world.

This leads us to the second major way in which we can be said to have a specifically Christian ethic. Namely, that our behavior, although it is materially oriented toward the merely human good, is existentially generated by a whole complex of peculiarly Christian motives. If it is asked why the good should be done, no doubt one can properly answer that it should be done simply because it is the good. That is, a thoroughly human rationale can (and probably should) be offered for the behaviors that are encouraged or proscribed. That, after all, is what natural law means: that one's value commitments are in principle communicable in human, this-worldly categories. But if it is asked why *I* do the good, the answer would probably be quite different. It might be that the personal experience of Jesus Christ, the Savior who has personal love for each of us, motivates my altruistic behavior. It might be that the Church asks for this behavior, and the Church has gifted me with the experience of Christian community. It might be that I sense this behavior to be more in accord with the vision and ideals of Scripture. All of these are most legitimate motives. Indeed, they are common if not universal motives. And to the extent that behavior is only well understood in the context of motivation, these motives rightly lead us to speak of a "Christian ethic."

This is no small thing to say. As we saw in our discussion of the sociology of knowledge in Chapter Seventeen, how one views a reality has tremendous reverberations on what one does about it. Indeed, in some ways "seeing makes it so"; vision is a fountainhead of behavior. For example, Christians may be doing the very same good deeds as their nonreligious neighbors. But Christians interpret their behavior very differently.

They see it as a sign of love for the loving God, as a response to the gifts of Christ. They see their behavior as profoundly religious. And because they see it thus, it is thus.

To put this another way, the life of Christians may be (or could possibly be) materially identical with the life of other people. But it has a radically different formality. The Christian life is a life of Eucharist, of thanksgiving, of response to divine initiative. And this is so precisely because and to the extent that we see it to be so.

This point has been powerfully developed by the Protestant ethicist James Gustafson, and his thoughts deserve a bit of attention. While granting the possibility of a theoretical (metaphysical) identity of Christian ethics and human ethics in the ideal, Gustafson reminds us that they are existentially quite different.

> It might be interesting to find out whether historically the moral teachings of the Christian community have been distinguishably different from the moral teachings of other communities. . . . My suspicion is that most historians of cultures are likely to claim some distinctiveness.[7]

This is all the more true if one focuses on the contemporary scene.

> It is almost ironic to ask this, for while the ablest moral theologians in the Catholic Church are working assiduously to indicate that Catholic ethics . . . are not radically distinguishable from general human ethics, most politicians, scientists, and physicians in North America would answer the question . . . with a resounding affirmative. My conjecture is that many persons would observe that the most distinctive moral community (with regard to its teachings) in North America is the Catholic Church.[8]

Why is this so? Gustafson makes a most significant contribution to our reflections when he states that "there are affective aspects to be accounted for. . . . I would in addition suggest that moral teachings . . . emerge out of *historic* human experience, and not simply out of a rational apprehension."[9] Having highlighted both the affective and the historical influences on the living of the Christian life, Gustafson concludes:

> If the affective and the historical are not merely accidental, or merely a source of error, some things follow. . . . One need not be so apologetic about the distinctiveness of Catholic . . . or any other ethics. . . . To make my point in a dramatic way, we are not going to get ethics unqualified until we get rational minds unqualified by affectivity, or persons unqualified by particular histories; or knowledge of a moral order unqualified by historical and embodied experience.[10]

These are precisely the ideas which we have meant to include under the umbrella terms of "Christian meaning" and "Christian motivations." And as is clear from Gustafson's development, they are highly significant. Indeed, these two terms could well serve as bases for the articulation of a Christian spirituality. Emphasis upon them is surely one of the hallmarks of spiritual theology as distinguished from moral theology as such.

In the end, then, what we have been developing in the pages of this book is a human ethic with tremendous Christian influence. We have been developing a Christian humanism, a vision which is in accord both with experience and with faith, and which is accountable to both of these. We have been articulating a vision which recognizes the interpenetration of the divine and the human in the lives we lead, and which reflects that interpenetration. On the basis of that vision we have tried to understand the principles of a morality which is human in its content and its source, but also a morality which is Christian in its essential meaning-conviction and its existential motivation.[11]

Christ and Natural Law

All this can be put another way, and a very important way. We have been developing an "incarnational" vision. And this vision has acknowledged that essentially and ultimately the natural law and the law of Christ are one and the same thing. Just as (and because) the divine and the human were conjoined in the person of Jesus, the Christ, so they are conjoined in the reality of this ethic.

This is no small thing. One often hears people speak of the law of Christ as if it were something quite different from the natural law, as if it were some additional or superrerogatory ethic. It is not, as we have seen. So it may be helpful to conclude this reflection on the question of a specifically Christian ethic be noting the four ways in which these two laws are really and profoundly one.

The natural law is, properly understood, nothing else than the law of Christ "ontologically." As we saw in Chapter Four, Christ is in no way the historical afterthought of creation. Rather he stands at the very head of creation. He is its exemplary cause, the model on which its reality is based. Thus Christ is the ground of all things; and all things are potential sacraments of Christ. The result of this ontological connection is that any good action is a potential avenue of relationship with the divine. "The good leads to God." The similarity of these two terms is not merely a matter of spelling; it is also ontological. And this because of the central function of the Logos, the Son of the Father, the exemplary cause of creation.

Secondly, the natural law and the law of Christ are identical "existentially." By this term we mean to take note of the fact that humans have always possessed a supernatural destiny. Our existence, as it has actually been lived, has always been a supernaturally oriented and supernaturally shaped existence. We may assert (and indeed we must) that the supernatural gifts which we affirm in faith are not due to us. They are truly gifts, undeserved and radically unrequired. But to say this is not to say that they have ever been withheld. Quite the contrary. The perspective of Christian history is that God has always been involved in his world, he has always intended more for us than we deserve. Even if we may speak of "pure nature," metaphysical nature viewed apart from any supernatural additions, such a nature has never actually existed. It is a mental fiction. The humanity which has existed is supernaturally endowed humanity, Christian humanity. Thus the natural law is existentially identical with the law which is Christ himself.

Thirdly, and following from the above, these two laws are synonymous "operationally." We saw in Chapter Nine that it is only with the aid of grace that we are able to adopt a fundamental stance that is positive and oriented toward the good. It is only grace that makes us able to be all that we should be. Paradoxically, therefore, it is only by means of grace that we are capable of becoming and remaining fully human. If this is true, then it follows that it is only grace, the grace that comes through and because of Christ, that makes us able to respond to the natural law, to perceive and obey the demands of our being and our world. It is grace that empowers, therefore, the achievement of even that natural morality which appears to be an utterly human thing. Without grace we are less than human, with grace we are more than human. There is no in-between. Thus, as the natural law operates in my life, calling me, challenging me, and guiding my response, it is really the law of Christ that lies hidden within.

Finally, the natural law and the law of Christ are united "historically." For it was in the historical event of the Incarnation that all of the above became apparent. Indeed, more than that, it was only in relation to the Incarnation that all of the above became real. When God became man, he ratified the human. He certified its dignity. He revealed and manifested its oneness with himself. He showed, as we have said before, that God does his saving thing "on our turf." Consequently, he made clear that the path to God is the path of this human world, that fidelity to the human is the sure promise of the presence of the divine. Thus Christ, in the Incarnation, made apparent the fact that there is no other law of Christ than the law of our own being.[12]

Conclusion

"To thine own self be true," said Shakespeare. And the words are more accurate than is usually suspected. For what are Christians called to do, as they live their human lives? They are called to do the good, as best they can. That is the natural law. But the natural law is, in the end, also the law of Christ. If we are true to our selves, if we are faithful to the selves which we understand and interpret in the light of the Gospel proclamation of human destiny, then we are true to the law of Christ.

At a much deeper level than is often surmised, then, we have been discussing a Christian ethic throughout the pages of this book. Not an ethic with sectarian demands, not a specifically Christian ethic in that sense, but a human ethic rooted in and shaped by the Christian vision that is our theological heritage. Not an ethic predicated on a fundamentalistic use of our scriptural and magisterial sources, but a rational ethic suffused and illumined by a vision of humans and their world that is deeply biblical and strongly, proudly traditional.

We have been discussing a human ethic, but a human ethic for Christian persons in an ultimately Christian world. And so we have been discussing a Christian ethic in the deepest and most exciting sense possible.

20

CATHOLIC MORALITY: TODAY AND TOMORROW

A s we come to the end of this enterprise, it is reasonable to ask two questions. What have we done? Where will it lead? In this brief concluding chapter, we wish to respond to these questions.

What Have We Done?

The simplest answer to this question is: Not everything, but something. In general, we have been attempting to develop a theology and philosophy of the Christian life. But to apply this rubric is really to overstate the project in which we have been involved. For the study of the Christian life involves three distinct tasks, and we have only been pursuing one of these. Christian living clearly involves the challenge to behave ethically and to develop an ethical commitment and sensitivity in one's life. But it also involves the development of an inner spirituality by which to nourish that life, and the participation in a liturgical community by which to express the posture of worship-response. Thus the "science" of the Christian life involves not only moral theology, but also spirituality and liturgy.[1]

We have neglected the latter two aspects. And the result of this is that our perspective has been only partial. We have, for example, spoken very little about the ascetical realities of the Christian life. We have neglected the profound truth that sacrifice of self is not merely an external religious command; it is also an inevitable, profoundly human, and potentially enriching correlate of commitment to the service of others. We have not spoken, therefore, of a most potent theme: the ascesis of love, which must surely play a role in the successful living of the Christian life.[2] Similarly, we have not dealt at length with the important reality of corporate living and worship. We have made brief references to this issue, speaking of the Christian life as communal in Chapter Ten, becoming conscious of the sociology of knowledge in Chapter Seventeen, and noting the significance of Christian motivations in Chapter Nineteen. But it has not been given nearly the attention it deserves. For liturgical worship-response functions, in the real world, as a most profound component in the living of the Christian life.[3]

So we have not done everything. It is important to say this, not only because it is true but also because unreasonable expectations can lead to unjustified criticisms. It is a rather common characteristic of students that they criticize a particular course, book, or lecture on the grounds that it does not deal with everything, that it does not solve all problems. And the only response to this criticism, of course, is agreement. But perhaps such objections can be forestalled by a free admission from the start. Moral theology is not everything. Indeed, from any truly Christian non-Pelagian point of view, it is not even the most important thing. It is at most one good thing.

Similarly, in this book we have not done everything, but we have done something. At least we have attempted to do something. We have taken a point of view, we have stood somewhere. Specifically, we have used as our starting point and our ongoing point of reference the moral person, the Christian seeking to respond to the gift and call of the Lord. From this point of view we have attempted to look everywhere. While we have not tried to exhaustively describe how the Christian life can and should be lived, we have tried to express what is going on in the living of that life. We have tried to look in all the important directions, to ask all the important questions, and to formulate responsible answers. Specifically, we have attempted to move from this consciously chosen individual and existential starting point to an internally coherent and experientially adequate theory of the moral life.[4] And we have tried to develop this theory in a way that maintains the linkage with the best of the Christian and Catholic tradition.

But doing this has presented problems of its own. Not least among these is the fact that as a comprehensive theory the argument of this book belongs to this author alone. Because of our decision to "stand someplace," to view things in a certain way, we have ended up disagreeing with just about everyone else in some particular or other. We have reserved our strong criticism for those who would trivialize God, the Christian person, or the Christian life. But inasmuch as these pages have been a sort of dialogue with others who take all the same issues seriously, whether they be members of the Catholic magisterium, fellow theologians, or Christian individuals, inevitable points of disagreement have emerged. And this raises the very serious question of theological diversity today.

Where Will It Lead?

Given the fact of this diversity, our second question naturally arises: Where does this particular synthesis lead? And where does the fact that it cannot represent a universally held position lead?

Of the fact that diversity exists there can be no doubt. Even prior to the personal and therefore unique synthesis that is this book, Catholic moral theology has been marked by substantial amounts of diversity.[5] And this book will not eliminate that. While we believe that this synthesis largely represents a collection of widely held convictions, and while we hope that bringing these convictions together in this way will facilitate communication and the search for agreement, still it is surely true that no one will agree with absolutely everything. And some will probably find themselves in disagreement with most of what has been said here.

In one sense this diversity is regrettable. Certainly the vision of the Church as a people one in mind and heart, as a place not only of common commitment but also of common conviction, is an ideal fondly to be hoped for. Indeed, it is a goal to be striven for.[6] Conversely, when a community which sincerely seeks this goal is nonetheless confronted with substantial areas of disagreement and contradictory diversity, a certain amount of pain is to be expected. At the same time, this phenomenon can be seen as good in that it reveals three things: honesty, sincerity, and humility.

For one thing, it is a manifestation that honesty is alive in the Church. Theology is an exercise of intellect, not of will; it is an effort to discern, not to command. And if the fact is that people see things differently, then the admission of these differences is a powerful proof of the honesty of all the participants. The one truly tragic thing would be to claim or exhibit unanimity before it is actually discovered, to accept common ways of speaking before they are truly understood, to proclaim common convictions before they are really affirmed. That God's people should always be an honest people, that the Church should be a "zone of truth," is something that must never be sacrificed.[7]

In the second place, this diversity is a good thing in that it demonstrates the sincerity of the members of the Church. It is one thing to speak privately about one's personal opinions, to express disagreement or complaint in the safe environment of personal conversation. It is quite another to articulate these things in a formal and public way, to state one's position and to present one's reasons, to exhibit one's convictions before the eyes of all who would see. To do this is to invite response, to permit others to disagree in turn, and to allow for the possibility of being found wanting or proved wrong. No human being takes such a risk lightly. Thus the fact that such risks are being taken in the Church today is *prima facie* proof of the sincerity and dedication of all who join in the theological debates of our time.

Thirdly, this diversity is an example, and a sacrament, of humility. If the central convictions of the Christian faith mean anything, they mean that God is in charge. As human persons, we are beings of great dignity; but we are also distinctly finite beings. Our perspectives are limited, our understandings are partial, our capacity for error is unremitting. Even as a Church, we do not escape this finitude, with all the dangers that are consequent. We are finite, and there is no avoiding that.

What is more, the Christian faith asserts, not only that we *are* finite but also that we *may* be finite. It is not necessary for us to find all the answers, to resolve all the doubts, to conquer all the ambiguities of life. God is in charge; and he who is larger than our thoughts and transcends our theories will care for us in his own loving way.

Finally, we *must* be finite. Despite all that has been said above, the fact is that the human mind yearns for truth. It seeks understanding and clarity of insight. It is unsatisfied with incomplete answers and unresolved questions. It is, in Augustine's term, restless. This desire for perfection is no doubt good, since it was put in us by God. But it can also be a temptation, since it can lead us to be dissatisfied with the being that is ours. In the extreme case, it can lead us to dream of being God; it can even deceive us into thinking we are God. But we are not. The truth for which we yearn is Truth itself. The life we would like to envision for ourselves is Life itself. And the way we really should walk is that Way which is the Lord himself. Augustine surely was speaking truth when he described our hearts as restless; he was deeply wise when he completed his thought: "Our hearts are restless till they rest in Thee."[8]

We are powerfully, even painfully, reminded of all this by the theological diversity of our day. We do not have all the answers, and we never will. Often enough we do not even know how to properly formulate the questions. We must search, to be sure. We cannot turn off our minds. But we must at least not be surprised when our efforts bear less than perfect fruit. We must in the end be humble.

Conclusion

So again we ask: Where will all this lead? We do not know. This author fondly hopes that the insights of this book will be a real service to the Church and to all those who share its life. He hopes that it represents a step forward, a move not toward greater division but toward deeper oneness of heart *and* mind. But he is under no illusions about the complete achievement of that goal. Diversity exists, and it will continue to exist. It may be a pain-causing reality. It may occasion a certain amount of embarrassment. Not confronted, it can even lead to rancor. But at the same time, and in a strangely paradoxical way, it is also a proper insignia to adorn the Christian uniform, an ultimate admission that God is God, that we are merely human and that such a situation is ultimately very good.

There is a sentence penned by St. Irenaeus in the second century, a sentence usually interpreted as high praise for human beings. And it is that, for it proclaims that we are very important to God himself. But the sentence is also, in a subtle way, an expression of this humility we have been considering. It says we are important, but it affirms that we are finite. It says that we are powerful, but it acknowledges that we are dependent. It says that we are humans and not animals, but it admits that we are humans and not God.

That sentence is central to the perspective of this book. It is the keystone of Christian morality as we understand it. Its realization in our minds and its achievement in our hearts is also central to the motivation of this book. And so, more than a hope, it is a prayer that brings this book to a conclusion.

May all the followers of Jesus Christ, and in a special way those followers who find their roots and meaning in the Catholic tradition of Christianity, more and more come to appreciate and celebrate and live the truth of the Incarnation proclaimed by Irenaeus: "The glory of God is man—fully alive."[9]

NOTES

For full data on books and articles cited in the Notes, see the Bibliography.

Chapter 1

1. E.g., B. Lonergan, *Method in Theology;* and D. Tracy, *Blessed Rage for Order.*

2. J. Daniélou, "Christianity and non-Christian Religions," p. 91f.

3. It is interesting that Aquinas parallels Paul's understanding by speaking of a "pastoral magisterium," the bishops, and a "teaching magisterium," the theologians. Cf. *Quodlibet* 3, Q. 4, art. 1; as reported in A. Dulles, "The Theologian and the Magisterium," p. 242.

4. This notion of theology as bridging revelation and culture is richly developed by P. Tillich, *Theology of Culture* (New York: Oxford University Press, 1959), esp. pp. 40–51. Tillich speaks of "religion and culture," but the insight is fundamentally the same as that described here.

5. In these pages the terms "moral theology" and "Christian ethics" will be used interchangeably.

6. The German language offers an interesting example of the relationship of these two moments, even linguistically connecting them: *Gabe*, "gift"; *Aufgabe*, "task."

Chapter 2

1. Of course, a thorough survey of the history of moral theology is more than we can attempt here. Even if we had the space, the task would remain problematic in view of the lack of appropriate resources. The literature on the history of moral theology falls neatly into two categories, with a huge chasm in between. On the one hand, there are the brief overviews found in textbooks and encyclopedias. On the other hand, there are highly detailed monographs on specific periods or figures. To the best of our knowledge there exists nothing in between, no book-length summary of our history. One can hope that this lacuna will soon be filled.

In developing the points that comprise our historical overview we have primarily followed the lead of Bernard Häring, *Law of Christ*, 1:3–33. This has been supplemented by material from articles in the *New Catholic Encyclopedia*, from T. Deman, *Aux origines de la théologie moral*, F. Murphy, *Moral Teaching in the Primitive Church*; and a number of other confirmatory sources.

2. Quoted in Häring, p. 7.

3. These two figures offer an interesting example of theologian David Tracy's distinction between analogical and dialectic thinking in theology. Cf. his "Presidential Address."

4. E.g., Häring, p. 8; G. Regan, *New Trends in Moral Theology*, p. 23.

5. E.g., A. Kosnik et al., *Human Sexuality*, p. 37.

6. In one other particular Augustine stands as significant for modern theology, and that is in his roots in Platonic philosophy. There is no doubt that Platonism is a philosophy which risks dualistic excesses, and some would probably say that Augustine himself is a contributor to such excesses. But in my view it need not be so. Platonism also offers the possibility of grounding a richer, more poetic and mystical approach to theology. Indeed, it seems to have done so in our time. So if it is true that much modern theology is Platonic, in the best sense of

the word, and if Augustine is a major representative of this theological approach, he is on that account particularly deserving of our attention. Cf. T. O'Connell, "Old Priest, New Theology: A Dilemma."

7. From his *Prologue to the Commentary on the Book of Sentences*; quoted by Häring, p. 11.

8. This same line of argument is used by John Courtney Murray to show that the American political vision logically requires a commitment to natural law, to the objectivity and discernibility of value. Cf. *We Hold These Truths.*

9. It was not only in moral theology that this permutation took place. Similar changes can be discerned in liturgical theology. From a science with clearly dogmatic roots and with implications for spirituality, it became a science of the correct, of the valid and licit, of rubrical propriety. Liturgy, too, developed an affiliation with canon law. And again, this was a development that has lasted to our day. Even today the Gregorian University in Rome publishes two journals: *Gregorianum*, a journal of theology, and *Periodica de re morali, canonica et liturgica*, a journal of moral, canonical, and liturgical matters.

Chapter 3

1. That this overall vision and sense of "Christian character" is the most significant contribution of the Bible to Christian morality is well argued in B. C. Birch and L. L. Rasmussen, *Bible and Ethics in the Christian Life.*

2. The significance of the idea of covenant for Christian moral theology has often been pointed out. Among others, it has been extensively used by theologian Enda McDonagh; for example, cf. *Invitation and Response*, pp. 43–47.

3. R. Schnackenburg, *The Moral Teaching of the New Testament*, p. 13. Much of the following material is based on Schnackenburg's excellent research.

4. The central significance of "reversal" not only in specifically ethical contexts but also in the parables is highlighted in J. Crossan, *In Parables.*

5. R. Bultmann, *Jesus* (1951), p. 79; quoted in Schnackenburg, p. 76.

6. A theme beautifully developed by R. McCormick, "Human Significance and Christian Significance," p. 234f.

7. E.g., J.T. Sanders, *Ethics in the New Testament*, pp. 91–100.

8. Schnackenburg, p. 15f.

Chapter 4

1. J. Fitzmyer, "Pauline Ecclesiology and Ethics," sec. 166.

2. E. Schillebeeckx, *Christ the Sacrament of the Encounter with God.*

3. On the vision of Christ developed here, cf. J. Fuchs, "The Law of Christ," in *Human Values and Christian Morality*, pp. 76–91; and K. Rahner, "On the Theology of the Incarnation."

4. Rahner, p. 115.

5. Ibid., p. 116.

6. This is not to say that "sacred space" is unimportant, of course. It is simply to say that its importance is psychological rather than theological. The function of sacred space is precisely to highlight and make explicit the presence of God that is to be found throughout his creation. Thus the church building is *our* house, not God's. Or perhaps better: it is God's house *because* it is ours.

7. This writer has been intrigued to notice, time and again, the way students of theology limit themselves to "historical Christology." When asked an open-ended question such as "What is the significance of Christ for moral theology?" they almost always respond in an

"historical" vocabulary. They will say that, by himself living a human life, Jesus (they often unconsciously replace the "Christ" of my question with the human name) has shown us how to live, that his loving style and wise teaching offer us guidance in our lives.

These two types of Christology are discussed by K. Rahner in his "The Two Basic Types of Christology."

Chapter 5

1. All of the ideas sketched here will be considered again in these pages. For now they are simply mentioned by way of introducing our present topic.

2. E.g., H. Davis, *Moral and Pastoral Theology*, 1:11. The entire presentation of this chapter is representative of Davis and other manuals such as J. Fuchs, *Theologia Moralis Generalis*, 2:1–43; and H. Noldin, *Summa Theologiae Moralis*, 1:15–100.

3. It is interesting to note that the distinction between "human acts" and "acts of man" is not only a datum of common experience, it is also a principle of law. Criminal trials often spend considerable effort determining the freedom and responsibility of the defendant at the time of the crime. The question of whether negligence was involved is raised. The legal distinction between "murder" and "manslaughter" is carefully protected. All these examples are expressions of this same fundamental insight; not everything that a person does is his or her responsibility.

4. Emotions can, of course, also function as eminently human thrusts toward action. They can be, as it were, the power plants of human behavior. So the inclusion of passion among a list of impediments should not be interpreted as supporting the Stoic idea that the ideal human being is totally "apathetic," untouched by emotion. Still, most people would readily concede that emotion can *also* dehumanize action in some circumstances.

5. A. Maslow, *Toward a Psychology of Being* (Princeton, N.J.: Van Nostrand, 1968), esp. pp. 21–70.

6. Cf. J. Fuchs, 1:155–56.

Chapter 6

1. The general understanding of fundamental option, though not the precise term, can be traced as far back as 1922. Cf. D. von Hildebrand, "Sittlichkeit und ethische Werterkenntnis." It entered the manual tradition in J. Fuchs, *Theologia Moralis Generalis*, 2:4. Both the concept and the term have been implicitly affirmed by the magisterium of the Catholic Church in the "Declaration on Certain Questions Concerning Sexual Ethics" of the Sacred Congregation for the Doctrine of the Faith (December 29, 1975), no. 10. The document criticizes certain distorted understandings of fundamental option, but in so doing it also indicates an appropriate understanding which is substantially the same as that presented here.

2. Cf. K. Rahner, "Guilt and its Remission: The Borderland between Theology and Psychotherapy," p. 269ff.

3. J. Fuchs, 2:147. This insight into the tentativity of human fundamental options has led some authors also to posit the existence of a "final option" made at the moment of death. This option, in contrast to all the others, is definitive and irrevocable. Cf. R. Troisfontaines, *I Do Not Die*, pp. 160–88.

4. There are many excellent presentations in English of this overall view of the human person. Among the best are: J. Fuchs, "Basic Freedom and Morality," in his *Human Values and Christian Morality*, pp. 92–111; id., "Sin and Conversion"; J. Glaser, "Transition between Grace and Sin: Fresh Perspectives"; R. McCormick, "The Moral Theology of Vatican II"; K. Rahner, "Some Thoughts on a 'Good Intention' "; id., "Theology of Freedom"; id., "Guilt–Responsibility–Punishment within the View of Catholic Theology"; F. Podimattam, "What Is Mortal Sin?"; R. Tapia, "When Is Sin Sin?"

Chapter 7

1. This linking of the "horizontal" and "vertical" dimensions of sin occasions some interesting reflections upon the practice of the Sacrament of Reconciliation in the Catholic Church. The point has often been made, with some justification, that past practice focused almost exclusively upon sin as an offense against God. The neighbor was largely overlooked. Recent renewal, both in practice and in catechesis, has attempted to remedy this imbalance. But in some cases it has seemed to move to the opposite extreme. This writer had occasion recently to talk with a group of high-school students who asserted that if their neighbor was the one they had offended by their sins, they should apologize to the neighbor rather than "go to confession." At first I was tempted to accuse the students of oversimplification. But then I realized they were right. If only the neighbor has been injured, then only the relationship with the neighbor requires reconciliation, and the sacrament serves no purpose. Only if we experience the reality of covenantal love relationships with *both* our neighbor and our God, and only if we experience these two as inextricably intertwined, does a sacramental ritual of reconciliation truly have meaning.

2. This idea that we do not achieve complete certitude regarding our moral state is well developed in K. Rahner, "Guilt–Responsibility–Punishment within the View of Catholic Theology," p. 204f.

3. This is beautifully expressed in J. Fuchs, "Sin and Conversion." This theory of fundamental (and final) option also gives a much more plausible justification to the theological concept of hell. Namely, the power of human freedom must include even the utterly perverse capacity to elect forever a living-in-isolation which frustrates and negates the person. Not to acknowledge this power is to undermine the significance of human freedom. And similarly, hell is to be understood not as something God does to us, but as something we are frighteningly capable of doing to ourselves. Cf. K. Rahner, "Guilt–Responsibility–Punishment within the View of Catholic Theology," p. 215.

4. Cf. K. Rahner, "The Theological Concept of Consupiscentia."

5. A line of argument usefully pursued by C. Curran, "Masturbation and Objectively Grave Matter," in *A New Look at Christian Morality*, pp. 201–32.

6. Some authors prefer to distinguish mortal sin, venial sin, and "serious sin" to deal with the very issue addressed in this paragraph. For them, serious sin is grave matter which has not yet functioned as a tool for a fundamental option but which, because of its seriousness, may very well be a preamble to such an option. The distinction may well have some pastoral utility. But we have avoided it because it blurs the anthropological differentiation between acts that mediate a fundamental option and acts that do not. Clarity regarding this differentiation seems to us the highest priority, particularly when the phenomenon of "venial sin with grave matter" can be explained as simply as it has been.

7. The implications of this understanding of man and of fundamental option for the administration of the sacrament of Penance have been developed at some length. Cf. T. O'Connell, "Sin and Reconciliation," and "Identification of Sin."

8. Many of the ideas developed in this chapter, and the one before, are also considered in T. O'Connell, "The Point of Moral Theology."

Chapter 8

1. This point is forcefully made by E. M. Pattison, "The Development of Moral Values in Children." Cf. also K. Rahner, "Guilt and Its Remission."

2. E.g., J. Fuchs, *Theologia Moralis Generalis*, 1:152–55. Other authors speak of two sorts of conscience, synderesis and syneidesis, and understand moral science as the methodical application of synderesis: e.g., H. Noldin, *Summa Theologiae Moralis*, 1:197f.

3. B. Häring, *The Law of Christ*, 1:151.

4. *IV Sent.*, dist. 38, art. 4.

5. *Human Life in Our Day* (Washington: USCC, 1968), p. 14.

6. Ibid., p. 14f.

7. J. Fuchs, 1:176.

8. A point recognized also by Protestant theologians. Cf. J. Gustafson, "Is There a Catholic and/or Christian Ethic?—A Response"; and L. Gilkey, *Catholicism Confronts Modernity.*

9. This expression of the matter is, of course, at variance with much recent writing which speaks, instead, of a Catholic's obligation to give "religious and internal assent of mind and will" even to noninfallible teachings. But as a number of authors have shown, recent practice has presumed a narrow, highly juridical conception of magisterium that is of recent origin and not consonant with the bulk of Catholic tradition. Thus this presentation seeks to reclaim and restate that broad tradition. Cf. Y. Congar, "Pour une histoire sémantique du terme 'magisterium,' " and "Bref historique des formes du 'magistere' et de ses relations avec les docteurs"; id., "The Magisterium and Theologians—a Short History"; A. Dulles, "The Theologian and the Magisterium"; R. McCormick, "Notes on Moral Theology—Theologians and the Magisterium," *TS* 38 (1977): 74-100 (where additional citations are offered).

10. We will return to this notion of historicity and develop it in greater detail in Chapter Fourteen.

11. Cf. G. Hughes, "Infallibility in Morals."

12. This is not to deny that the Church, like any human institution, may need to protect its identity and effectiveness through the exercise of external discipline. All the more so in that values are, as we have seen, fragile. They too, need care and protection. Thus there is a place for such a thing as excommunication. But if such a practice is plausible, it should also be rare, invoked only when the very life or mission of the community is at stake.

Chapter 9

1. Needless to say, these presentations cannot be exhaustive. We will indicate literature in which these ideas are further developed.

2. C. S. Lewis, *The Problem of Pain* (New York: Macmillan, 1945), p. 3.

3. *Humani Generis* (New York: Paulist, 1950), p. 18f.

4. K. Rahner, "Theological Reflexions on Monogenism," esp. pp. 280-85.

5. K. Rahner, "The Sin of Adam," p. 252. Cf. also "Evolution and Original Sin," for Rahner's first brief statement of his new position.

6. For further discussions of original sin cf., in addition to Rahner, H. Rondet, *Original Sin*; P. Schoonenberg, *Man and Sin*; E. Maly, *Sin: Biblical Perspectives.*

7. This line of thought, which has a long history going back at least to Augustine, is presented here in dependence upon C. Meyer, *A Contemporary Theology of Grace*; and R. Gleason, *Grace.* For a related presentation cf. T. O'Connell, "Grace, Relationship and Transactional Analysis."

8. Indeed, the theological concepts of fundamental option and fundamental stance were at least partly developed by dogmatic theologians seeking to understand the mystery of grace more profoundly. Cf., for example, S. Dianich, "La corruzione della natura e la grazia nella opzioni fondamentali"; M. Flick and Z. Alszeghy, *Il Vangelo Della Grazia*, esp. pp. 141-67, 192f; P. Fransen, "Towards a Psychology of Divine Grace"; and H. Rondet, *The Grace of Christ.*

9. Meyer, p. 180.

Chapter 10

1. One of the hallmarks of contemporary moral theology is the attempt to take time seriously. We will return to this aspect of reality in Chapter Fourteen. Both here and in that later context we are greatly dependent on the insights of B. Lonergan, "The Transition from a Classicist World-View to Historical-Mindedness"; also J. Walgrave, "Is Morality Static or Dynamic"; and B. Häring, "Dynamism and Continuity in a Personalistic Approach to Natural Law."

2. S. Hauerwas, *Character and the Christian Life*, p. 11. Cf. also his *Vision and Virtue*. In both these works Hauerwas admirably develops the theme of "character" as central to Christian ethics.

3. E.g., G. Gutierrez, *A Theology of Liberation;* the various works of J. Segundo; and G. Baum, *Religion and Alienation*.

4. E.g., P. Lehmann, *Ethics in a Christian Context;* and J. Gustafson, *The Church as Moral Decision-Maker*.

5. The work being done at the National Opinion Research Center at the University of Chicago is particularly notable in this regard.

6. For example, the clinical task of child psychology is in many places giving way to "family counseling." For it is being realized that healthy individual growth can take place only in a healthy family unit.

7. The uniqueness of the individual Christian life, and therefore also of some moral obligations, is particularly developed by K. Rahner. Cf., especially, "On the Question of a Formal Existential Ethics."

Chapter 11

1. M. Heidegger *Being and Time* (New York: Harper & Row, 1962). Cf. also L. Binswanger, *Being in the World;* May, Angel, Ellenberger (eds.), *Existence*.

2. D. von Hildebrand, *Ethics* (Chicago: Franciscan Herald Press, 1953).

3. It is no accident that we are describing values in terms similar to those we used in Chapter Five in discussing evaluative knowledge. The similarity of these two notions is more than semantic. Speaking ontologically, evaluative knowledge is the way by which the human person perceives the values of our world. And speaking historically, the two notions were developed by the same group of scholars as aspects of the same essential insight. Note, for example, that J. Fuchs cites von Hildebrand in his discussion of "cognitio aestimativa" (*Theologia Moralis Generalis*, 1:156). This approach is characteristic of a school of moral philosophy and theology, *Wertethik* (value-ethics), whose central figure is Max Scheler. Cf. also A. Deeken, *Process and Permanence in Ethics: Max Scheler's Moral Philosophy*.

4. This presentation is typical of that found in the manuals. Cf., for example, H. Noldin, *Summa Theologiae Moralis*, 1:104–29; and H. Davis, *Moral and Pastoral Theology*, 1:117–58.

5. A number of these questions are discussed in depth in J. Fuchs, *Natural Law: A Theological Investigation*. This book involves some very noteworthy advances over the typical manual; it is, however, still fundamentally within that tradition.

6. An example of the first position would be H. Noldin, p. 111. The second position was adopted by H. Davis, p. 127.

7. This idea of three levels of natural law will serve as the starting point for our own consideration of the "knowability" of the natural law in Chapter Seventeen.

Chapter 12

1. The formulation of these various types of law exhibits distinguishable varieties, too According to a widely held distinction, generally associated with exegete Albrecht Alt, there are apodeictic and casuistic laws. The former are clearly proclaimed, universal prohibitions They are deductive laws, as it were. The latter work inductively, from cases to a principle. Casuistic laws are much more common in nonbiblical literature (cf., for example, S. Freyne. "The Bible and Christian Morality"). Another distinction, particularly applied to the New Testament, is that which differentiates paranetic and explanatory discourse. The former has a homiletic quality, not meant to be taken literally and not intended to be really exceptionless The latter is literal and technical. Thus, "Thou shalt not kill" is an example of paranetic discourse, since people have always recognized that it is sometimes sadly necessary to kill. Cf., for example, R. McCormick, "Notes on Moral Theology," *TS* 37 (1976): 72–74, where he uses this distinction in a very helpful way to respond to an article of this author.

2. M. O'Connell, "Some Aspects of Commandment in the Old Testament," p. 12f.

3. J. Michener's novel, *The Source*, beautifully captures the flavor of this love-motivated legalism.

4. J. J. Stamm and M. E. Andrews, *The Ten Commandments in Recent Literature*, p. 68f.

5. Thus people should not be surprised, as they often are, to notice that the biblical text of the Decalogue (unlike the version learned in school) includes a statement of the first commandment so extended that it is almost as long as the other nine put together. Indeed, Commandments IV–X, the more "practical" dictates, occupy less than a third of the text!

6. On these topics we are primarily dependent on Stamm and Andrews; cf. also E. Nielsen, *The Ten Commandments in New Perspective*. I cannot resist one further comment. Recent catechetical practice in Catholicism has tended to avoid teaching the Ten Commandments to children. The hope, I suppose, was that by avoiding these texts a more positive and loving approach to ethics might be developed. But on the basis of the understanding presented here, I would suggest that the Decalogue should be taught. Not as if it could function as a sufficient ethical framework for life, nor as divine commands which the good Catholic docilely accepts and blindly follows, but rather as a sacred poem, as a collection of wisdom and love, which "our people" have been reciting and proclaiming for three thousand years.

7. R. Schnackenburg, *The Moral Teaching of the New Testament*, p. 95. This last point Schnackenburg distills from the Lukan version of this event. For there Jesus moves right from the proclamation of the two great commandments into the story of the Good Samaritan.

8. *In Epistolam Joannis*, tract. 7, cap. 4, PL 35, 2044.

9. We have not attempted to discuss all the many, quite specific moral dictates to be found in Paul's writings. Almost all of the Epistles include a section dealing with how the Christian should behave, and Paul was not above getting into considerable detail. We have avoided discussing these for several reasons. First, a comprehensive consideration would be far beyond what could be attempted here. Second, to fairly assess these norms at this point in the book would require the development of a theology of revelation and inspiration which is, again, beyond the scope that is possible. The brief references to that area of theology which have already appeared and which will appear as we proceed will have to suffice. And third, in due course we shall establish the proper way to understand *all* specific moral dictates, whether found in the Bible or elsewhere.

10. There are many fine sources available on the topic of the biblical understanding of law and commandment. In addition to those cited in the course of this chapter, the following should be noted: J. Blank, "Does the New Testament Provide Principles for Modern Moral Theology"; K. Berger, "Law"; J. Fitzmyer, "Pauline Ecclesiology and Ethics," secs. 157–66; G. Schneider, "The Biblical Grounding of the Ethical Norms"; R. Collins, "Scripture and the Christian Ethic"; and responses to Collins by J. Dedek and V. Peter in *Proceedings*, pp. 243–46 and 247–54.

Chapter 13

1. The fact that the prevailing understanding of natural law is at least in part a function of the character of the wider cultural scene is noted and exemplified by B. Häring, *Morality is For Persons*, p. 146ff.

2. *De Republica*, lib. iii, c. xxii, 33; as cited in C. Ryan, "The Traditional Concept of Natural Law: An Interpretation," p. 15. Ryan contrasts this view with the more passive understanding of the Stoics.

3. The fact that natural law can have these two meanings, that the historical debate has involved them, and that one must eventually choose to emphasize either the world as fact or right reason has often been noted. For example, P. Delhaye, " 'Droit naturel' et théologie morale," p. 140, speaks of the opposition between the visions of natural law as *cosmos* and as *logos*. R. Troisfontaines, "L'insémination artificielle: Problèmes éthiques," distinguishes natural law as conformity to nature and as communion of persons. And K. Rahner, "The Experiment with Man," p. 215f., establishes that how one answers this natural law question will determine what one considers permissible in the area of biological and genetic manipulations. C. Ryan, p. 15, also points out what he calls "two possible strands in the concept of natural law."

4. Our own answers to these questions will be developed in Chapter Fourteen.

5. C. Curran, "Natural Law and Contemporary Moral Theology," in *Contemporary Problems in Moral Theology*, p. 106. In much of the data summarized in this historical survey we are dependent on Curran's work. Cf. also his "Absolute Norms in Moral Theology," in *A New Look at Christian Morality*, pp. 75–84; J. Arntz, "Natural Law and its History"; and G. Watson, "Pagan Philosophy and Christian Ethics."

6. A fact noted by M. Crowe, "Natural Law Theory Today."

7. Cf. T. O'Connell, "Grace, Relationship and Transactional Analysis."

8. L. Bernstein, *The Unanswered Question* (Cambridge: Harvard University Press, 1975).

9. It is interesting, if not amusing, that the great chronicler of our culture, *Time* magazine, devoted a major article to the "rebirth" of natural law: "The Rediscovery of Human Nature," April 2, 1973, pp. 79–81. The article was part of a series entitled, "Second Thoughts About Man."

Chapter 14

1. The first two of these characteristics would, I think, be supported by all Catholic moral theologians as well as magisterial teaching. The latter three are increasingly controversial, though it is safe to say that even they have widespread theological support. In any case, the effort here will be to argue to the validity and necessity of all five characteristics on intrinsic grounds. References will be made to other moral theologians, and to the various controversies, where appropriate.

2. As was said by manualist H. Davis, *Moral and Pastoral Theology*, 1:127.

3. This confusion of "experiential" with "empirical" and even with "utilitarian" is not uncommon. Cf., for example, J. Connery, "Morality of Consequences: A Critical Appraisal," though Connery's objections arise more directly from the next characteristic we shall discuss: consequentialism. In any case, it should be said clearly that an understanding of natural law as experiential differs from "naive empiricism" on at least three counts. (1) It recognizes the validity of a far wider range of knowledge-objects, consciously accepting value knowledge as we saw in Chapter Eleven. (2) With regard to knowledge-modes, it explicitly rejects the "technological bias" of utilitarianism and instead affirms what we previously called evaluative knowledge (Chapter Five). (3) It gives considerable emphasis to the social nature of moral

perception and thus acknowledges the role of tradition in accumulating and transmittin insight into moral value. However, our position is one with empiricism in a single significan way: we assert that knowledge of moral value must *ultimately* be based on objective experienc and not on any subjective or legal premise.

4. This presentation of the experiential quality of natural law is dependent upon a grea deal of contemporary theological literature. One of those most responsible for stimulating th discussion is J. G. Milhaven. Although the understanding presented here does not conforr completely to Milhaven's and although we have chosen to avoid his use of the word "empiri cal" for reasons indicated above, his work has been most helpful and provocative. Cf. his "Towards an Epistemology of Ethics," and "Objective Moral Evaluation of Consequences.'

5. In this I am disagreeing with a position ably argued by R. McCormick in "Humar Significance and Christian Significance." It appears that Fr. McCormick no longer holds the position developed in that article; cf. his "Notes on Moral Theology," *TS* 33 (1972): 78, 82f Still the earlier article raises important points which deserve the attention given here.

6. This objection is particularly formulated by J. Connery, "Morality of Consequences A Critical Appraisal." Somewhat similar lines are pursued, with much less scholarship, in ; foray into theology by physicist P. Quay, "Morality by Calculation of Values."

7. It should be pointed out that a macroconsequentialist approach also involves attempt ing to discern the consequences of particular action *both* upon the outer world and upon the agent himself. In certain ethical issues this second aspect is extremely important. Take, for example, the case of the terminally ill patient and the question of whether he should be killed or whether, on the contrary, we should limit ourselves to making him comfortable while no resisting the process toward death. In other words, consider the question of whether there is any *meaningful* difference between active euthanasia and passive euthanasia. If one looks only at the consequences upon the recipient of the action, the dying patient, then one might conclude that there is no difference. For in either case the patient will die. But if one looks also to the consequences upon the agent, if one also asks the question "Who do I become if I act in this way?" then the distinction between active and passive euthanasia may be very important.

8. This idea that a consequentialist ontology can still recognize the legitimacy of moral rules is exemplified and enriched in a fascinating way by psychiatrist D. Campbell. He points out that the presumption of all scientific method is that truth is best sought by a cumulative process of trial and error in which an hypothesis is subjected to the test of experience to see if it, indeed, works out. Campbell suggests that, even according to the canons of scientific method, the accumulated wisdom of religious tradition deserves high respect. For while various psychological and sociological theories have been tested only for periods ranging from years to decades, many religious guidelines for living have survived centuries of "testing." Thus, for example, if a psychologist suggests I give full vent to my feelings and a religious tradition urges me to control myself at least to the extent of being genuinely concerned for the other, an honest scientist would have to hold that the religious tradition is more likely to be correct. And this for thoroughly scientific reasons. Cf. D. Campbell, "On the Conflicts Between Biological and Social Evolution and Between Psychology and Moral Tradition," *American Psychologist* 30 (1975): 1103–1126.

9. We have already discussed this vision, particularly in Chapter Four. We shall give it further, extended attention in Chapter Nineteen.

10. Connery's objection has also elicited responses from other theologians. The points made here were developed partly in independence, partly in dialogue with them. Beyond the responses made here, these authors offer several other excellent observations. Cf. R. McCormick, "Notes on Moral Theology," *TS* 36 (1975): 93–100; and B. Schüller, "Neuere Beiträge zum Thema 'Begründung sittlicher Normen,' " which McCormick also discusses.

11. It should be acknowledged that in this assertion, and in the arguments for it that will now be developed, we are opting for a Roman, rather than a Greek, conception of the natural

law. For we are giving acquiesence to "the facts" a subsidiary role, and we are emphasizing the intelligent selection of means to a humane end.

12. A point often wisely emphasized by C. Curran. Cf., for example, "Dialogue with Social Ethics: Roman Catholic Ethics—Past, Present and Future," in *Catholic Moral Theology In Dialogue*, pp. 111–49.

13. This idea of experiment, and the risks it implies, are powerfully outlined by K. Rahner, "The Experiment with Man."

14. In addition to the article of Rahner already cited, the concept of historicity is admirably developed in the following sources: B. Lonergan, "The Transition from a Classicist World-View to Historical-Mindedness"; J. C. Murray, "The Declaration on Religious Freedom"; B. Häring, "Dynamism and Continuity in a Personalistic Approach to Natural Law"; C. Curran, "Natural Law and Contemporary Moral Theology, in *Contemporary Problems in Moral Theology*, pp. 97–158; J. Walgrave, "Is Morality Static or Dynamic?"; and M. Crowe, "Human Nature: Immutable or Mutable." The notion of historicity as this affects Catholic magisterial teaching, particularly in the area of morality, is pursued by G. Hughes, "Infallibility in Morals"; and Hughes' views are critiqued by B. Tierney, "Infallibility in Morals: A Response," *TS* 35 (1974): 507–17.

15. This idea of proportionality as a central and paramount principle of objective morality has been developed by a number of theologians in recent years. Of particular importance has been the work of B. Schüller. Cf. his "What Ethical Principles Are Universally Valid?" Indeed, the aphorism "Maximize the good and minimize the evil" has come to be known as "Schüller's Preference Principle."

16. An extremely fine critique of the manualist vision of natural law is that of Edward Malloy. His comments, and alternative proposals, have influenced what is said here. Cf. E. Malloy, "Natural Law Theory and Catholic Moral Theology."

Chapter 15

1. In Chapter Eleven we summarized von Hildebrand's understanding of values as things which are "important in themselves." We noted that there are intellectual, aesthetic, and moral values. And then we focused on the nonnegotiable importance of moral values. But the broader meaning of the word "value," which is being developed here, is also recognized by von Hildebrand. For he distinguishes "qualitative value," the value that some things have because of their excellence, their special importance (and intellectual, aesthetic, and moral values would be included here), from "ontological value," the value that all things have simply because they exist. It is the reality of ontological value that we are observing and discussing here. Cf. D. von Hildebrand, *Ethics*, pp. 129–39.

2. This term comes from J. Fuchs, "Absoluteness of Moral Terms." Others express the same insight in alternative vocabularies. L. Janssens speaks of "Ontic Evil and Moral Evil," in an article of that title. P. Knauer distinguishes moral evil and physical evil in his "The Hermeneutic Function of the Principle of Double Effect." And D. von Hildebrand, pp. 265–81, discusses moral values and morally relevant values.

3. That, indeed, is the function of Special Moral Theology. As this book pursues General Moral Theology in trying to develop appropriate principles, so Special Moral Theology seeks to accurately assess the ethical importance of the various specific premoral values of our world.

4. We do speak of a "just wage," a "fair deal," an "honest statement." But in so doing we use the terms analogously and with a conscious narrowing of our focus. And even in these usages, we can use the value terms only because persons are involved. A just wage, for example, is a wage appropriate to the dignity and the contribution of a person. Still this loose, analogous usage can be confusing.

5. Some may find the example of stealing a bit difficult. I have found that in some circle "stealing" is a term used to describe taking another's possession with or without a good reason Thus some would argue that "Do not steal" is a material norm. This is a perfectly acceptabl understanding as long as one is clear about the implications. If stealing is understood in thi material way, then a distinction would have to be made between justified and unjustifie stealing. The norm would have to be understood as admitting exceptions, as indicating : premoral value to be attended to, not as proclaiming an absolute to be always observed. But i there is this sort of clarity, then the difference is merely semantic. And with consisten definition it should cause no problem. Still most moral philosophers and theologians woulc use the term as I have in the text.

6. Cf. T. O'Connell, "The Question of Moral Norms." I am grateful for the critique o this article in R. McCormick, "Notes on Moral Theology," *TS* 37 (1976); 72–74. Although I cannot altogether agree with McCormick, his insightful comments have led to a somewha different formulation of the matter here.

7. The danger of this, of course, is that the preacher can settle for empty platitudes tha evade the real issues of people's lives. So there is need to speak the language of materia norms, too. In certain instances the preacher may need to point out the evil of refusing to sel one's house to another purely on the basis of race, of the proliferation of pornography, o allowing young people to wander about at all hours of the night, and so on. But the one thing the preacher cannot do is draw proportional conclusions. He cannot determine how thes premoral disvalues will interact with other factors in the lives of his people. That judgmen they alone can make.

8. At the beginning of Chapter Fourteen we indicated that, as we proceeded through the successive characteristics of the natural law, we would be moving into more and more controversial issues of contemporary moral theory. The strategy we have developed in this current chapter, the understanding of values and norms that we have articulated, should make clear how this is so. Really the pivotal insights of contemporary moral theology derive from the last two characteristics of the natural law: historicity and proportionality; and they are certainly the most hotly debated. On the one hand, contemporary theory looks at the moral world as at least potentially mutable; and this because it takes seriously the historical nature of man. And on the other hand, it sees that world as essentially conflictual, where values compete for the agent's allegiance and where morality is constituted by the humane resolution of their claims; and this because it takes seriously the finite nature of the human person. Objections to this understanding of moral theology usually follow one of three lines. Either they object straightforwardly to viewing people as historical or the world as conflic-tual, or they reject this vision because of a prior allegiance to some biblical testimony or other, or they judge that commitments already made by the magisterium of the Church do not leave room for this theory. In the last two cases, the issue is really not moral theology at all; it is the theology of revelation or the theology of Church, respectively. Obviously, neither of these topics can be completely discussed in this book. But we have tried to give each our attention in the appropriate places.

9. In addition to the sources cited in this chapter, these ideas are also deeply pursued by R. McCormick in the various editions of his "Notes on Moral Theology" in *Theological Studies*. Cf., especially, 32 (1971): 80–97; 33 (1972): 68–90; 36 (1975): 85–100; 37 (1976): 71–87; 38 (1977): 74–84. In these pages McCormick both presents his own views and summarizes most all of the significant contributions of others. Also very helpful is McCormick's monograph *Ambiguity in Moral Choice*. For a very interesting, consistent, and thoughtful application of the theory developed in this chapter, cf. P. Keane, *Sexual Morality: A Catholic Perspective*. Keane employs Janssens' terminology, which distinguishes moral evil and ontic evil. And he works out all his specific judgments in the area of sexual morality by asking, first, what the ontic evils present might be and, second, in what situations these evils might be outweighted by the goods

(and therefore be morally good) or not outweighed (and therefore be morally bad). Keane also presents an excellent brief summary of the ideas we have been considering throughout this book in his Chapter III: "Some Pertinent Themes in Fundamental Moral Theology," pp. 35–56.

Chapter 16

1. E. Schillebeeckx, *Marriage: Human Reality and Saving Mystery*.

2. These sacramental and dogmatic issues continue to be pursued by theologians, though no clear resolution has yet appeared. Cf. W. Bassett and P. Huizing, eds., *The Future of Christian Marriage*; L. G. Wrenn, ed., *Divorce and Remarriage in the Catholic Church*; the entire issue of *The Jurist* 30 (January, 1970); D. Doherty, *Divorce and Remarriage: Resolving a Catholic Dilemma*; C. Curran, "Divorce: Catholic Theory and Practice in the United States," in *New Perspectives in Moral Theology*, pp. 212–76, and "Divorce in the Light of a Revised Moral Theology," in *Ongoing Revision*, pp. 66–106. The two articles by Curran also review a good deal of the other literature on this topic.

3. This analysis using the example of capital punishment is derived from D. Schüller, "What Ethical Principles are Universally Valid?" though he analyzes the example differently.

4. It should be noted that this entire section is oriented toward refuting the notion that there are acts which are intrinsically *morally* evil (or better, morally wrong). In contrast to this, the assertion that there are acts which are intrinsically premorally evil is quite correct. Indeed, it is a correlate of the fact that value is truly objective. Killing, for example, always involves a premoral disvalue: namely, the death of the victim. And so killing is intrinsically evil in the premoral sense. The question is whether it is also intrinsically morally evil in every case. And this we deny. But the point being made here is that there is, in fact, a very legitimate place for a rehabilitated concept of *intrinsice malum*.

5. J. Fuchs reaches a similar conclusion, and we are dependent on his work, in "Absoluteness of Moral Terms," p. 450.

6. This analysis was first developed by P. Knauer, "The Hermeneutic Function of the Principle of the Double Effect." My presentation differs from that of Knauer in several particulars, but it is nevertheless indebted to him. Also very worthwhile is C. Curran, "The Principle of Double Effect," in *Ongoing Revision*, pp. 173–209.

7. After composing the preceding paragraphs I discovered a somewhat similar analysis of Watergate in J. Fletcher, "Situation Ethics, Law, and Watergate."

Chapter 17

1. In K. Rahner and H. Vorgrimler, *Theological Dictionary* (New York: Herder and Herder, 1965), p. 305.

2. The examples given in this paragraph include both formal and material norms. This may confuse things. But the fact of the matter is that the manuals did not clearly distinguish these two, so in our summary of their thought neither shall we. And if this does raise some questions, perhaps that will just prove again how important the distinction is.

3. For typical manualist presentations of these three levels of the natural law, cf. H. Noldin, *Summa Theologiae Moralis*, 1:113; and J. Fuchs, *Natural Law*, pp. 117, 151.

4. A point made and impressively developed in P. Ramsey, "The Case of the Curious Exception."

5. Words can take on new meanings, of course. But that only adds to the confusion. For it results in the possibility that we may grossly misinterpret the actual meaning of formulations from an earlier, different era. Hence the need for hermeneutics, a science whose very existence testifies to the difference between formulations and understandings.

6. An insight somewhat appreciated in more recent scholastic writings; e.g., J. Fuchs *Theologia Moralis Generalis*, 1:81ff., where the author asserts that the very term "natural law" refers primarily to an inner reality and only secondarily to formulations.

7. Cf., for example, Marx's *Critique of Hegel's Philosophy of Right* (Cambridge: Cambridge University Press, 1970).

8. Cf., for example, W. Stark, *The Sociology of Knowledge*.

9. J. S. Mill, as quoted by H. R. Niebuhr, *Christ and Culture*, p. 238.

10. On the idea of human nature as a *Restbegriff*, cf. K. Rahner, "Concerning the Relationship Between Nature and Grace," p. 313f.; J. Fuchs, *Natural Law*, p. 45: E. McDonagh, *Invitation and Response*, p. 34.

11. A point made by K. Rahner, "The Experiment with Man," p. 218f.

Chapter 18

1. These are points very well argued by J. C. Murray, "Should There Be A Law? The Question of Censorship," in *We Hold These Truths*, pp. 155–74.

2. Cf. J. Fuchs, *Theologia Moralis Generalis*, 1:113.

3. Cf. H. Noldin, *Summa Theologiae Moralis*, 1:123f.

4. Cf. J. Fuchs, pp. 117–20; H. Noldin, pp. 132–36.

5. This entire section is dependent on the work of J. Fuchs, "Auctoritas Dei in Auctoritate Civili." A general understanding of Fuchs's argument can be derived from the digest of the above article: "The Authority of God in Civil Authority."

6. That the common good and not "legitimate source" justifies positive law is emphasized by K. Rahner, "The Dignity and Freedom of Man," p. 256.

7. Thus fidelity to one's judgment in the fact of continued enforcement of the letter of the law can lead to tragedy. This point is acknowledged and discussed by K. Rahner, p. 252.

8. On the twin risks of anarchy and tyranny (totalitarianism), and the tensions that these cause in human living, cf. K. Rahner, pp. 235–64.

Chapter 19

1. R. Collins, "Scripture and the Christian Ethic," p. 240.

2. C. Curran, "Dialogue with the Scriptures: The Role and Function of the Scriptures in Moral Theology," in *Catholic Moral Theology in Dialogue*, pp. 23–64. This article includes considerable additional bibliography on this topic.

3. A point made by, among others, D. Maguire, "Moral Absolutes and the Magisterium," p. 80.

4. The fact that this approach changed somewhat in the last hundred years, and the reasons for the change, are discussed by Y. Congar, "The Magisterium and Theologians—A Short History."

5. How this understanding is to be reconciled with the declaration of Vatican I is a serious question. I am impressed with the suggestion of G. Hughes, "Infallibility in Morals," even though that theory is responsibly challenged by B. Tierney, "Infallibility in Morals: A Response."

6. A very apt phrase I once heard sociologist and theologian Andrew Greeley use.

7. J. Gustafson, "Is There A Catholic and/or Christian Ethic?—A Response"), p. 155.

8. Ibid., p. 156.

9. Ibid., p. 158.

10. Ibid., p. 158f.

11. In addition to the sources cited thus far, this topic has been helpfully pursued by the following: J. Fuchs, "Human, Humanist and Christian Morality," in *Human Values and Christian Morality*, pp. 112–47; id., "Gibt es eine specifisch christliche Moral?," which is summarized in "Is There a Specifically Christian Ethic?"; C. Curran, "Dialogue with Humanism: Is There a Distinctively Christian Ethic?" in *Catholic Moral Theology in Dialogue*, pp. 1–23; J. Gustafson, *Can Ethics Be Christian?*.

12. This fourfold identity of the natural law and the Law of Christ is derived from a similar development by J. Fuchs, *Theologia Moralis Generalis*, 1:100–109.

Chapter 20

1. In a Catholic context it is also sometimes seen to include the study of canon law. And the justification for this is that the Christian life is lived socially, that society needs structuring, and that canon law is the means by which the Catholic community structures itself in order to facilitate the living of that life.

2. Moral theology, because it is a limited thing, often neglects this theme. One author who has attempted to address it is G. Gilleman, *The Primacy of Charity in Moral Theology*.

3. One author who has attempted to address this truth is E. McDonagh, "Liturgy and Christian Life," in *Invitation and Response*, pp. 96–108.

4. These two ideas: internal coherence and external adequacy, are seen as the two characteristics of any successful theory by J. Macmurray, *The Self as Agent*, p. 25.

5. C. Curran, "Moral Theology: The Present State of the Discipline."

6. A point made in an otherwise disturbing article: T. Dubay, "The State of Moral Theology: A Critical Appraisal." Here Dubay responds to the article of Curran cited above. Their discussion in print has continued, an interesting example since it is a disagreement about disagreement.

7. The phrase comes from Charles Davis, *A Question of Conscience* (New York: Harper & Row, 1967), pp. 64–77.

8. *Confessions*, trans. by F. Sheed (New York: Sheed & Ward, 1944), p. 1.

9. Irenaeus, *Adversus Haereses*, Book IV, chap. 20, section 7.

BIBLIOGRAPHY

Books

Bassett, William, and Huizing, Peter, eds. *The Future of Christian Marriage (Concilium* 87). New York: Seabury, 1974.

Baum, Gregory. *Man Becoming.* New York: Herder and Herder, 1970.

———. *Religion and Alienation: A Theological Reading of Sociology.* New York: Paulist, 1975.

Binswanger, Ludwig. *Being in the World.* New York: Harper Torchbooks, 1968.

Birch, Bruce C., and Rasmussen, Larry L. *Bible and Ethics in the Christian Life.* Minneapolis: Augsburg, 1976.

Böckle, Franz. *Law and Conscience.* New York: Sheed & Ward, 1966.

Crossan, John. *In Parables.* New York: Harper & Row, 1973.

Curran, Charles. *A New Look at Christian Morality.* Notre Dame: Fides, 1968.

———. *Catholic Moral Theology in Dialogue.* Notre Dame: Fides, 1972.

———. *Contemporary Problems in Moral Theology.* Notre Dame: Fides, 1970.

———. *New Perspectives in Moral Theology.* Notre Dame: Fides, 1974.

———. *Ongoing Revision.* Notre Dame: Fides, 1975.

———. *Themes in Fundamental Moral Theology.* Notre Dame: University of Notre Dame Press, 1977.

Davis, Henry. *Moral and Pastoral Theology.* 4 vols. 7th ed. New York: Sheed and Ward, 1958. Vol. 1, *Human Acts, Law, Sin, Virtue.*

Dedek, John. *Contemporary Medical Ethics.* New York: Sheed & Ward, 1975.

———. *Contemporary Sexual Morality.* New York: Sheed & Ward, 1971.

———. *Human Life.* New York: Sheed & Ward, 1972.

———. *Titius and Bertha Ride Again: Contemporary Moral Cases.* New York: Sheed & Ward, 1974.

Deeken, Alfons. *Process and Permanence in Ethics: Max Scheler's Moral Philosophy.* New York: Paulist, 1974.

Delhaye, Philippe. *The Christian Conscience.* New York: Desclée, 1968.

Deman, Thomas. *Aux origines de la théologie morale.* Montreal: Institut d'Études Médiévales, 1951.

Doherty, Dennis. *Divorce and Remarriage: Resolving a Catholic Dilemma.* St. Meinrad, Ind.: Abbey Press, 1974.

Flick, Maurizio, and Alszeghy, Zoltan. *Il Vangelo Della Grazia.* Rome: Lib., Editrice Fiorentina, 1964.

Fransen, Peter. *Divine Grace and Man.* New York: Mentor–Omega, 1965.

Fuchs, Josef. *Human Values and Christian Morality.* Dublin: Gill & Macmillan, 1970.

———. *Natural Law: A Theological Investigation.* New York: Sheed & Ward, 1965.

———. *Theologia Moralis Generalis.* 2 vols. Rome: Gregorian University Press, 1963 and 1967.

Gilkey, Langdon. *Catholicism Confronts Modernity.* New York: Seabury, 1973.

Gilleman, Gerard. *The Primacy of Charity in Moral Theology.* Westminster, Md.: Newman, 1959.

Gleason, Robert. *Grace.* New York: Sheed & Ward, 1962.

Guindon, André. *The Sexual Language.* Ottawa: University of Ottawa Press, 1976.

Gustafson, James M. *Can Ethics Be Christian?* Chicago: University of Chicago Press, 1975.

———. *Protestant and Roman Catholic Ethics: Prospects for Rapprochement.* Chicago: University of Chicago Press, 1978.

———. *Christ and the Moral Life.* Chicago: University of Chicago Press, 1976.

———. *The Church as Moral Decision Maker.* Philadelphia: Pilgrim, 1970.

Gutierrez, Gustavo. *A Theology of Liberation.* Maryknoll, N.Y.: Orbis, 1973.

Häring, Bernard. *The Law of Christ.* 3 vols. Westminster, Md.: Newman, 1961–1966. Vol. 1, *General Moral Theology.*

———. *Morality is for Persons.* New York: Farrar, Straus & Giroux, 1971.

Hauerwas, Stanley. *Character and the Christian Life.* San Antonio: Trinity University Press, 1975.

———. *Vision and Virtue.* Notre Dame: Fides, 1974.

Keane, Philip. *Sexual Morality: A Catholic Perspective.* New York: Paulist, 1977.

Kosnik, Anthony, et al. *Human Sexuality.* New York: Paulist, 1977.

Lehmann, Paul. *Ethics in a Christian Context.* New York: Harper & Row, 1963.

Lonergan, Bernard. *Method in Theology.* New York: Herder and Herder, 1972.

Macmurray, John. *The Self as Agent* and *Person as Relation.* London: Faber Papercovered Editions, 1969, 1970.

Macquarrie, John. *Three Issues in Ethics.* New York: Harper & Row, 1970.

Maly, Eugene H. *Sin: Biblical Perspectives.* Dayton: Pflaum, 1973.

May, Rollo; Angel, Ernest; and Ellenberger, Henri; eds. *Existence.* New York: Clarion–Simon & Schuster, 1958.

McCormick, Richard A. *Ambiguity in Moral Choice.* Milwaukee: Marquette University, 1973.

McDonagh, Edna. *Gift and Call.* St. Meinrad, Ind.: Abbey Press, 1975.

———. *Invitation and Response.* New York: Sheed & Ward, 1972.

Meyer, Charles R. *A Contemporary Theology of Grace.* Staten Island: Alba House, 1971.

———. *The Touch of God.* Staten Island: Alba House, 1972.

Milhaven, John G. *Toward a New Catholic Morality.* Garden City, New York: Doubleday, 1970.

Murphy, Francis. *Moral Teaching in the Primitive Church.* New York: Paulist, 1968.

Murray, John Courtney. *We Hold These Truths.* New York: Sheed & Ward, 1960.

National Conference of Catholic Bishops. *Human Life in Our Day.* Washington: U.S. Catholic Conference, 1968.

———, *To Live in Christ Jesus.* Washington: U.S. Catholic Conference, 1976.

Niebuhr, H. Richard. *Christ and Culture.* New York: Harper Torchbooks, 1956.

———. *The Responsible Self.* New York: Harper & Row, 1963.

Nielsen, E. *The Ten Commandments in New Perspective.* Naperville, Illinois: Allenson, 1968.

Noldin, Hieronymous. *Summa Theologiae Moralis.* 3 vols. Innsbruck: Rauch, 1957–1960. Vol. 1, *De principiis, de poenis ecclesiasticis, de castitate.*

O'Connell, Timothy. *Changing Roman Catholic Moral Theology: A Study in Josef Fuchs.* Ann Arbor: University Microfilms, 1974.

———. *A Contemporary Meditation on Personal Holiness.* Chicago: Thomas More, 1975.

———. *What a Modern Catholic Believes About Suffering and Evil.* Chicago: Thomas More, 1972.

Regan, George M. *New Trends in Moral Theology.* New York: Newman, 1971.

Rondet, Henri. *Original Sin.* Staten Island: Alba House, 1972.

———. *The Grace of Christ.* Westminster, Md.: Newman, 1967.

Salm, C. Luke. *Readings in Biblical Morality.* Englewood Cliffs, N.J.: Prentice-Hall, 1967.

Sanders, Jack T. *Ethics in the New Testament.* Philadelphia: Fortress, 1975.

Schelke, Karl. *Theology of the New Testament.* 4 vols. Vol. 3, *Morality.* Collegeville, Minn.: Liturgical Press, 1973.

Schillebeeckx, Edward. *Christ the Sacrament of the Encounter with God.* New York: Sheed & Ward, 1963.

———. *Marriage: Human Reality and Saving Mystery.* New York: Sheed & Ward, 1965.

Schnackenburg, Rudolf. *Christian Existence in the New Testament.* 2 vols. Notre Dame: University of Notre Dame Press, 1968 and 1969.

———. *The Moral Teaching of the New Testament.* New York: Seabury, 1973.

Schoonenberg, Piet. *Man and Sin.* Notre Dame: University of Notre Dame Press, 1965.

Shea, John. *What a Modern Catholic Believes About Sin.* Chicago: Thomas More, 1971.

Stamm, J. J., and Andrews, M. E. *The Ten Commandments in Recent Literature.* Naperville, Illinois: Allenson, 1967.

Stark, Werner. *The Sociology of Knowledge.* London: Routledge and Kegan Paul, 1967.

Tracy, David. *Blessed Rage for Order.* New York: Seabury, 1975.

Troisfontaines, Roger. *I Do Not Die.* New York: Desclée, 1963.

Van der Marck, W. H. *Toward a Christian Ethic.* New York: Newman, 1967.

Van der Poel, Cornelius J. *The Search for Human Values.* New York: Newman, 1971.

Von Hildebrand, Dietrich. *Ethics.* Chicago: Franciscan Herald Press, 1953.

Wrenn, Lawrence G., ed. *Divorce and Remarriage in the Catholic Church.* New York: Newman, 1973.

Bibliography Articles

Arntz, Joseph. "Natural Law and Its History." *Concilium* 5 (1965): 39–57. New York: Paulist.

Berger, Klaus. "Law." In *Encyclopedia of Theology,* edited by K. Rahner, pp. 822–30. New York: Seabury, 1975.

Blank, Josef. "Does the New Testament Provide Principles for Modern Moral Theology." *Concilium* 25 (1967): 9–22. New York: Paulist.

Collins, Raymond. "Scripture and the Christian Ethic." *Proceedings of the Catholic Theological Society of America* 29 (1974): 215–41.

Congar, Yves. "Pour une histoire sémantique du terme 'magisterium' " and "Bref historique des formes du 'magistere' et de ses relations avec les docteurs." *Revue des sciences philosophiques et theologiques* 60 (1976): 85–112.

———. "The Magisterium and Theologians—A Short History." *Theology Digest* 25 (1977): 15–20.

Connery, John. "Morality of Consequences: A Critical Appraisal." *Theological Studies* 34 (1973): 396–414.

Crowe, Michael. "Natural Law Theory Today." In R. McCormick et al., *The Future of Ethics and Moral Theology,* pp. 78–105. Chicago: Argus, 1968.

———. "Human Nature: Immutable or Mutable." *Irish Theological Quarterly* 30 (1963): 204–31.

Curran, Charles. "Moral Theology: The Present State of the Discipline." *Theological Studies* 34 (1973): 446–67.

Daniélou, Jean. "Christianity and non-Christian Religions." In *The Word in History* edited by T. P. Burke, pp. 86–101. New York: Sheed & Ward, 1966.

Dedek, John. "Scripture and the Christian Ethic: A Response." *Proceedings of the Catholic Theological Soceity of America* 29 (1974): 243–46.

Delhaye, P. " 'Droit naturel' et théologie morale." *Revue théologique de Louvain* 6 (1975): 137–64.

Dianich, Severino. "La corruzione della natura e la grazia nella opzioni fondamentali." *Scuola Cattolica* 92 (1964): 203–20.

Dubay, Thomas. "The State of Moral Theology: A Critical Appraisal." *Theological Studies* 35 (1974): 482–506.

Dulles, Avery. "The Theologian and the Magisterium." *Proceedings of the Catholic Theological Society of America* 31 (1976): 235–46.

Fitzmyer, Joseph. "Pauline Ecclesiology and Ethics," *Jerome Biblical Commentary* 79:157–166. Englewood Cliffs, N.J.: Prentice-Hall, 1968.

Fletcher, Joseph. "Situation Ethics, Law, and Watergate." *Cumberland Law Review* 6 (1975): 35–60.

Fransen, Peter. "Towards a Psychology of Divine Grace." *Lumen Vitae* 12 (1957): 203–32.

Freyne, Seán. "The Bible and Christian Morality." In *Morals, Law and Authority*, edited by J. P. Mackey, pp. 1–38. Dayton: Pflaum, 1969.

Fuchs, Josef. "Absoluteness of Moral Terms." *Gregorianum* 52 (1971): 415–58.

———. "Auctoritas Dei in Auctoritate Civili." *Periodica de Re Morali, Cononica, Liturgica* 52 (1963): 3–18.

———. "Gibt es eine specifisch christliche moral?" *Stimmen der Zeit* 185 (1970): 99–112.

———. "Is there a Specifically Christian Ethic?" *Theology Digest* 19 (1971): 39–45.

———. "Sin and Conversion." *Theology Digest* 14 (1966): 292–301.

———. "The Authority of God in Civil Authority." *Theology Digest* 12 (1964): 104–9.

Glaser, John. "Transition Between Grace and Sin: Fresh Perspectives." *Theological Studies* 29 (1968): 260–74.

Gustafson, James M. "Is There a Catholic and/or Christian Ethic?—A Response." *Proceedings of the Catholic Theological Society of America* 29 (1974): 155–60.

———. "Context vs Principles: The Misplaced Debate in Christian Ethics." In *New Theology #3*, edited by M. E. Marty and D. G. Peerman, pp. 69–102. New York: Macmillan, 1966.

Häring, Bernard. "Dynamism and Continuity in a Personalistic Approach to Natural Law." In *Norm and Context in Christian Ethics*, edited by G. H. Outka and P. Ramsey, pp. 119–218. New York: Scribner, 1968.

Hughes, Gerard. "Infallibility in Morals." *Theological Studies* 34 (1973): 415–28.

Janssens, Louis. "Ontic Evil and Moral Evil." *Louvain Studies* 4 (1972): 115–56.

Knauer, Peter. "The Hermeneutic Function of the Principle of Double Effect." *Natural Law Forum* 12 (1967): 132–62.

Lonergan, Bernard. "The Transition from a Classicist World-View to Historical-Mindedness." In *Law for Liberty*, edited by J. E. Biechler, pp. 126–33. Baltimore: Helicon, 1967.

Maguire, Daniel. "Moral Absolutes and the Magisterium." In *Absolutes in Moral Theology?*, edited by C. Curran, pp. 57–107. Washington, D.C.: Corpus, 1968.

Malloy, Edward. "Natural Law Theory and Catholic Moral Theology." *American Ecclesiastical Review* 169 (1975): 456–69.

McCormick, Richard. "Human Significance and Christian Significance." In *Norm and Context in Christian Ethics*, edited by G. H. Outka and P. Ramsey, pp. 233–64. New York: Scribner, 1968.

———. "Notes on Moral Theology." *Theological Studies* 32 (1971): 80–97; 33 (1972): 68–90; 36 (1975): 85–100; 37 (1976): 71–87; 38 (1977): 70–100.

———. "The Moral Theology of Vatican II." In R. McCormick et al., *The Future of Ethics and Moral Theology*, pp. 7–18. Chicago: Argus, 1968.

Millhaven, John G. "Towards an Epistemology of Ethics." *Theological Studies* 27 (1966): 228–41.

———. "Objective Moral Evaluation of Consequences." *Theological Studies* 32 (1971): 407–30.

Murray, John Courtney. "The Declaration on Religious Freedom." *Concilium* 15 (1966): 3–16. New York: Paulist.

O'Connell, Matthew. "Some Aspects of Commandment in the Old Testament." In *Reading in Biblical Morality*, edited by C. L. Salm, pp. 9–29. Englewood Cliffs, N.J.: Prentice Hall, 1967.

O'Connell, Timothy. "Grace, Relationship and Transactional Analysis." *Thought* 48 (1973) 360–385.

———. "Identification of Sin." *Reconciliation Background Papers*. Chicago: Liturgy Training Program, 1976.

———. "Old Priest, New Theology: A Dilemma." *American Ecclesiastical Review* 167 (1973) 236–51.

———. "Sin and Reconciliation." *Reconciliation Resources II*. Chicago: Liturgy Training Program, 1975.

———. "The Point of Moral Theology." *Chicago Studies* 14 (1975): 49–66.

———. "The Question of Moral Norms." *American Ecclesiastical Review* 169 (1975): 377–88.

Pattison, E. Mansell, M.D. "The Development of Moral Values in Children." In *Conscience: Theological and Psychological Perspectives*, edited by C. Nelson, pp. 238–62. New York: Newman, 1973.

Peter, Val. "Scripture and the Christian Ethic: A Response." *Proceedings of the Catholic Theological Society of America* 29 (1974): 247–53.

Podimattam, Felix. "What Is Mortal Sin?" *Clergy Monthly* 36 (1972): 57–67.

Quay, Paul. "Morality by Calculation of Values." *Theology Digest* 23 (1975): 347–64.

Rahner, Karl. "Concerning the Relationship Between Nature and Grace." *Theological Investigations I*, pp. 297–318. Baltimore: Helicon, 1961.

———. "Evolution and Original Sin." *Concilium* 26 (1967): 61–73. New York: Paulist.

———. "Guilt and Its Remission: The Borderline between Theology and Pscychotherapy." *Theological Investigations II*, pp. 265–82. Baltimore: Helicon, 1963.

———. "Guilt–Responsibility–Punishment within the View of Catholic Theology." *Theological Investigations VI*, pp. 197–217. Baltimore: Helicon, 1969.

———. "On the Question of a Formal Existential Ethics." *Theological Investigations II*, pp. 217–34. Baltimore: Helicon, 1963.

———. "On the Theology of the Incarnation." *Theological Investigations IV*, pp. 105–20. Baltimore: Helicon, 1966.

———. "Some Thoughts on a 'Good Intention.'" *Theological Investigations III*, pp. 105–28. Baltimore: Helicon, 1967.

———. "The Dignity and Freedom of Man." *Theological Investigations II*, pp. 235–64. Baltimore: Helicon, 1963.

———. "The Experiment with Man." *Theological Investigations IX*, pp. 205–24. New York: Herder and Herder, 1972.

———. "The Sin of Adam." *Theological Investigations XI*, pp. 247–62. New York: Seabury, 1974.

———. "The Theological Concept of Consupiscentia." *Theological Investigations I*, pp. 347–82. Baltimore: Helicon, 1961.

———. "The Two Basic Types of Christology." *Theological Investigations XIII*, pp. 213–23. New York: Seabury, 1975.

———. "Theological Reflexions on Monogenism." *Theological Investigations I*, pp. 229–96. Baltimore: Helicon, 1961.

———. "Theology of Freedom." *Theological Investigations VI*, pp. 178–96. Baltimore: Helicon, 1969.

Ramsey, Paul. "The Case of the Curious Exception." In *Norm and Context in Christian Ethics*, edited by G. H. Outka and P. Ramsey, pp. 67–135. New York: Scribner, 1968.

Ryan, Columba. "The Traditional Concept of Natural Law: An Interpretation." In *Light on the Natural Law*, edited by I. Evans, pp. 13–37. Baltimore: Helicon, 1965.

Schneider, Gerhard. "The Biblical Grounding of Ethical Norms." *Theology Digest* 22 (1974): 117–20.

Schüller, Bruno. "Neuere Beiträge zum Thema 'Bergründung sittlicher Normen.' " *Theologische Berichte* 4: 109–181. Einsiedeln: Benziger, 1974.

———. "What Ethical Principles are Universally Valid?" *Theology Digest* 19 (1971): 23–28.

Tapia, Ralph. "When Is Sin Sin?" *Thought* 47 (1972): 211–24.

Tierney, Brian. "Infallibility in Morals: A Response." *Theological Studies* 35 (1974): 507–17.

Tracy, David. "Presidential Address." *Proceedings of the Catholic Theological Society of America* 32 (1977): 234–44.

Troisfontaines, Rogers. "L'insémination artificielle: Problèmes éthiques.' *Nouvelle Revue Théologique* 95 (1973): 764–78.

Von Hildebrand, Dietrich. "Sittlichkeit und ethische Werterkenntnis." *Jahrbuch für Philosophie und phänomenologische Forschung* 5 (1922): 463–602.

Walgrave, Jan. "Is Morality Static or Dynamic?" *Concilium* 5 (1965): 22–38. London: Burns & Oates; New York: Paulist.

Watson, Gerard. "Pagan Philosophy and Christian Ethics." In *Morals, Law and Authority*, edited by J. P. Mackey, pp. 39–57. Dayton: Pflaum, 1969.